The
SWING
VOTE

Also by Linda Killian

The Freshmen: What Happened to the Republican Revolution?

The

SWING
VOTE

The Untapped Power of Independents

Linda Killian

St. Martin's Press ☙ New York

Library of Congress Cataloging-in-Publication Data

Killian, Linda.
  The swing vote : the untapped power of independents / Linda Killian.
      p. cm.
  Includes bibliographical references and index.
  ISBN 978-0-312-58177-0 (hardcover)
  ISBN 978-1-4299-8944-2 (e-book)
  1. Voting—United States.   2. Elections—United States.   I. Title.
  JK1967.K56 2011
  324.973—dc23

                                                        2011026065

First Edition: January 2012

10 9 8 7 6 5 4 3 2 1

For all the Independent and Swing voters who
love this country and want to make it better

CONTENTS

CONTENTS

The
SWING
VOTE

PREFACE

Common Sense

IN JANUARY 1776, ONLY a little more than a year after arriving in America from England, Thomas Paine published a sixty-page pamphlet titled *Common Sense*, which became one of the most important documents in American history. Addressing his tract "to the inhabitants of America," Paine spoke directly to the people, rather than to the political and intellectual classes, and used clear, simple, and straightforward arguments—as he put it—"in language as plain as the alphabet" to make the case for American independence and the creation of a democratic republic to be governed by the people. It was, he said, "nothing more than simple facts, plain arguments, and common sense."

Paine's call for not only independence but also political participation by the people and a truly representative system of government was revolutionary in its language and its thinking. Paine argued that the populace could shape its own destiny through the fight for independence and create something entirely new. *Common Sense* mobilized public support for the idea of independence and paved the way for the Continental Congress's ratification of the Declaration of Independence six months later. It became one of the founding documents of a new form of government—of, by, and for the people.

The reason I begin with Thomas Paine and his *Common Sense* is that Paine's call for real, participatory democracy still resonates and in many ways is needed now just as badly as it was at the birth of our nation. Americans today are faced with a dysfunctional and polarized political system, controlled by political and party elites and special interests, that seems incapable of dealing with the serious issues and choices facing this nation. The necessity for a revolt by the people is no less great than it was at our founding.

Throughout his life and writings, Paine believed in the possibility of change and the idea that the citizenry could take control of its own government. "I saw an opportunity in which I thought I could do some good, and I followed exactly what my heart dictated," he wrote of his mission.

In some small way, I hope the spirit of Thomas Paine and *Common Sense* is evoked in this book because this moment in our national political life is so critical. We have a choice of continuing to do things the way we have been doing them and expecting a different result—not likely—or making a fundamental change that will benefit all citizens, improve our democratic institutions, and ensure the future strength and prosperity of this nation.

I have covered American politics and government at the local, state, and national levels for many years, and increasingly I have become more concerned about the partisanship, the mounting influence of special interests and money on the legislative process, and the inability of the two parties to work together to solve our problems. I have also become aware that a great many Americans don't feel truly represented by their politicians and the system, especially the Independent voters, who now account for a larger portion of the electorate than either Democrats or Republicans. This disconnect between so many voters and the people elected to represent them is eroding trust in our political system and its effectiveness.

This nation faces so many serious problems: unemployment at its highest level in twenty-five years, a shrinking manufacturing base, a dependence on foreign oil and high energy prices, a crumbling infrastructure, a failing education system, and a federal debt and deficit that are driving the nation to the edge of a cliff. Our financial system and tax code serve those at the top but penalize the middle class and have increased the income gap between rich and middle-class wage earners to the largest disparity since the Census Bureau began keeping records, more than forty years ago. In 2010, CEO pay of Fortune 500 companies was up an astronomical 24 percent, at a higher level than in 2007, before our near economic collapse, and corporate profits were up 81 percent. But most Americans weren't feeling the benefits of this economic success—it was reserved for those at the top.

Our political system and elected officials seem incapable of dealing with these serious issues. In the eyes of the Independent voters, our politicians are fiddling while Rome burns. They can't seem to stop fighting long enough to do anything and aren't willing to make the compromises and tough choices that might solve some of our problems but might also jeopardize their own political careers.

Why has this happened, and what can be done about it? I hope that this book helps to answer those questions.

I wanted to tell the story of the Independent/Swing voters—the centrist voters who decide elections and represent more voters than those at the conservative and liberal ends of the political spectrum. Most of them are undeclared or unaffiliated—Independent voters. Some of them still remain registered Democrats and Republicans but they feel disconnected from the political parties and the government. They are not hard left or hard right and don't consistently identify with one political party. They are fiscally conservative and socially tolerant. They are in the middle. They "swing" back and forth, voting for candidates from both parties, largely because they are seeking change, aren't getting it from their elected leaders, and are increasingly disgusted with a system they don't believe truly represents them. I use the term *Independent/Swing voter* here to refer to those centrist voters who are Independents as well as to swing voters still belonging to a political party. Throughout the book, for clarity and simplicity, I will use the term *Independent voters* in referring to this group.

I was determined to talk with as many Independent voters as I could and use their own words to explain how they feel let down by the system. I wanted to give voice to these voters—the people to whom American politics should also belong.

Journalists from time to time interview or hold focus groups with "average voters" and feature them in stories. But this is mostly just a garnish. The meat and potatoes of political coverage are the political parties, their leaders, and the horse race—who's up and who's down, who's going to win either the next fight in Congress or the next election. Media stories about the presidential campaign begin long before any politicians have even declared their candidacies and dominate political coverage.

Republicans and Democrats, the left and right, are whom the American people consistently hear from even though a plurality of voters don't consider themselves one or the other. And the fundamental structural problems in our political system, the disenfranchisement of many of these Independent voters, gets ignored.

If a minority group were getting shut out of full participation in the political process, there would be a huge outcry. But Independent voters are far from a minority group. There are more of them than either Democrats or Republicans. Yet they are still woefully unrepresented within the political system. And they are just expected to take it. To sit back and enjoy the scraps thrown to them by the two political parties who have a stranglehold on the electoral and political process.

The conventional wisdom is that these voters pay less attention and participate less frequently, not to mention that they tend not to be regular or large financial donors to campaigns. Politicians and academics say they tune in and out. Some of that may be true, but the reason for that relative lack of engagement is our flawed political system.

What I heard over and over from the Independent voters I interviewed, who were by and large extremely politically aware and well informed, is that our current politics doesn't give them much of a reason to care. They don't see much difference between the two political parties, and they don't see things changing, no matter who gets elected.

To be sure, in addition to the Independent voters I talked with, I also interviewed hundreds of local, state, and national officials, party leaders, academics, and policy experts for this book. Not to have done so would have been like writing a book about baseball and interviewing only the fans and not the players and managers. But I talked to these politicians to understand how they operate in the system, the frustrations they also have, and what they think can be done to improve things.

I decided the best way to get at this story was to focus on four key swing states from different regions of the country, each representing a crucial group of Independent/Swing voters I wanted to describe. There were many states I considered, including Florida, Indiana, Missouri, Nevada, North Carolina, and Pennsylvania. But after much deliberation, I finally determined that New Hampshire, Virginia, Ohio, and Colorado were the best and most interesting examples of the nation's important swing states. Each state is unique to its region and illustrates a key swing voter demographic, and together they effectively tell the story of Independent/Swing voters throughout the country.

I reached out to Independent voters in those states in a variety of ways—I obtained lists of registered unaffiliated voters from voter registration offices and polling organizations and called up strangers on the telephone to ask them about their politics. Amazingly, most of them were willing to talk with me, even eager to do so. They were happy someone was listening. I also contacted universities and civic groups to find the perfect blend of Independent voters. I am incredibly grateful for all the time these voters shared with me. This book wouldn't have been possible without their cooperation.

I conducted focus groups in all four states before and after the 2010 election, and what I heard during these sessions was strikingly similar, no matter where I went. Many Independent voters were concerned about the spending and growth of government under President Barack Obama and the Democratic Congress, but they also weren't convinced things would improve if the Republicans were in charge. They were incredibly pessimistic about the political system, did not feel well represented by it, and believed the average person has almost no impact on what happens. They believe the two parties with their ideological extremism and special interests have a stranglehold on the system. All these interviews and conversations convinced me I was on the right track and the story of the Independent/Swing voters needed to be told.

When I began this project in early 2010, and especially after I interviewed so many voters in the fall of that year and spring of 2011, I knew there was a great deal of anger and frustration out there that needed to be explained. But I had no idea how much worse things would get. As I concluded the final revisions for this book last summer, and the crisis over the debt ceiling erupted, followed by the public disgust over the spectacle and the inability of our elected officials to effectively address our nation's challenges, it seemed everyone, including President Barack Obama, was talking about the dysfunction of the system and the public's loss of faith in Congress and our political leaders. But I knew there was much more to be said.

I would expect this book to be read by those who follow politics closely—the officials, activists, academics, and journalists as well as the political junkies. But I hope that Independent voters—those who feel ignored, fed up, and shut out of the system—will also find and enjoy this book and recognize themselves in its pages. It is my hope that while reading, at some point they will stop and say, "Finally someone gets it—that's exactly how I feel." And I hope it motivates them to get involved and to speak out.

I think this book says a lot about where we are as a country right now. I'm afraid it's not all that good. But I do have some hope. Mostly because I believe in the Independent/Swing voters, and I don't think the center in American politics is gone forever.

1

Who Are the Independent Voters?

A government of our own is our natural right.
—Thomas Paine

Ninety-year-old betty Hall lives in the 1850s farmhouse in Brookline, New Hampshire, where her grandmother was born. After graduating from Barnard College in 1943, working as an engineer with the Western Electric Company during World War II, and getting married, she returned to New Hampshire with her husband to start a textile manufacturing company and raise their five children.

Back then, only about eight hundred people lived in Brookline, which is about fifteen miles west of Nashua, and Hall's children were educated in the town's two-room schoolhouse. She felt the school needed improvement and better resources and decided to try to do something about it, so she ran for town school board and then selectman, explaining her reason for getting into politics.

She started out as a Republican. Most people in New Hampshire were. She first got elected to the New Hampshire House of Representatives in 1970 and served a total of twenty-eight years. "Liberal Republicans were fairly common then. I had a lot of great liberal Republican colleagues, but eventually they got pushed out." In the 1980s, she found she was voting more often with the Democrats so she decided to change

7

her party registration and was reelected to the legislature as a Democrat. But eventually she realized, "I was so sick of both parties, I decided I was going to be an Independent and escape from them telling me how to vote because I felt the most important thing was the responsibility to my constituents."

Four years ago, she officially became an Independent and made a couple of unsuccessful runs for the state legislature in 2008 and 2010. "I called myself an Independent moderate. I knew the odds were going to be against me."

Looking and sounding much younger than her ninety years, Hall recalls some of her political experiences, like the time she ran for a state senate seat by riding her bicycle one thousand miles around the district to campaign door-to-door. When President George W. Bush came to New Hampshire to speak in 2004, she protested outside the event with a sign that said BUSH IS BAD FOR AMERICA. A pen had been set up for protestors, but Hall refused to stay behind the barriers, and authorities arrested her and charged her with disorderly conduct. "They wanted me to do a plea bargain for twelve hours of community service, but I said no—I was not disorderly and I was going to defend myself. The judge totally exonerated me." Hall was a member of the legislature at the time and introduced a bill to impeach Bush. "Don't you think that didn't stir up a hornet's nest," she says with a laugh.

"They call me a firebrand. Nobody knows what to make of me," says Hall, who is something of a true New England eccentric. She says her children, along with twelve grandchildren and six great-grandchildren, "kill themselves laughing at me, but they're very supportive of what I'm doing."

Her hero and role model is Doris "Granny D" Haddock, the political activist who at the age of eighty-eight began walking across the United States to advocate for campaign finance reform. Granny D's march took more than a year and ended in Washington, D.C., in 2000. The Bipartisan Campaign Reform Act, also known as McCain–Feingold for its two sponsors, Senators John McCain and Russell Feingold, passed two years later.

In 2004, at the age of ninety-four, Granny D became the Democratic candidate for U.S. Senate from New Hampshire against incumbent Republican Judd Gregg, a campaign that was the subject of an HBO documentary called *Run Granny Run*. Granny D died in 2010 at the age of one hundred.

Hall says she is trying to follow in Granny D's footsteps and is a strong supporter of election reform. "If the primaries were reformed, maybe there would be hope for the two parties. The whole system—the primary system—is functionally bankrupt. The only candidates that can prevail in a primary have to have tons of money. It's all about money. I don't like that the parties can tell people how to vote, and if they don't toe the party line they won't get elected again, because they won't get the money and the party support."

Using what she has learned from her many years in politics, Hall's mission now is to push for more campaign-finance and election-law reform and encourage more Independent candidates to run for office.

"I'm not afraid to speak truth to power. I've always been a maverick. I'm going to live to be a hundred years old and I'm going to give them trouble all the way."

Dr. James Squires was a moderate Republican all his life. The seventy-three-year-old retired physician lives in Hollis, a town of about seven thousand people in southeastern New Hampshire on the Massachusetts border. For twenty years, he has been the moderator of the annual town meeting, a New England tradition that began with the first Puritan settlers even before the United States was founded and which represents the purest form of democracy. Citizens gather in the spring to take up matters of interest to the town and to debate and approve the town budget. Anyone can speak, and everyone has the same vote.

Squires was elected to the state senate in 1996 and served for four years. "I kept trying to maintain that I was there to represent everyone in the state, not just the party that nominated me." When he ran for reelection, Squires faced a primary challenge on the right. "I was confused, thinking there might be some middle ground in the Republican

Party, but it was going away. The Republican Party moved past me to some new place I didn't understand or agree with."

In 2000, Squires ran for governor but lost the Republican nomination to a much more conservative candidate who was defeated in the general election. "The Republicans have made a mistake in being so extreme and exclusionary," Squires believes. In a state where a majority of voters, like Squires, are pro-choice and favor gay marriage rights, the Republican Party demands complete allegiance and opposition to those positions.

"We're becoming so polarized, there isn't any room for a middle ground. My political philosophy is not based on ideology—I'm more pragmatic. I think each issue needs to be looked at and evaluated."

Two years ago, Squires became what New Hampshire calls an "undeclared" voter, joining many moderate Republicans who have become Independents.

Scott Clinger is a forty-seven-year-old policeman in Columbus, Ohio, born and raised not far from where he lives now. He served in the Marine Corps for ten years before joining the force. His wife is an elementary school teacher, and they've got two grown children. She's a Democrat, but he has always considered himself an Independent.

In 1984, he voted for Ronald Reagan. He liked Reagan's vision of a strong America, and a strong military is important to him. He voted for George Bush in 1988 and '92, but went for Bill Clinton in 1996. "I was happy with him. The main thing was that we had a balanced budget and a surplus."

He voted for George W. Bush in 2000 and says, "That was a mistake." In 2004, he voted for John Kerry. "When we invaded Iraq, I thought it was the worst thing ever—the dumbest thing we had ever done. I knew how expensive and long it would be."

In 2008, Clinger liked McCain and says it was a tough choice for him. "I think the country was going in the wrong direction under George Bush. When McCain picked Sarah Palin, at first I thought she sounded pretty sparky, but then when she started talking, you said, 'Oh my gosh, she doesn't know anything.'

"I wasn't a hundred percent sold on Obama, but I thought we did need some sort of change." Clinger credits Obama for getting Osama bin Laden, but he's not sure if he will vote for him again. "I have to look at who runs against him."

Clinger says he likes to vote for both Democrats and Republicans because "I like to see balance—it forces them to come together and maybe come up with a better plan. With what's been happening—it's like the parties have gone just crazy. I don't get why they can't work with each other."

As a member of a two-union household, Clinger is very concerned about the anti-union efforts around the country and especially the passage in Ohio of Senate Bill 5, which strips public unions of their collective bargaining rights. He says it would never have happened if the Republicans didn't control both houses of the legislature and the governorship.

Depending on what kind of cuts take place as a result, he said he's worried about being able to afford his mortgage payments. "This is nothing but a union-busting bill." Clinger has never been politically active before, but now he spends weekends with his wife collecting signatures on petitions to repeal SB 5. Many union members in Ohio like Clinger have voted Republican in the past, but he thinks the Republicans "have committed political suicide."

Ryan Ayers, thirty, and Allen Wells, thirty-one, live in Canton, Ohio, and have known each other since high school. I met them during the 2010 campaign at the North Canton Community Center, where they were attending a town hall meeting featuring the two candidates for Congress in Ohio's Sixteenth District. Ayers and Wells are both married. Wells has three children and works at a factory that builds furnaces and electromagnets for steel mills. Ayers, a quality manager at a structural steel fabrication company, was expecting a baby.

Both men described themselves as Independent voters who lean to the right but vote for both Democrats and Republicans. Ayers is a member of the National Rifle Association. In 2008, they both voted for John McCain for president and for John Boccieri, the Democratic candidate, for Congress. Two years later, they were unhappy with the Democratic Congress and on the fence about whether Boccieri deserved another term. Ultimately, Wells voted for Republicans Jim Renacci for Congress and Rob Portman for Senate but supported Democrat Ted Strickland for reelection to the Ohio governorship. Ayers voted mostly for Republicans, including John Kasich for governor, a vote he said he regretted a few months after the election.

Wells was happy at first that the Republicans won the U.S. House and the Democrats held on to the Senate because he thought it might force the two parties to work together. But by the spring of 2011, he had become pessimistic. "It's the same as usual in my opinion, they're just putting on a big dog and pony show and not doing anything. . . . The Republicans don't want government to do anything, and the Democrats want the government to do everything. . . . I don't see much change. I hope they're going to get this out of their system and start to work together.

"Most people you talk to, they think the election was about listening to what the voters have to say," said Wells. "We were trying to tell the Democrats to slow down and listen to other views, but it wasn't just a total endorsement of Republican conservative positions."

"The American people have just had enough. They're tired," said Ayers. "Politicians are out of touch with us and they're not listening to what we want. I don't feel that the politicians really do what's best for us. . . . In my household—you only pull in so much money. You can't spend more than you bring in. The government can't sustain deficit spending for a long time. They've been spending and spending and spending, and we've got to rein that in. We've got to concentrate on our own country, developing our own infrastructure to get people back to work." Ayers lost one job when the plant he was working at moved from Ohio to North Carolina.

"The economy is the biggest thing right now, it's hitting us hard in Ohio," said Wells. "I'd like to see them sit down and look at trade agreements with other countries. There's got to be a way to bring domestic jobs back. . . . Let's hit companies that keep moving jobs overseas, hit them with a tariff or tax incentive to create jobs and punish them for sending jobs overseas. . . . But I think the American people have to step up too and say we're buying only American-made stuff—instead of buying cheap stuff made in China at Walmart."

"We need a true swing party," Ayers believes. "I was hoping the Tea Party would do it, but they've gone too far to the right." Having viable Independent candidates would make a difference, "but they don't have funding or a way to get their names out."

Even though neither of them voted for Obama in 2008, they were somewhat pleased with what they perceived as his course correction after the midterm election.

"I think he's gone more than halfway," said Wells. "I look at my job, and if they tell me I'm doing something wrong, I'm going to change—I'm not going to keep doing it my way and risk getting fired. I'm going to do what I need to do to keep my job. The voters are his boss."

"This election was a wake-up call," said Ayers. "It was 'do what your constituents want or we're going to get rid of you.'"

Twenty-five-year-old Adam Gray lives in Broomfield, Colorado, located between Denver and Boulder. He's an engineer who works for a small composite technology company that does advanced applications for the aerospace industry with clients including NASA and the Department of Defense.

Like so many young people, he moved to Colorado to attend college and never left. His parents are Republicans, and Gray says he started out as a Republican, voting for George W. Bush and John McCain for president, but then became an Independent. In 2010, he voted for Democrat John Hickenlooper for governor. "I thought when I first started to vote that you had to pick a side, but I got a little older and found myself disappointed with both sides."

Gray says he is more economically Republican but more socially Democratic. "This whole debt thing scares the hell out of me. . . . People my age get it. You're just starting out on your own, you know you can't spend more than you make. It's something most people my age can relate to—not overspending your bank account."

Gray is pro-choice, and believes gays should have the right to marry. "I think those are human rights," he explains. He watches Fox News, but also likes to check out the websites of CNN and the BBC. Like a lot of young people, he also picks up a lot of his political ideas from talking with his friends.

He doesn't understand why there should be only two parties in the United States and has some frustration about being a registered Independent because "You don't really have a voice if you don't side with one of the two big dogs."

But he is sick of what he sees going on in Washington. "There's no real compromise. It's like this tug-of-war match—it's not constructive. It's all a power play."

Gray has friends who worked on the Obama campaign who now say they are a bit disappointed, and he thinks "the Obama sheen has worn off." When I ask if he can see himself voting for a Democrat for president, he instantly responds, "Oh, sure," and says what he is really looking for in a candidate is, "Someone willing to admit their mistakes. I really hate that no one owns up to any mistake they make. I really want someone to be honest, tell it straight, and move forward. Candidates always make the safe play. I'd like to see someone just throwing it out there."

Jeanna Grasso, who lives in Denver, is a twenty-nine-year-old single mother of a six-year-old boy. She says she has already had some ups and downs in her life. Her father is a carpenter, and the grandmother who raised her is a receptionist at a car dealership. She took time off when her son was born to be with him but has since gone back to school at the

University of Colorado–Denver and was on track to finish her political science degree in 2011.

She knows a lot of people who are unemployed and looking for work, and she is worried about finding a job when she graduates. She has been an Independent voter since she first registered to vote at eighteen and says it's because she has both liberal and conservative views. Some of her family members supported Ross Perot when he ran for president, and she says her favorite politicians are Bill Clinton and Colorado Governor John Hickenlooper. Grasso mostly votes for Democrats, although she's not always sure exactly what they stand for and usually doesn't think the options offered by either party are all that good.

I first met Grasso a few weeks before the 2010 election when she participated in a focus group I held in Denver and she expressed very negative feelings about Congress. "I don't feel a connection between them and real people. I definitely don't think they're relatable," she told me.

Grasso is concerned about the corrupting influence of money in politics and thinks being in Congress is "a purchased job. Who spends a hundred million dollars to get a job that pays a hundred fifty thousand? There's a reason why.

"All they are concerned about is, How do I stay in office? They are worried about protecting themselves and making sure they have a job rather than doing what's right."

Michael Sciulla is a sixty-year-old retired lobbyist who lives in Vienna, Virginia, in the suburbs just outside Washington, D.C. He's married, with two teenage children, and says he has been an Independent all his life. In 1980, he voted for John Anderson, an Independent candidate who was running for president. Usually, when he's trying to decide whom to vote for, Sciulla feels like he is forced to pick "the lesser of two evils."

"Economically I should be voting Republican, but I can't seem to do it because of their social agenda and their hypocrisy about the budget deficit and all of the spending they did for all of those years."

As a lobbyist, Sciulla ran a political action committee (PAC) and says, "I gave out thousands of dollars in campaign contributions and I became so disgusted with the system, I threw up my hands and got out." Sciulla says he thinks both parties are more interested in getting and holding on to power than in working on real solutions, and the cost of campaigns and the fund-raising politicians have to do to finance them are some of the biggest problems with the system.

Even though a lot of his friends and neighbors make their living working for or with the government, Sciulla says most of them, no matter their political philosophy, believe government spending and waste, fraud, and abuse are huge problems.

Sciulla says he thinks most people voted for Barack Obama because they wanted hope and change and "We haven't had much of either and that is so disappointing.

"Politics is an emotional sport as well as an intellectual endeavor. There's a keg of dynamite under a lot of people, and it can be set off if provided the right match."

Fifty-two-year-old Sue Thomas lives in Great Falls, Virginia, another Washington suburb. She has two children and owns a small company that does information technology management consulting. Her husband works in government relations.

She considers herself a fiscally conservative, socially liberal Independent. She votes in general elections but not in primaries. "I really feel like I'm representative of the nonpolitical American who has a business and a family and cares about what things mean for their parents and children and who's looking around and says this political system doesn't make sense to me." Her family has had some serious health issues, and Thomas is very aware of the problems with our health care system and the crisis that comes with not having health insurance.

Thomas voted for Ronald Reagan and Bill Clinton. She voted for Barack Obama in 2008 but says, "He was not my first or second choice, but I didn't feel comfortable with McCain." She thinks Hillary Clinton has done a terrific job as Secretary of State and likes Virginia Senator Mark Warner for his business background and also because "He's willing to step out there and work with Republicans on the right way to tackle the deficit. I'm really glad that he's my senator. I would like to see more people acting like Warner."

Thomas thought it was "stupid" that the government almost shut down last year and says it just proved "it's all about the parties" and that politicians aren't really working for the country. "The notion of fair is lost right now, it's about labels, it's about reelection, and it's about campaign contributions."

These are the Independent/Swing voters.

They are not reliably conservative or liberal. Many of them never registered with a party and have been Independent voters their entire lives. Others are former Republicans and Democrats who became disaffected with the parties because of social or economic policies. Many Independents say they have been driven from the two parties by their extremism and a failure to focus on the nation's most important issues. Independent voters think the parties care more about winning elections than about solving the nation's problems, and they have largely lost faith in the two-party system. Nearly two-thirds of these voters say they believe both parties care more about special interests than about average Americans.[1]

These voters swing back and forth, supporting candidates from both parties, often in the same election. They live all over the country but are most important and sought after when they reside in swing states that also move back and forth from the Democratic to Republican column—especially the battleground states of New Hampshire, Colorado, Ohio, Virginia, Florida, and Pennsylvania. In closely contested elections, their votes usually determine the winner. The 2000 presidential contest was famously one of the closest elections in U.S. history with Al Gore winning the popular vote and, after a partial recount in Florida, George W. Bush winning the electoral vote and the state of Florida by fewer than one thousand votes. In 2008, Barack Obama carried North Carolina by only fourteen thousand votes and Virginia by a little more than five thousand votes.[2] In congressional and local elections, the margin of victory can be as low as triple and even double digits in tight races in swing districts.

The number of Independent voters, along with their disaffection with the two-party political system, is growing exponentially. About 40 percent of all American voters now call themselves Independents, which is a bigger group than those who say they are either Democrats or Republicans and is the largest number of Independent voters in seventy years[3]. In some states, Independents are a majority of the voters.

Polling by various organizations from Gallup to Pew verifies the significance and growth of the Independent voters. The American National Election Studies at the University of Michigan has been charting voting behavior and party identification in this country since 1952. Back then, about 25 percent of those polled identified themselves as Independent or Independent leaning. In 2008, the figure was up to 40 percent.[4] The Pew Research Center in its most recent surveys also puts the number of Independents at around 40 percent.[5]

Among these Independent voters, about half say they have not thought of themselves as either a Democrat or Republican in the last five years.[6] I believe this figure comes close to the true number of Independent/Swing voters in this country—about 20 percent of the electorate. And the role of this 20 percent of swing voters, especially in recent presidential elections, has been critical. Every election since World War II has been determined by voters in the middle. They are the voters who cast their ballots on issues and in favor of the candidate rather than for the party; and it is these voters who determine who will be president and which party will control Congress.

These are the voters who elected Ronald Reagan, Bill Clinton, and George W. Bush. In the 1992, 1996, and 2000 presidential elections, roughly a third of the voters were swing voters.[7] They also elected Barack Obama. The margin by which Obama carried the Independent vote in crucial swing states around the country was one of the significant factors in his victory and will undoubtedly be critical to whether or not he is reelected. Obama carried 60 percent of the "moderate" vote, which made up 44 percent of the electorate in 2008.[8]

The Republican victories in the 2010 midterm election were also decided by these voters. Independents supported Democrats by 18 points in 2006. But driven by their concern about the nation's economy and strong opposition to Democratic spending and health care initiatives, they supported Republican congressional candidates in 2010 by the overwhelming margin of 56 to 38 percent, a 36-point swing from 2006.[9] These Independent voters cannot all be classified as one thing or said to have all the same interests and views. They are diverse in age, race, gender, and income level. But I have divided them into four distinct and important demographic groups which comprise most of the Independent/Swing voters.

Those voters who are socially moderate and fiscally conservative and who used to be known as Rockefeller Republicans became Independents because of a growing disaffection with their natural party home. These were traditional, socially moderate, country club Republicans named because their political philosophy was in line with New York Governor and Vice President Nelson Rockefeller, a liberal Republican who supported abortion rights and many other socially liberal positions and declared, "I do not believe it right for one group to impose its vision of morality on an entire society." But Rockefeller has been dead for more than thirty years, and it is time for a new label for these voters. I call them *NPR Republicans*. Betty Hall and James Squires of New Hampshire are examples of NPR Republicans, and many of them can be found in New England, especially in New Hampshire. These voters moved away from the GOP in large numbers during the George W. Bush years because of the war in Iraq, Republican overspending, and what they perceived to be their party's general mismanagement of the government and a loss of focus on important issues. They were also turned off by the GOP's alignment with the religious right and its conservative stands on social issues like abortion and gay rights. The NPR Republicans tend to be affluent, well-educated, older voters. They believe in balancing the budget and holding the line on tax increases, but they also believe the government should stay out of people's personal lives. Although there are many NPR Republicans in New England, they can be found all over the country. Increasingly, these voters are being driven out of the Republican Party and out of political office by primary challenges from the right and by those who want the GOP to be a conservative, ideologically pure party.

Another group of Independent/Swing voters is the group I call *America First Democrats.* They used to be known as Reagan Democrats, but just like the moniker Rockefeller Republicans, that title is also outdated. While many in this group admired Reagan and his call for a strong America, many others are too young to have had the chance to vote for Ronald Reagan and were just children when he was president. The America First Democrats are largely male, working- and middle-class voters who are concentrated in the Midwest and Rust Belt of the country. Scott Clinger, Ryan Ayers, and Allen Wells of Ohio are America First Democrats. It would make more economic sense for America First Democrats to be solidly aligned with the Democratic Party. Republican taxation and trade policies have put the squeeze on them and the rest of the middle class in recent decades. But they perceive a reluctance on the part of many Democrats to stand up for traditional American values both at home and abroad and usually tend to be more conservative than the Democratic Party on social issues. They lean toward populism, and are more protectionist, more religious, and more socially conservative than the NPR Republicans. They voted in large numbers for Bill Clinton, and many supported Hillary for president. Because they are persuadable and are often ticket splitters, they are actively pursued by both Republican and Democratic strategists and candidates.

Another significant Independent voter demographic are those under thirty-five—which includes a portion of what is often referred to as Generation X along with Generation Y—or the Millennials who were born after 1980. I call them the *Facebook Generation*. Adam Gray and Jeanna Grasso of Colorado are Facebook Generation voters. These young voters are not joiners and are mistrustful of groups except for those organized online. They are often more comfortable communicating via a computer screen than face-to-face and are used to having hundreds of choices when it comes to entertainment and most other aspects of their life, so they don't understand why they should be forced to choose between just two political parties.

They see themselves as unique and special and don't think they can be pigeonholed in just one political party. They do not like party labels and are similar to the NPR Republicans in their social libertarianism and fiscal conservatism, especially since they haven't yet experienced the need for many government programs except for student loans and education aid, which they strongly favor.

They were captivated by the transformational nature of Barack Obama's 2008 candidacy and voted for him in large numbers, but they are disenchanted with the partisan gridlock in Washington and Obama's inability to bring about the fundamental changes to the political system that he promised in the campaign. They are also far less reliable than other groups when it comes to turning out to vote, as was evidenced in the 2010 election.

Finally, the largest and most important of the Independent/Swing voting groups, aggressively pursued by both parties, are the suburban and exurban voters. I call these voters the *Starbucks Moms and Dads* because they rarely live very far from a strip mall with a Starbucks and they usually have children. Sue Thomas and Michael Sciulla of Virginia are a Starbucks Mom and Dad.

These are the real power voters—up for grabs and deciding elections in every region of the country. They too tend to be skeptical of big government, socially moderate, concerned about education and national security. In 2006, suburban voters went 50 percent in favor of Democrats and 48 percent for Republicans, but in 2010 only 42 percent of suburban voters chose Democrats versus 55 percent who voted Republican.[10]

There can be overlap among these groups, and they do not represent the only Independent voters in the country, but they do comprise the majority of swing voters that really matter. Academics often use the term *swing voters* to refer to persuadable voters who haven't made up their minds a few months or weeks before the election and show up in pre-election polling as undecided voters. But I am focusing here not on the voters who might predict or explain the outcome of a single election, but on the longer-term national implications of voters who are known by academics as *party switchers* or *floating* voters.[11] These voters swing back and forth between parties from election to election and often split their tickets voting for candidates from both parties and, in so doing, decide election outcomes.

In addition, party affiliation is an ever-moving target because party allegiances and preferences shift constantly. Voters' views change over time and are affected by national events. Someone may start voting for one party more frequently but not change their original voter affiliation. Or they may register as a Democrat in the South to vote in local and state primaries where the candidates are more plentiful but vote Republican in national races. Or they may call themselves an Independent but consistently vote for one party over another. Because of all these factors, some academics who study voting behavior insist the number of true Independent voters is smaller than 40 percent.

The crucial Independent voters that I am describing here are ideologically "middle of the road" or centrist, and their views reflect the feelings of more Americans on national issues than either liberals or conservatives. They tend to be fiscally conservative, more skeptical about government, and more concerned about deficits, which is more in line with

Republican Party positions. But they do believe some government pro-grams are important and agree more with the positions of the Democratic Party on issues like abortion and gay rights. They want the government to stay out of their personal lives and they want Congress and the president to spend their tax dollars wisely and conduct foreign policy and defense in a way that will protect American interests and keep the country safe.[12]

In several Pew Research Center polls over the past few years, more Independents say the Republican Party comes closer to their views on foreign policy, national security, and economic issues. But they say the Democratic Party is closer to their views on social issues.

> In this regard, more than twice as many Independent voters than Republican voters favor allowing gays and lesbians to marry legally (45% vs. 20%).[13]

> As a group, independents remain difficult to pin down. They are clearly left-of-center when it comes to religiosity and issues of moral values—independents' views on homosexuality, gender roles, censorship and the role of religion in politics are clearly closer to those of Democrats than Republicans. At the same time, their views on broader economic issues have taken a turn to the right. In particular, they are now more conservative on questions relating to the role of government in providing a social safety net and the government's overall effectiveness and scope.[14]

They are concerned about the federal deficit, government spending, and the American economy. They are extremely angry with Congress, frustrated with the way things are going in Washington, and mistrustful of a Democratic expansion of government, and these feelings determined their votes in the 2010 election.[15]

There is no doubt this ever-growing bloc of voters is significant. But calculating its size is not an exact science. In twenty-nine states, citizens register to vote by party and the number of unaffiliated voters in those states is a matter of public record. But in the other twenty-one states—including Alabama, Illinois, Indiana, Georgia, Michigan, Minnesota, Missouri, Ohio, South Carolina, Virginia, and Wisconsin—voters do not have to specify their party affiliation when registering, which can make calculating party affiliation in these states a bit tricky. These are, however, the states where Independents can participate in the primary process.

In every New England state, Independents—or what most voter registration offices call unaffiliated or undeclared voters—outnumber Republicans or Democrats. In Massachusetts, more than half of all the voters are Independents.[16] In Maine, where Eliot Cutler, the Independent candidate for governor, narrowly lost the 2010 election by less than 2 percent to Republican Paul LePage, Independents number about 35 percent of the electorate.[17] In Connecticut and New Hampshire, more than 40 percent of the voters identify as unaffiliated.[18] In Rhode Island, where former moderate Republican Senator Lincoln Chafee left the Republican Party in 2007 and successfully ran as an Independent candidate for governor of the state in 2010, about 48 percent of the voters are Independents.

But it's far more than just a New England phenomenon. In Alaska, more than 53 percent of the state's voters are registered as "nonpartisan or undeclared."[19] In New Jersey, more than 46 percent of the voters are undeclared, more than twice as many as are registered Republicans, and significantly more than are registered as Democrats,[20] making it clear that GOP governor Chris Christie's election in 2009, the first time a Republican had won statewide office in New Jersey in a dozen years, was thanks to his winning the state's Independent vote.

There has also been a growth of Independent voters in many other states, including Iowa and Colorado, where they outnumber both Democrats and Republicans. About 30 percent of the voters in Arizona are Independents, a 15 percent increase between 2008 and 2010.[21]

Independent voters represent the largest and most important group of voters in this country. They are not part of a temporary phenomenon or fad, they have been around for decades, and their numbers are growing. They are angry and frustrated over the problems of the political system, but they don't march on the capitol or show up screaming at congressional town hall meetings and so don't get the attention they deserve.

Despite their critical role in election outcomes, these Independents have little to say about whom the parties select to run for office. That's because in half the states in the country, the primary process is closed to them. An electoral system that all Americans pay for with their tax dollars is run solely by and for the two major political parties. Which means the American electoral system is not fully democratic. In many states, Independent voters are shut out from the start. Polls show that Independent voters are usually less satisfied with their choice of candidates than Republicans and Democrats and frequently say they are voting against something or someone rather than for someone.[22] As a result, Independents are typically less engaged in the political system.

But in general elections, politicians need the Independent voters to win. Candidates seek the votes of Independents and woo them with attention in November. But once they have their victory or—to use the vernacular—get what they want, Independent voters are forgotten as quickly as a one-night stand. That has left them feeling a bit used—disconnected and disillusioned with a government they do not believe truly represents them. Independent voters feel ignored, fed up, and shut out of the system.

Once candidates are in office and looking toward their next reelection, Democratic and Republican office holders are beholden to their base supporters, the special interests who donate time and money to them and the parties that control both candidate selection and the agenda.

Independent voters are getting tired of being taken for granted. They're tired of partisan wrangling, which all too often results in either gridlock and a lack of action on the most important issues the nation faces, or unsatisfactory, extreme legislative outcomes, pushed through by one political party with little input from the other.

Independent voters have determined the outcome and sought change in each of the last three national elections, but they haven't yet seen the change they are looking for. Recent polls show that most Americans do not believe the country is on the right track and confidence in government is at an all-time low.[23] That feeling is even stronger among the ever-growing group of Independent voters, especially those I spoke with in focus groups around the country.

Many think a third- or multi-party system might work better in representing a wider number of political views. They believe campaign contributions from special interests and lobbyists and political ads control and pervert the system, making it extremely hard for the average citizen to make his voice and views heard. They believe most politicians are simply interested in getting reelected and will do whatever it takes to win. These voters also think politicians consider their own reelection more important than the average person's problems.

Not surprisingly, polls taken after the 2010 election showed that Independents believed both parties should move toward the center and that President Obama should work harder to find common ground with Republicans.[24] They believe governing is about compromise, and they want elected officials to work with the other side to pass good legislation on important issues.

But even as the number of voters who consider themselves at the ideological center of American political opinion continues to grow, the number of moderates in both parties in Congress, the ones needed to achieve compromise, shrinks with every passing election, and the political parties become ever more extreme.

Political scientist Morris Fiorina of Stanford has written about this in several books—*Culture War? The Myth of a Polarized America* and *Disconnect: The Breakdown of Representation in American Politics.* "There is little doubt that the political class in the United States is significantly more polarized today than it was a generation ago. But a close examination of the general population finds little or no sign of a comparable increase in polarization," writes Fiorina.[25] "In both red and blue states a solid majority of voters see themselves as positioned between two relatively extreme parties."[26]

Most Americans are in the center and actually agree on a great deal. We're not so deeply divided a nation as either the two parties or the political pundits would have us believe. They just need to listen to the Independent voters. These voters at the ideological center of national political thought represent the way forward for the political parties and a new way of thinking and trying to solve problems. These voters want compromise and common sense, and they want Republicans and Democrats to work together on centrist solutions to the most difficult issues we face as a nation. Only by listening to these voters and reforming the political process can we revitalize our politics and our country.

2

A Brief History of the "Passionate Center" and How the Two Parties Lost It

I was no party man myself, and the first wish of my heart was, if parties did exist, to reconcile them.

—GEORGE WASHINGTON, LETTER TO
THOMAS JEFFERSON, JULY 6, 1796

T HE NATION'S FIRST PRESIDENT was the only one in our history not to be a member of a political party. George Washington was extremely skeptical and critical about political parties. In Washington's farewell address written to "The People of the United States" in 1796 to announce that he would not seek a third term in office and published in newspapers around the country, Washington warned against the dangers of political parties.

> They serve to organize faction, to give it an artificial and extraordinary force; to put, in the place of the delegated will of the nation, the will of a party, often a small but artful and enterprising minority of the community; and, according to the alternate triumphs of different parties, to make the public administration the mirror of the ill-concerted and incongruous projects of faction, rather than the organ of consistent and wholesome plans digested by common counsels, and modified by mutual interests.

Washington believed political parties would become

> potent engines, by which cunning, ambitious, and unprincipled
> men will be enabled to subvert the power of the people, and to usurp
> for themselves the reins of government; destroying afterwards the
> very engines, which have lifted them to unjust dominion . . . the
> common and continual mischiefs of the spirit of party are sufficient
> to make it the interest and duty of a wise people to discourage and
> restrain it.[1]

Unfortunately, Washington's advice went unheeded. The U.S. Constitution does not explicitly mention political parties, but our nation's two-party system began to develop shortly after its adoption with the creation of the Federalist Party, founded by Alexander Hamilton, and the Democratic-Republican Party, founded by Thomas Jefferson and James Madison.

Political parties continued to grow in their power and control over the reins of government. In the 1830s, the party that has become today's Democratic Party was formed out of the Democratic-Republican Party to support the populist policies of Andrew Jackson, the first Democratic president. Around the same time, the opposition Whig Party was formed, and its chief supporters were Henry Clay and Daniel Webster. The Whig Party evolved into the anti-slavery Republican Party in 1854 and elected its first president, Abraham Lincoln, in 1860. Since the mid-nineteenth century, the Democratic and Republican parties have dominated our national politics, controlling Congress and winning every presidential election.

There have, however, been several noteworthy third-party and Independent political campaigns for president, reflecting dissatisfaction with the two existing political parties. In 1912, Theodore Roosevelt mounted the most successful Independent presidential campaign of the modern era. Concerned with the conservative direction of the Republican Party, he founded the Progressive "Bull Moose" Party to run for a third term as president on a moderate, anti-corruption platform including greater rights for women, labor unions, and environmental stewardship. Roosevelt finished second in the election, to Democrat Woodrow Wilson, and won more than 27 percent of the vote and half a dozen states, including Pennsylvania, California, and Michigan.

In 1924, U.S. Senator Robert La Follette of Wisconsin formed his own Progressive Party and ran for president as a populist candidate on an antiwar platform that called for government ownership of railroads and electric utilities, the outlawing of child labor, stronger laws to help labor unions, and more protection of civil liberties. He won the strong support of labor unions and former Bull Moose Progressives and 17 percent of the popular vote, winning Wisconsin and coming in second in eleven Western states.

In the years since, there have been several significant Independent presidential candidacies. In 1968, opposition to the Democratic Party's policies on civil rights spurred Democratic Alabama Governor George Wallace to run as the conservative American Independent Party candidate. Wallace was a pro-segregationist populist who won five Southern states and 14 percent of the national vote.

Ten years later, liberal GOP congressman John Anderson, who first ran for the Republican Party nomination that year but then decided to mount an Independent campaign, won 7 percent of the popular vote.

The most recent, quixotic, and self-indulgent example is perennial candidate Ralph Nader, who in 1996 ran as a Green Party candidate for president, qualifying for the ballot in only about half the states and winning less than 1 percent of the vote. In 2000, he ran again as the Green Party's candidate. He won just under 3 percent of the vote, but many consider him a spoiler and blame him for Al Gore's defeat because of the percentage of the vote Nader won in several key swing states like Florida and New Hampshire. In 2004 and 2008, Nader ran as an Independent candidate for president, winning only about one-half of 1 percent of the popular vote.

The most successful and significant contemporary Independent presidential candidacy was that of Texas billionaire H. Ross Perot. In 1992, during another time of economic instability with high voter anxiety and anger, Perot campaigned on reducing the deficit, reining in government spending, and balancing the budget—all issues that were of great concern to Independent voters.

Anxiety over federal spending and the deficit as a symbol of what was wrong in Washington was so high and Perot's message resonated so well, especially with Independent voters, that in the summer of 1992, Perot led both President George Bush and Bill Clinton in national polls. However, in July, Perot unexpectedly dropped out of the race and then in October just as unexpectedly reentered the campaign. Despite this erratic behavior and his personal idiosyncrasies, Perot obviously tapped into something significant and was able to win about 19 percent of the vote, an indication of how seriously unhappy many American voters were with the two parties. Former President Bill Clinton, appearing at a Washington event focusing on the national debt in 2010 said that Perot's candidacy had "highlighted the problems of the deficit" and overall "had a very positive effect" on the 1992 campaign. In 1996, Perot ran again, this time as the candidate of the Reform Party, and won only 8 percent of the vote, although he still enjoyed the support of many Independent voters.

The Perot voters were angry about the deficit and felt it was "a symbol of the mess in Washington." Moreover, they were "deeply anti-political" held "deep antipathy to Congress," and were "anti-government and anti-establishment," according to a Democratic Leadership Council study conducted at the time by Democratic pollster Stan Greenberg.[2]

Driven by the deep recession, the nation's economic situation, and massive deficit, the Tea Party followers have focused on many of the fiscal issues that were at the heart of "Perotism." But there are significant differences between the Perot voters and Tea Partiers. Unlike Perot voters, who realized that tax increases might be necessary to deal with the deficit and other fiscal issues, Tea Party members oppose tax increases at all costs and focus only on cutting government. The demographics of Perot supporters and Tea Partiers are different as well. Tea Party supporters are overwhelmingly upper-middle-class white Republicans who are trying to push the GOP to the right and defeat Republicans deemed insufficiently committed to the cause. Perot voters were consciously breaking with both the Republican and Democratic parties and were far less conservative, more socially libertarian, less wealthy, and significantly younger than Tea Partiers. Sixty-three percent of Perot voters were ages eighteen to forty-four, and more than two in three called themselves Democrats or Independents. More than half the Perot supporters described themselves as moderate, about a quarter said they were conservative, and 20 percent considered themselves to be liberal.[3] A CBS–*New York Times* survey found 75 percent of those who identified as Tea Party activists considered themselves conservative and were forty-five or older, and more than half had incomes of fifty thousand dollars or more.[4]

One thing the Perot candidacy proved is that it is possible for an Independent candidate to mount a serious campaign for president and to motivate the large number of Independent voters in this country. However, the hurdles that exist in our current two-party system make such a run almost impossible for anyone except candidates wealthy enough to self-finance their own campaigns.

Independent candidates have had slightly more luck running for other offices, especially three high-profile governors in the 1990s. Lowell Weicker of Connecticut was a liberal Republican who served in the U.S. Senate for eighteen years. Ironically, he lost his bid for a fourth term in the Senate in 1988 to Democrat Joseph Lieberman, who was to Weicker's right on many issues. Lieberman would be forced to mount his own Independent campaign to retain the seat in 2006 when he failed to get the Democratic Party's nomination.

Weicker decided to run for governor in 1990, at a time when the state was facing serious budget problems. He created his own party, called "A Connecticut Party," and stressed government reform and fiscal responsibility. Weicker won the election but had to come up with a plan for getting the state out of its more than $2 billion deficit. He took on both parties and instituted the state's first income tax, becoming wildly unpopular as a result. But Weicker, who had pledged to serve only one term, managed to balance the state's budget in just two years.

In 1994, Angus King, the owner of an energy conservation business, a television host, and former Democrat, was elected the Independent governor of Maine, and in 1998 he was resoundingly reelected. Maine has a tradition of independence. In 1974, James Longley had been elected governor as an Independent and Ross Perot received 30 percent of the vote here—his highest vote total in the country. The state is also known for its two senators—Olympia Snowe and Susan Collins—the most moderate Republicans in the Senate.

Undoubtedly the most flamboyant of the Independent governors of the '90s was Minnesota's Jesse Ventura, the former professional wrestler, actor, and radio talk show host. Ventura was elected in 1998 as the candidate of the Reform Party. Ventura promised to shake up the system but found working inside it frustrating and did not run for reelection.

In the U.S. Senate, moderate Jim Jeffords of Vermont left the Republican Party to become an Independent in 2001, an especially momentous move because at the time the Senate was split 50–50 between the Republicans and Democrats. Jeffords agreed to caucus with the Democrats in exchange for being appointed chairman of the Environment and Public Works Committee.

The other Independent from Vermont is Bernie Sanders, a Socialist who is to the left of the Democratic Party but organizes and usually votes with them. He served in the U.S. House of Representatives for sixteen years and won Jeffords's Senate seat when he retired in 2006.

That was also the year that Connecticut's Lieberman successfully ran on the "Connecticut for Lieberman" party ticket for the Senate after losing the Democratic primary to the more liberal, antiwar candidate Ned Lamont, primarily over Lieberman's support of the war in Iraq. Lieberman was not particularly popular with Democrats before the move, and although he caucuses with them, he also votes with Republicans. He endorsed John McCain for president and spoke at the 2010 Republican convention. Undoubtedly realizing he would face an uphill battle getting reelected as an Independent, Lieberman announced he would not run for reelection in 2012.

In 2010, Eliot Cutler narrowly lost an Independent bid for governor of Maine, and Rhode Island Independent Lincoln Chafee, a former moderate Republican senator, was elected governor.

The highest-profile Independent politician in the country is New York City Mayor Michael Bloomberg, who has been mentioned as a potential presidential candidate but has consistently denied any interest in running for president. The billionaire businessman was a Democrat who switched his registration in 2001 to Republican to run for mayor. He won reelection in 2005 but left the Republican Party in 2007 to become an Independent. He successfully pushed for a change in the city's term-limits law to allow him to run for a third term in 2009 but spent more than $85 million, more of his own money than any other person in U.S. history, to win. Adding up all three of his races, Bloomberg has spent more than $250 million of his own money on his mayoral campaigns, according to *The New York Times*.[5]

Following Perot's presidential campaigns, Independents have not had any real success either in mounting a national campaign or in unifying and mobilizing the political center.

In December 1995, at the height of the government shutdown brought on by the showdown between President Bill Clinton and House Speaker Newt Gingrich's Republican Congress over the budget, a group of independent-minded politicians and their supporters held a conference in Minneapolis called the Future of Independent Politics. It didn't get much national attention, especially given what else was going on at the time, but one of its programs, called "Locating the New Political Center in America," was televised on C-SPAN. It featured presentations by Democrat Paul Tsongas, who had unsuccessfully challenged Clinton for the Democratic nomination in 1992, stressing the issue of deficit reduction and budgetary reform, and former Colorado Governor Richard "Dick" Lamm.[6]

The group had come up with an eleven-point plan focused on balancing the federal budget that was endorsed by a group of centrist politicians including Tsongas, Lamm, Weicker, and former Colorado Senator Gary Hart. Their stated goal was to "define a political center around which all Americans can unite."

Tsongas, who had previously served in the House and Senate from Massachusetts, was also a cofounder of the Concord Coalition, a nonpartisan group whose mission is to stress the dangers of federal budget deficits and promote entitlement reform.

"We believe there is a centrist instinct in the American people. . . . Ross Perot plugged into that in 1992," Tsongas told those assembled in Minneapolis. He decried the loss of Senate centrists like Republicans Nancy Landon Kassebaum, Mark Hatfield, Alan Simpson and Democrats Sam Nunn, David Pryor, David Boren, and Bill Bradley, who he said were "the people who make it work."

While the parties were getting more extreme, Tsongas said, "what's happening in the country is the opposite." Tsongas described a "passionate center" of Americans who believed in being fiscally responsible, socially tolerant, in favor of environmental protection, and who favored campaign finance reform.

"Cynicism is part of the system," said Tsongas. He said the Democrats didn't really believe in balancing the budget, and what the Republicans were most interested in was a tax cut for the wealthy and draconian budget cuts to pay for it.

It's amazing how little fundamental change there has been in American politics since Tsongas made that presentation in 1995.

Tsongas was always thoughtful and honest, perhaps too much so to be a successful national politician. His '92 presidential campaign had been about stressing hard truths like the budget deficit and the need for entitlement reform. He won the New Hampshire primary and several others and though he lost the nomination fight to Bill Clinton, he emerged from the contest a national figure of greater stature.

Tsongas had fought non-Hodgkin's lymphoma before running for president and died just a year after his appearance in Minneapolis. In 1996, Lamm, who said what was needed was a "substantial rethinking of all American public policy" unsuccessfully challenged Ross Perot for the presidential nomination of the Reform Party.

Tsongas and Lamm's effort to create a political reform movement was not successful, but there has been a major national party realignment, resulting in a significant increase in the number of swing voters in the country. The American National Election Study of voter behavior in presidential elections is a fascinating record of the behavior and growth of swing and ticket-splitting voters in the United States. In 1972, a year in which Democratic presidential candidate George McGovern carried only one state, 25 percent of those surveyed voted for a Republican for president and a Democrat for Congress. In both 1980 and 1984, when the "Reagan Democrat" voter was created, 20 percent of voters cast their ballot for Ronald Reagan and a Democrat for Congress.[7]

Since the 1960s, the two political parties have been undergoing both a demographic and geographic realignment, which has contributed to the increase in the number of Independents. Democratic Party support for civil rights legislation, which brought African American voters into the Democratic fold, drove many staunch Democratic Southern white voters out of the party. In addition to the Democratic Party's support for civil rights, its opposition to the Vietnam War, identification with protest movements, and positions on social issues, including abortion rights, feminism, and gay rights, chipped away at support for the Democrats among working- and middle-class, middle-American voters around the country, especially men. The Democrats were seen as the party that appealed to the urban poor and minorities, union members and the well-educated elite, but not ordinary people.

The country's racial problems, Vietnam, Watergate, and a recession shook Americans' belief in their institutions and even the American way of life. Ronald Reagan, with his message of optimism and strength, successfully renewed their faith in the country and the power of America. The voters who came to be known as the Reagan Democrats—white blue-collar and largely male middle-class voters—had grown alienated from the Democratic Party because of civil rights, national security, patriotism, and values issues and Reagan capitalized on this.

Bill Clinton was able to win their votes because they did not see him as a "pointy-headed liberal" the way they did many of the party's other presidential candidates, and he could reach out to this group of voters and speak to them in a language they could understand about religion and issues they cared about. Bill Clinton brought many of the Reagan Democrats home and was able to attract Independent and even some Republican votes. In 1996, the number of voters who cast their ballot for a Republican for president and a Democrat for Congress fell to only 4 percent—its lowest level since the NES survey began in 1952.[8] Conversely, the number of people who voted for Clinton and a Republican for Congress that year was 13 percent, the highest level of split-ticket voting for a Democrat for president and Republicans for congress in the history of the survey.

But the liberal elite of the Democratic Party never fully embraced Bill Clinton or his budget compromises with Republicans and the tensions between moderate and liberal Democrats that had existed for 25 years were intensified during the Clinton years and showcased in the 2008 Democratic primaries in the fight between Hillary Clinton and Barack Obama. When Obama made his remark about small-town voters in Pennsylvania and the Midwest being bitter and clinging to "guns and religion" and Michelle Obama said in a campaign speech, "For the first time in my adult lifetime, I'm really proud of my country," the McCain campaign jumped on the remarks and wouldn't let voters forget them. The Republicans knew how important swing and Reagan Democrat voters would be to the outcome of the election and how vulnerable the Democratic Party was on the issue of patriotism. Ultimately however, the failed Bush presidency and the war it created combined with an economy teetering on the brink of collapse trumped whatever misgivings enough Reagan Democrats had to convince some of them to vote for Barack Obama.

The Republican Party's emphasis on social and racial issues to win votes started with Barry Goldwater's candidacy in 1964 and escalated in 1968 with Richard Nixon's "Southern strategy," emphasizing "law and order" and appealing to rural white Southerners who had previously been solid Democratic voters. The Republicans exploited the racial and social divisions within the nation, and the GOP has attempted to use issues of race, values, and patriotism against Democratic candidates ever since.

In the years following the Civil War and into the first half of the twentieth century, the South was solidly Democratic, with Southern voters famously having the reputation that they would vote for a "yellow dog" before they would vote for a Republican. But the South has swung to become a solidly Republican region and now represents the most significant base of support for the Republican Party. About 40 percent of the GOP's supporters are now concentrated in the South, and Republicans are the majority in the congressional delegations of every Southern state. Most Democratic members of Congress from the South are either minority or urban representatives. Virginia, Florida, and North Carolina remain swing states, won by Barack Obama in 2008, but he will undoubtedly have to fight hard to carry them again in 2012.

In the 1980s and '90s, the Republican strategy shifted from overtly focusing on race to social and religious issues, which won it voters in the South and Midwest, especially among Evangelical Christians, but lost the party support in other parts of the country. Of the ten most religious states in the country, only one, North Carolina, voted for Barack Obama. And among the ten least religious states, only Alaska voted for John McCain.[9]

There are now just a handful of Republicans in Congress from New England and the Northeast, not only because of the decline in Republican Party membership in the region but also because of GOP primary challenges from the right, which have eliminated moderate candidates who can appeal to general election voters. Many moderate and libertarian-leaning Republican voters, turned off by the party's alignment with the religious right, its emphasis on conservative moral and social issues, its fiscal irresponsibility in the past decade and by the administration of George W. Bush, have become Independents who voted for Barack Obama in 2008.

In addition, the Republican Party is facing significant demographic challenges that could further reduce its numbers and drive up the number of Independent voters. It is predominantly composed of non-Hispanic whites (88 percent) compared with just 56 percent of the Democratic Party.[10] The GOP is also largely male, and the average Republican voter is almost fifty years old compared with the average Democrat, who is around forty-seven, and the average Independent, who is about forty-four.[11] The Republicans have moved to the right as they try to woo their older, conservative religious supporters who predominate in the South and focus on social issues that appeal to them, but this has turned off more traditional, moderate Republicans and Independents.

"The Republicans have widened their tent—but in widening it, they've also caused people to walk out of it," says former moderate Republican Congressman Jim Leach. "The party of the country club is in many ways more a party of the people, but a Goldwater Republican today would be the most liberal of Republicans."

That's exactly how the libertarian Goldwater described himself in the 1980s when he said he was one of "the new liberals of the Republican Party." The man known as "Mr. Conservative," whose 1964 campaign laid the groundwork for the election of Ronald Reagan and the development of the modern GOP, was later in his life harshly critical of the religious right's "frightening influence" on the party and spoke out in favor of abortion and gay rights.

Tom Davis is a former congressman from northern Virginia, first elected to the House of Representatives in 1994, who served for fourteen years before leaving Congress in 2008. When I asked Davis, a moderate Republican, if he regrets what is happening to the GOP, he said if the

Republican Party wants to be "a national party instead of a regional club with a list of requirements," they should focus on economic issues and forget the social agenda. "It's become the rural party of dumb white guys," he said.

The social issues that hurt the Democratic Party with many white middle-class voters in the past no longer seem so important to most voters, especially at a time of economic insecurity when fiscal issues are front and center. Much of the country has evolved over the past few decades and has moved to the center on many social positions, especially on issues like gay rights. It would appear the nation has caught up with the Democratic Party's positions on these things, and the social conservatism that dominated the national political debate for the past several decades is on the wane. The Pew Research Center has documented that over the past twenty years, the number of voters who support traditional social and family values has been trending downward.[12] In 2008, Obama managed to convince voters to put aside racial and values concerns and vote Democratic because the real problems facing this country were so great.

In fact, the very issues and positions that had been an electoral liability for the Democrats for the past forty years made the nomination and election of Barack Obama possible and became an advantage for the Democrats with new young and minority voters, who are the antithesis of Reagan Democrats. The Republicans tried constantly to focus on the old tired issues of race, values, and patriotism in 2008, but they were using an outdated playbook. Obama took pains throughout the campaign and on election night to make it clear he was elected not by a series of groups but by a majority of Americans and that he would be the president of all of America. Relying on the traditional Democratic base of union members, women, minorities, and urban voters, Obama successfully added to their support by building a new majority coalition, winning much larger percentages of the Latino and under-thirty vote than George Bush did in 2004, increasing African American turnout, and decisively winning college-educated urban *and* suburban voters.[13]

But Obama and the Democrats' honeymoon with Independent voters was short lived. Nervous about their own economic situations, these voters opposed the growth of government spending under the Democrats and massive deficits. And instead of ushering in a new kind of politics, during Barack Obama's first years as president, the situation between Republicans and Democrats was just as politically polarized as ever.

Even though most Americans are focused on the nation's economic future and moving the country forward, the two parties don't seem to have gotten the message and don't appear willing to make the significant compromises necessary to make that happen. They are still playing to their base and can't make the tough decisions—whether it's cuts in military spending, tax increases, and elimination of corporate tax loopholes for the Republicans or significant entitlement reform for the Democrats.

The rise of the Tea Party on the right has manifested the anger over government failures and spending and has received an enormous amount of attention from the media and the Republican Party. Tea Party supporters were a major force in the 2010 election and will undoubtedly continue to be influential in 2012 GOP primaries. However, they will be far less important in the 2012 general election, when turnout is higher and their numbers are diluted.

But the Tea Party is not the only group looking for change. A number of other independent groups that want to promote civility, bipartisanship, and solutions to the nation's problems have been springing up in recent years, more evidence that Independents feel left out of the political system and want something different.

The Coffee Party is the brainchild of Annabel Park, a soft-spoken but very determined forty-two-year-old documentary filmmaker who volunteered for the Obama campaign and, like so many Americans, was fed up not only with what is happening in Washington but also with the rhetoric coming out of the Tea Party movement. So she posted a notice on her Facebook page in early 2010—let's start our own movement and call it the Coffee Party.

Park and the Coffee Party took a page out of the Obama presidential campaign playbook and used the web and social media to organize their movement. There are Democrats, Republicans, and plenty of Independents in the group, and Park says what unites them is frustration with the inability of the Democrats to get things done, the Republicans' obstructionism, and the heightened political polarization in Washington.

We will give voice to Americans who want to see cooperation in government. We recognize that the federal government is not the enemy of the people, but the expression of our collective will, and that we must participate in the democratic process in order to address the challenges that we face as Americans. As voters and grassroots volunteers, we will support leaders who work toward positive solutions, and hold accountable those who obstruct them.[14]

Park says while her group is very different from the Tea Partiers, what both groups have in common is dissatisfaction with the seeming inability of government to deal with important problems. "Something's got to change. There's a consensus that our process is broken down."

IndependentVoting.org is a group pushing for structural election reform like open primaries and a more fair redistricting process to open up the electoral system to Independents and third-party candidates.

The organization of this sort that has gotten the most national attention is probably No Labels, launched with much fanfare in New York City in December 2010 at an event that featured Evan Bayh, David Gergen, MSNBC's Joe Scarborough, Michael Bloomberg, Charlie Crist, Mike Castle, and many others. No Labels wants to promote centrism and bipartisanship and support politicians who practice those principles. No Labels has set a goal of recruiting 1 million members around the country by 2012, organizing chapters in all 435 congressional districts, setting up 150 chapters on college campuses, establishing a rating system to hold elected officials accountable for their actions, monitoring them for bipartisan behavior, raising money for its own political action committee, and supporting candidates who are in line with the No Labels bipartisan mission.[15]

At a time of extreme party polarization and political dysfunction when the two political parties seem to offer less and less of value, the rise of groups like the Coffee Party and No Labels is one small hopeful sign for the Independent voters that maybe they can have a greater voice in the political process and things can change. The heavy lifting still has to be done by the two major political parties, since they control the levers of government. There are so many things wrong with the system and so much that needs to change for it to work better. Since the Republicans and Democrats don't seem to be willing or able to make the changes that are needed, it's going to be up to the Independent voters in the "passionate center" to register their opposition to the status quo and push for a transformation of our political system.

3

Our Broken Political System—"Ridiculous and Embarrassing"

A long habit of not thinking a thing wrong, gives it a superficial appearance of being right, and raises at first a formidable outcry in defense of custom.

—THOMAS PAINE

FORMER SENATOR EVAN BAYH, the moderate Indiana Democrat who left Congress in 2010, has been one of the most outspoken critics of what he calls our "dysfunctional" political system. "The political process is not delivering the outcome that most Americans want. . . . There's no question our democracy is not working as it should.

"It's going to take all of us, moderates and pragmatists in both parties, standing up and saying 'enough.' Americans want action. We need people that are going to stand for reform of the process. The public needs to stand up and insist upon it. We need raging moderates. I think the public is ahead of the political class on this," says Bayh.

Jim Leach, the former fifteen-term Republican member of Congress from Iowa who was defeated for reelection in 2006, actually fears for the future of our democracy. Leach endorsed Barack Obama for president, and now heads the National Endowment for the Humanities. On his lapel he frequently wears a pin bearing the word CIVILITY. In March 2010, almost a year before the attack on U.S. Representative Gabrielle

Giffords in Tucson, he gave a speech at New York University titled "Civility in a Fractured Society." In that speech, he bemoaned what has happened to political discourse in this country. "Stirring anger and playing on the irrational fears of citizens inflames hate. When coupled with character assassination, polarizing rhetoric can exacerbate intolerance and perhaps impel violence."[1]

Many politicians and political activists think of politics as a sport with winners and losers. "The public must be on guard and prepared to throw flags when politicians overstep the bounds of fairness and decency. As athletes compete to win, they learn to respect their opponents. Is it asking too much for candidates and their supporters to do the same?" asked Leach.

Ridiculous and *embarrassing* are two words frequently used by Independent voters to describe many of our political leaders and their antics. More than half of those questioned in a recent Pew Research study said the two political parties have not done a good job of addressing the problems facing this nation.[2] More than three quarters of Independent voters are dissatisfied with the way things are going in this country, and their approval of Congress is even worse.[3] The public is especially skeptical about government's ability to solve important problems. Just 22 percent say they trust the federal government to do what is right most of the time, among the lowest such measures in half a century.[4]

Twenty years ago, *Washington Post* columnist and Brookings Institution Senior Fellow E. J. Dionne wrote a book called *Why Americans Hate Politics*, in which he said, "Because of the particular myopias of left and right, American politics came to be mired in a series of narrow ideological battles at a time when much larger issues were at stake. . . . Thus when Americans say that politics has nothing to do with what really matters, they are largely right.

"Responsive mainly to the needs of their various constituencies, liberalism and conservatism *prevent* the nation from settling the questions that most trouble it. On issue after issue, there is consensus on where the country should move or at least on what we should be arguing about;

liberalism and conservatism make it impossible for that consensus to express itself," wrote Dionne.[5]

Sadly, very little has changed since *Why Americans Hate Politics* was published. In fact, the situation is worse now, and there are more Independents expressing their dissatisfaction with the system.

The public's patience seems nearly exhausted. What follows is part of a response to a column about health reform that I wrote for *U.S. News and World Report* in 2010 from a reader who identified himself as Larry from California.

> Republican vs. Democrat—does it really matter? If anyone votes for "ANY" incumbent you are just asking for more of the same. "We the people" need to make a "No Incumbent" stance for the next six years and cycle every one of them out of office. Go back a few years to when the Republicans held the House and Senate, they spent money like a bunch of drunk sailors. And guess what—a lot of the same Republicans are still there. If we do not hold OUR representatives accountable then this is our fault, no one else's. VOTE NO TO INCUMBENTS IN 2010, 2012, & 2014[6]

And yet, the political parties don't seem able to respond and aren't making the substantive changes that would improve both our politics and our government. Both parties are constantly in self-protection mode. Their mission is to win elections by any means possible, and the professional class of political consultants, pollsters, party activists, and special interest groups whose livelihood depends on these politicians is always trying to highlight their differences, driving the parties and political leaders even further to the extreme ends of the political spectrum. In recent years, large amounts of campaign spending by outside groups has also served to weaken party influence, making the parties even more insecure and frantic about their relevance and importance.

Increasingly, the election process is driving the business of governing. During a campaign, candidates and parties appeal to their extreme base and paint the other side as out of touch and wrongheaded, which makes reaching out to them after the election far more difficult.

The American political system is alarmingly bipolar, and the current ideological divide between the two political parties is enormous. As the parties become more ideologically cohesive and extreme, more voters feel left out and fall outside the party structure. But within the parties, ideology matters more than ever.

As Fiorina writes, "Many of today's representatives minimize common ground, deny that there is any acceptable middle ground, and insist that a victory for their side is the only acceptable solution to a problem. Facts give way to ideology."[7]

Democratic and Republican Party politicians and activists who have a stake in perpetuating the existing broken system of struggle and stalemate seem interested only in continually fighting for control and advantage. But Independent voters want the two parties to listen and to work together on compromises that will result in better policy and solutions to the nation's most difficult problems.

The Democratic and Republican Parties and Congress are further apart in ideology and more polarized now than at any time since the end of the nineteenth century. Those elected to Congress are primarily at the ends of the political spectrum and are beholden to their party leaders and supporters. As a result, Congress is held in lower esteem by the public than it has been in a hundred years.[8] Many members of Congress acknowledge the problems and say they feel trapped in the system.

Senator Jim Webb of Virginia is a pro–gun rights, centrist Democrat. He is a graduate of the U.S. Naval Academy and a Vietnam combat veteran who served as Secretary of the Navy in the Reagan Administration. He is fiercely independent and has supported both Republican and Democratic candidates in Virginia. He was an early opponent of military action in Iraq and was narrowly elected to the Senate in 2006, giving the Democrats their majority. After serving one term in the Senate, he announced in 2011 that he would not be running for reelection.

Prior to his announcement, Webb told me in an interview that he had tried to reach across the aisle to solve problems but found it was not always easy. "I'm doing what I can to try to work cooperatively. The Senate is like a hundred scorpions in a jar, and party considerations always seem to win out, sometimes over good policy," Webb told me.

"People want results—they want us to govern. People took a gamble on the Democrats in 2008. They wanted to see people who cared about the problems working people in this country have and could do something about it. There's an enormous frustration out there," said Webb.

An overwhelming 93 percent of Americans have said there is too much partisan fighting between Democrats and Republicans and very little cooperation in Congress, and 84 percent say special interests have too much influence over legislation.[9] Americans believe strongly in the nation's democratic traditions and institutions. Every spring and summer, schoolchildren and families from all over the country make a pilgrimage to Washington, D.C., to visit the national monuments, the White House, and the U.S. Capitol. Foreign visitors also make sure to see the home of American democracy, an inspiration to so many other democracies around the world. But increasingly, although they are still proud of the nation's democratic institutions, Americans feel let down by their elected officials and question the job they are doing carrying out the nation's business.

A big part of the problem is the stranglehold that the two parties have on the political process, driving their move away from the political center and toward the extremes of the political spectrum. *National Journal*, a policy magazine that ranks members of Congress based on their voting records on an ideological scale from the most liberal to the most conservative, determined that the 2010 Congress was the most polarized in the thirty years it has been keeping track.[10] Every Senate Democrat had a more liberal voting record than every Senate Republican. And every Senate Republican was more conservative than every Senate

Democrat. In the House, only five Republicans were rated more liberal than the most conservative House Democrat, and only four Democrats were more conservative than the most liberal Republican. And most of those moderates lost their elections in 2010, making the House even more polarized.

There are a number of reasons for the hyperpartisanship and polarization in Congress that have resulted in a loss of moderate voices.

- The growing influence of special interest lobbyists

- The small number of truly competitive congressional districts, which means that to get elected, most members of the House of Representatives have to worry about keeping only their base supporters happy and not those voters in the middle

- The financial pressure to raise huge sums of campaign cash, which is a big reason to be beholden to party leaders and core supporters as well as to special interest campaign donors

- State election laws that prevent Independents from voting in most primary elections

- An ever more partisan, opinion-driven, and shrill media that rewards the most outrageous and partisan players with airtime and positive coverage while often ignoring those who are working in a bipartisan way to solve problems.

In 2010, Congress passed the Wall Street reform legislation. The much-needed law established standards and supervision to protect the economy and American consumers and investors, provided for an advance warning system on the stability of the economy, created rules on executive compensation and corporate governance, and eliminated the loopholes that led to the economic near collapse in 2008. Despite the obvious need for the legislation, it was almost universally opposed by Republicans. Speaking to Wall Street leaders, who spent an estimated

$1.4 million a day trying to fight and water down the financial reform legislation, President Barack Obama talked about how the political system is weighed down by special interest lobbying and partisan rancor. "We have seen battalions of financial industry lobbyists descending on Capitol Hill, firms spending millions to influence the outcome of this debate. We've seen misleading arguments and attacks that are designed not to improve the bill but to weaken or to kill it. We've seen a bipartisan process buckle under the weight of these withering forces," said Obama. "We've seen business as usual in Washington, but I believe we can and must put this kind of cynical politics aside."[11]

The legislation passed with the votes of only four Republican senators: Scott Brown of Massachusetts, Olympia Snowe and Susan Collins of Maine, and Charles Grassley of Iowa. In the House, only three Republicans voted for the measure—Anh Cao of Louisiana, Mike Castle of Delaware, and Walter Jones of North Carolina—and of this group, only Jones still remains in the House.

"You would think this would be a bipartisan issue," Obama said at the time. "This is the same financial crisis that led to the loss of nearly eight million jobs, the same crisis that cost people their homes, their life savings."[12]

But as Obama said, it was "business as usual," with special interests lobbying heavily and the two parties ultimately failing to work together on the legislation.

The health care reform effort was another example of the inability of Democrats and Republicans to work together on a major national problem. From the beginning, especially in the House, Republicans were shut out of the legislative process, and even though some Republican ideas were ultimately folded into the final legislation, the process had broken down. Neither side trusted the other, and each retreated to its own corner with the Republicans refusing to participate in the final product. By the time the House of Representatives voted on final passage, Congress was completely polarized. Sullen Republicans sat on their side of the chamber while weary but jubilant Democrats cheered and claimed victory. For such a monumental change affecting every American to pass without a single Republican vote says a great deal about the state of our political system. It was another missed opportunity for the two parties to work together to address a major national challenge.

The Republicans used their opposition to the health care reform bill to bludgeon the Democrats in the 2010 election. Had they instead worked together on a bipartisan piece of legislation that could have been stronger and more effective in reducing health care costs, we would have a better health reform law, but the Republicans would have lost a campaign issue. And in the end, that seems to be largely what it's all about for the two parties.

In the same kind of tit-for-tat election blame game, the Democrats attacked the Republican plan to reform and privatize Medicare during a special election in May 2011 in an upstate New York congressional district. The tactic worked, and the Democrats won the solidly Republican House district, which had not been held by a Democrat since the 1960s. Seeking to capitalize on the win and score some political points, the Democratic-controlled Senate held a vote on the Republican budget plan and its Medicare provisions the very next day. The Republican budget was defeated, as was the budget offered by President Obama, which didn't get a single vote. In fact, Senate Democrats voted on four separate budget proposals that day, and not a single Democrat voted for any of them. Congressional Democrats had no budget plan of their own to present. Everything was at stalemate, with each side blaming the other for a refusal to deal responsibly with the nation's fiscal problems.

That same day, former President Bill Clinton spoke to Republican House Budget Chairman Paul Ryan, the author of the Republican budget plan, backstage at a fiscal summit being held in Washington to talk about the national debt. Clinton told Ryan while he was glad the Democrats had won the House seat, he hoped they wouldn't use the victory "as an excuse to do nothing on Medicare"[13] reform and the debt. But all the signs pointed to that being exactly what would happen.

After the 2010 election, a Washington-based group called Third

Way, which promotes centrist solutions to national problems and is a support group for moderate Democrats, conducted a poll of one thousand people who voted for Barack Obama in 2008 but either didn't vote at all or voted Republican in 2010. Forty percent of this group was made up of Independent voters, and a majority of them said too much government spending was a reason for the change. When asked the most important thing they would like to tell the new Republican Congress, responses involving bipartisanship and compromise were the most common answer. Typical responses included such advice as "cooperate with the Democrats to get things done"; "we need to put partisan issues aside and work together"; and "compromise and get our economy moving."[14]

However, a post-election Gallup poll revealed that most voters weren't optimistic it would happen. Just one in five (22 percent) said they expected relations between Republicans and Democrats to improve.[15]

A big part of the problem involves who gets elected to Congress and how. Independent voters are shut out of the primary process in a majority of states in the nation. Primary elections, party caucuses, and conventions that select the candidates who will be on the general election ballot typically draw a very small number of often extreme party activists. The base of the Republican Party and its core supporters—including the religious right, anti-tax, business groups, the NRA, and most recently the Tea Party—have been pushing the GOP to the right for decades. Primary challenges aimed at weeding out politicians not deemed sufficiently pure are increasingly common and serve to force Republican members of Congress who are worried about a potential primary challenge even further to the right.

Arizona Senator John McCain was just one of those who faced a primary challenge from the right in 2010. The idea that the Republican Party's 2008 standard bearer and presidential candidate would be challenged just two years later in his quest for renomination to the Senate is a good illustration of what is going on. McCain did manage to win by moving to the right and disavowing many of his previous positions on issues like immigration reform.

Perhaps the biggest target for conservatives in 2010 was Delaware's Mike Castle, who in 2008 was ranked the least conservative Republican in the House by the Club for Growth, which promotes low taxes and smaller government. A former governor and nine-term House member who was extremely popular in Delaware, where there are more than twice as many Democratic and Independent voters as Republicans, Castle was running for the U.S. Senate seat previously held by Vice President Joe Biden.

Tea Party and other national conservative GOP groups made it clear they didn't care whether they won the general election; they just couldn't stand the thought of seeing Mike Castle elected to the Senate. So they poured millions of dollars into the race and selected Christine O'Donnell as their nominee. O'Donnell defeated Castle in a GOP primary in which fewer than sixty thousand votes were cast and went on to lose the general election by 17 points in a race that Castle probably would have had no trouble winning.

O'Donnell, who was endorsed by Sarah Palin, ran somewhat odd campaign ads on television in which she declared, "I am not a witch," and was an unconventional choice, to say the least. A woman who had never held political office but who had run for the Senate three times— including 2006, when she finished third in the Republican primary— she had defaulted on her mortgage and had no discernible income in 2010, when the Internal Revenue Service filed a lien against her for back taxes.[16] She was accused by a group called CREW, Citizens for Responsibility and Ethics in Washington, of using $20,000 of campaign funds in 2009 and 2010 for personal expenses and the group filed a complaint with the Federal Election Commission on this charge.[17]

"A travesty" is what former New Jersey governor Christine Todd Whitman calls the primary defeat of fellow moderate Republican Castle. "If you're trying to be ideologically pure, you're going to lose elections."

Not that the Tea Partiers and other conservatives who opposed Castle care what Whitman thinks. She's exactly the kind of Republican they are trying to drum out of the party. The author of a book titled *It's My Party Too: The Battle for the Heart of the GOP and the Future of America*,

Whitman told me she is considered "the devil" by "the far right." Whitman has her own political action committee called It's My Party Too (IMP-PAC) to support moderate Republicans, which is allied with pro-choice, environmentalist, and gay rights GOP groups. Whitman says she has never thought about leaving the GOP and considers herself to be a loyal and "traditional Republican" who simply believes that alternative viewpoints should be allowed to be heard within the party.

Another flame-out for Tea Party conservatives and Sarah Palin in 2010 was the challenge to incumbent Alaska Senator Lisa Murkowski, who defeated their candidate by running as a write-in. Her victory over Tea Party candidate Joe Miller has somewhat emboldened and liberated Murkowski from the Republican Party, and she is extremely articulate about her disregard for the far right's tactics.

Murkowski was originally appointed to the Senate seat by her governor father but won it outright two years later in 2004. She voted with the Republican leadership in the Senate "just" 80 percent of the time in the last Congress and was considered too moderate by the Tea Party supporters who backed Miller, an Alaska attorney who defeated her in the Republican primary. Murkowski decided to run as a write-in candidate in the general election and is only the second person in history to successfully mount a write-in campaign for the U.S. Senate. The first was segregationist Strom Thurmond of South Carolina, who was denied the Democratic nomination and successfully ran as a write-in candidate in 1954.

"The decision to run as a write-in was an extraordinarily difficult one for me and my family," Murkowski told me in an interview in early 2011. But she said Mike Castle's defeat in Delaware was one of the things that motivated her decision. "To read the newspapers after my primary and see what was going on in Delaware and it was like reading what was going on in my own primary race."

Not only was there a large influx of out-of-state money from Tea Party supporters in the race, but Murkowski says "personal attacks and out-and-out lies" were used against her. "If they start in Alaska and they go to Delaware and pick us off one by one and if we roll over and accept that—what happens to the Republican Party?" Murkowski wondered. "The whole notion that it would be this small fringe group that would be defining what a Republican is got my dander up."

Murkowski won the general election, getting ten thousand more votes than Miller.[18] But her victory was not certified until the end of December, because of legal challenges by Miller paid for in part by conservative supporters, including Senator Jim DeMint of South Carolina. DeMint created the Senate Conservatives Fund, a political action committee associated with the Tea Party, which raised over $9 million to support conservatives running for the U.S. Senate in 2010.[19]

Almost 54 percent of the voters in Alaska are registered as nonpartisan or undeclared, and many of them voted for her, but Murkowski makes it clear that she has not left the Republican Party. In fact, she says she took great offense at the suggestion by Tea Party supporters that somehow she wasn't a real Republican. "You have this group that is adhering to these hard-and-fast guidelines that make it difficult to achieve any level of compromise. It's not so much what they stand for but how they are so absolute about what they feel has to happen and so insistent that their viewpoint is the only viewpoint."

Murkowski doesn't shrink from criticizing Palin, who has been at odds with the Murkowski family since she challenged and defeated Lisa's father Frank Murkowski for governor in the 2006 GOP Alaskan primary. When Palin resigned from the governorship before her term was completed, Lisa Murkowski was critical of the decision, and when Murkowski announced her write-in campaign, she pointedly said it was time for the state's voters to see "one Republican woman who won't quit on Alaska."

When I asked Murkowski what she thought of Palin and her potential as a national leader, Murkowski didn't mince words about what she perceived to be Palin's intolerance.

I'm looking for a leader in the Republican Party that will unite us and help to build us as a party. I think those candidates that would marginalize us are not good for us. When you move in a direction that says it's my way or the highway—that's not really governing. That borders on dictating. If you don't meet her [Palin's] definition of what an American patriot is, then she says you aren't one.

We are tolerant and respectful of others in this nation, and that's what I think the Tea Party has forgotten. . . . When we become intolerant and bigoted in our approach, then we become less of what this nation was founded on.

There's no doubt the conservative challenge to Murkowski backfired in a big way. Now she says she is free to do what she thinks is right, vote the way a majority of her constituents want her to, and occasionally join a handful of the most moderate Senate Republicans in voting with the Democrats. Murkowski says she also will not hesitate to work with Democrats on legislation for the next six years, since she knows she doesn't owe her seat to the Republican Party.

I don't think whether it's on the right or on the left that purity tests are worth wasting any time on. There is no standard definition of what it means to be a Republican or Democrat. . . . Nobody I have ever met has the monopoly on the good ideas. If you're smart, you look at the good ideas that other people have and you try to build something with the good ideas you have. . . . That's my concept of governing. . . . To suggest that there is only one path denies the greatness of what this country is about—our diversity has defined us as a nation.

That concept is very much at the heart of what makes America special. Unlike Murkowski, most politicians pay lip service to this idea, but they don't really practice it. You're either part of the political team or you're not, and members who try to work with the other side get little support for their efforts.

Another moderate Republican who was challenged from the right in

2010 was Florida Governor Charlie Crist, who didn't wait to be defeated in the primary, but announced that he would instead run as an Independent candidate for the U.S. Senate after facing the prospect of losing the nomination to former Florida House Speaker Marco Rubio. Crist, who came in second in the general election, far behind Rubio but ahead of Democratic candidate Kendrick Meek, told me what he learned from the experience is that it is "very, very hard" to run as an Independent candidate.

On the Democratic side, incumbent congressional Democrats faced only a handful of primary challenges in 2010, and there was almost none of the attempted ideological cleansing that Republicans were engaging in. However, many of the Democrats who were defeated were moderates, significantly reducing the number of centrist Democrats that remain in the House.

Senator Blanche Lambert Lincoln was the highest-profile Democrat who faced a primary challenge from the left. Arkansas Lieutenant Governor Bill Halter, a more progressive Democrat, challenged Lincoln in the primary, and his candidacy was supported by the liberal MoveOn.org group as well as unions, who felt the more centrist Lincoln, who had served in the Senate for two terms, was not supportive enough of union causes. Lincoln managed to win the primary but was seriously weakened by the challenge and lost the general election to Republican John Boozman.

There are many things that Independent voters find discouraging and disappointing about the political system and even more ways that they are treated unfairly by it.

In talking with Independent voters around the country, one of the things I heard most often from them was their concern and disgust about the influx of money into politics and the undue influence of special interests and lobbyists who contribute that money. Because of the link between money and access, many Independent voters believe the system is rigged against the average person, that big money talks, and while campaign donors have ready access to members of Congress, the average person is often ignored and has no voice.

According to the Center for Responsive Politics, the total amount spent on congressional campaigns in 2010, including money spent by outside groups, was $3.7 billion.[20] That's right—billion with a *B*. The average cost of winning a House seat in 1986 was around $360,000 compared to $1.4 million in 2010, and the average cost of winning a Senate seat was $3 million in 1986 and almost $9 million in 2010, according to the Campaign Finance Institute.[21] Special interest groups and political action committees spent more than $900 million trying to influence the 2010 election.

Former Kansas Congressman Dan Glickman, who served as Secretary of Agriculture in the Clinton Administration after being defeated in 1994, is now the head of the Aspen Institute's Congressional Program and a senior fellow at the Bipartisan Policy Center in Washington. He is firmly convinced that the explosion in the growth of government, federal spending, and the national debt that started around 1980 is tied directly to the growth in campaign contributions and spending.

> Money is the driving force in the American political system today, much more so than thirty years ago . . . it's everything. It's not just the mother's milk of politics—it's the cottage cheese and yogurt too.
>
> People put money into the system to get government to do things—either spending money or providing tax breaks. You can spend a couple of million in campaign money and get a billion in benefits.
>
> Both political parties are on the take. Both parties are raising money from the same people—they're the people who want things from the government. . . . It defies the laws of nature to think that you can take their money one day and then kick them in the butt the next day.

Glickman, who also served as Director of the Institute of Politics at Harvard University's Kennedy School of Government and as the head of the Motion Picture Association of America after leaving Congress, says this money cycle "breeds cynicism" with voters, especially Independents. "The money is corrupting. It does erode people's trust in government—it's corrosive."

You'd think with all this fund-raising and campaign spending going on that members of Congress are continually fighting for their political lives, but in reality, most of them are virtually assured of reelection. Only about 10 percent of the seats in the House of Representatives are in truly competitive "swing" districts that have a decent chance of being won by either a Republican or a Democrat. In what was considered a massive change election in 2010, only about sixty House incumbents were defeated—fewer than 15 percent of the 435 members of the House of Representatives.

Most of the congressional districts are drawn to strongly favor either a Republican or Democratic candidate, by including a majority of voters of one party within their boundaries. This practice is called *gerrymandering*, a label coined in 1812, when the Massachusetts legislature redrew the boundaries of state legislative districts to favor the party of the state's Governor Elbridge Gerry.

Every ten years after the national census results are released, congressional and state legislative districts are redrawn. The size of the House is capped at 435 seats, so states with the biggest proportional decline in population lose seats in Congress, and states whose populations have increased the most gain congressional districts. Following the 2010 census, it was determined that 10 states would lose congressional seats, almost all of them Democratic-leaning states in the Northeast and Midwest. Pennsylvania, New Jersey, Missouri, Michigan, Massachusetts, Louisiana, Iowa, and Illinois all lost one congressional seat, and Ohio and New York each lost two.

Eight states gained House representation, all in the South and West and most Republican leaning. Washington, Utah, South Carolina, Nevada, Georgia, and Arizona each gained one congressional district, Florida got two new districts, and Texas got four new House seats.

Only about a dozen states in the country, including California, Washington, Alaska, Arizona, and Idaho use independent commissions to handle their legislative redistricting; however, in most of those states the members of the redistricting commissions are appointed by the governor and members of the legislature. In the rest of the states, the re-apportionment process is controlled by the two parties through the legislature and the governor's office, and many of them do not even have public meetings on their redistricting plans. Independents and nonaffiliated voters are pretty much ignored and have virtually no say in the drawing of congressional and state legislative districts. The process is almost always a matter of backroom dealing and horse-trading, with Republicans and Democrats fighting over a map they hope will be the most advantageous to their own party.

"You have politicians choosing their voters rather than the other way around," says J. Gerald Hebert of Americans for Redistricting Reform. The result is mostly safe seats and districts where representatives don't have to appeal to the middle but instead cater to the extreme ends of the spectrum to get elected.

And once the districts are drawn, election laws heavily favor Republicans and Democrats and seriously disadvantage both Independent voters and candidates. As a result, it's no surprise that there are only about fifteen Independents holding office in Congress and all the state legislatures combined, according to Harry Kresky of IndependentVoting.org.

Probably the biggest impediment to electing more Independent and centrist candidates is the lack of open primaries. Fewer than half the states in the country have open primaries where unaffiliated or Independent voters can participate. In the other states, voters must be a registered Democrat or Republican to vote in the primary. Independent candidates are also extremely disadvantaged by laws governing ballot access and campaign contributions.

"As more and more people become Independent, parties have less and less support, and they become more aggressive in trying to control the process. Is it right to have a society where more and more people are

Independents and the parties have more and more control?" asks Kresky. "The parties want our votes in November, but they don't want us to participate in the primary elections where the choices about which candidates will run are determined."

Ask any politician about hyperpartisanship, party polarization, and the decline in civility in this country, and they inevitably mention the media as a big part of the reason for why things have gotten so bad. Cable television talking heads, talk radio hosts like Rush Limbaugh, and Internet bloggers who are vehicles of extremes, acrimony, and often misinformation and untruths stoke the flames that are licking at our democracy.

The media loves talking about and featuring people like Donald Trump, who flirted with a run for the presidency in 2011, and Sarah Palin—part politician, part media figure, and part entertainer. What she specializes in is division—keeping track of those who are with her and against her and suggesting not very subtly that those in the second category are not real Americans, including Barack Obama. The media can't seem to get enough of her.

The rise of polarizing and controversial media celebrities and the explosion of a blogosphere that appeals to a narrow constituency of either liberals or conservatives who want to hear their own views and opinions reinforced in the most inflammatory way and the other side demonized, has had a significant impact in debasing political discourse in this country. As substantive political discussion without name-calling becomes rare in the media and public life, Americans' view of politics and politicians grows more cynical and negative and their desire to be involved decreases.

Centrist politicians who are trying to work seriously in a bipartisan way on important issues say they are rarely asked to be guests on national television, while a polarizing but extremely colorful figure like Minnesota Republican Congresswoman and presidential candidate Michele Bachmann is a media darling. It's not really hard to see why. Bachmann suggested in a television appearance on MSNBC in 2008 that Barack Obama and Democratic members of Congress who don't think like her have "anti-American views." She also said that the Obama Administration was running "a gangster government."[22]

The founder of the House's Tea Party Caucus, Bachmann spent $11.6 million to get reelected in 2010,[23] more than any other House of Representatives candidate. But for someone who is always extolling patriotism, liberty, and the Founding Fathers, she seems to have an extremely limited knowledge of American history. In one speech, she insisted that the Founders "worked tirelessly until slavery was no more" and then on a visit to New Hampshire in 2011 she said, "You're the state where the shot was heard around the world in Lexington and Concord," an attempted reference to the Massachusetts battles that launched the Revolutionary War, a fact that any American schoolchild would be expected to know.

If there's one thing people in New England take seriously, it is their own history, and the ridiculous gaffe did not go unnoticed. "Seriously, the real question is whether she knows she [got it wrong], I suspect not," one New Hampshire Republican told *Politico*. "There is no Lexington in New Hampshire," said another.[24]

Confusing Massachusetts with New Hampshire is a big no-no in the Granite State, but Bachmann didn't seem at all concerned about her lack of American history knowledge and instead turned the whole thing into another volley in her culture war. "So I misplaced the battles of Concord and Lexington by saying they were in New Hampshire," she wrote on Facebook. "It was my mistake, Massachusetts is where they happened. New Hampshire is where they are still proud of it!"

Suggesting that Massachusetts residents are not proud of the role their state played in the fight for independence is ridiculous on the face of it. But it's just the kind of gibe Bachmann and Palin specialize in. There are good states and bad states—and only the states where most people think like they do represent the real America in their view.

Early in her presidential campaign, Bachmann was getting the lion's share of media attention but she also came in for criticism from her competitors. In a July 2011 appearance on "Meet the Press", fellow Minnesotan and former Governor Tim Pawlenty said of Bachmann, who is in her third term in the House of Representatives, "Her record of accomplishment in Congress is non-existent."[25]

The colorful Palin also seems to have some trouble keeping American history straight and is good at twisting it for her own purposes. Over Memorial Day weekend and in early June 2011, Palin launched what she called a "One Nation" bus tour, a publicity stunt that started in Washington, D.C., with a visit to the National Archives where the Declaration of Independence and U.S. Constitution are on display. From there she headed north to the Gettysburg battlefield, Independence Hall in Philadelphia, the Statue of Liberty in New York, and on to Boston, where she visited the Paul Revere House, Old North Church, and Bunker Hill Monument on the Freedom Trail. In Boston, when a reporter asked her about her visit, Palin said Paul Revere "warned the British that they weren't gonna' be takin' away our arms."[26]

It was an interesting but incorrect depiction of American history and Revere's role in the American Revolution.

Paul Revere's famous ride on April 18, 1775, immortalized by poet Henry Wadsworth Longfellow, was a horseback ride from Boston to Lexington to warn American patriots, including Samuel Adams and John Hancock, that the British would be marching on Lexington and Concord. Palin characterized the reporter's benign question, which was, "What have you seen so far today, and what are you going to take away from your visit?" as a "gotcha type of question" in the same way that she believed that CBS news anchor Katie Couric asking her during the 2008 campaign which newspapers she read was a "gotcha type of question."

On her SarahPAC website,[27] where the first link one encountered was a request to donate money to help pay for her jaunt through American history, Palin wrote this about her trip:

It's interesting when (for the 100th time) reporters shout out, "Why are you traveling to historical sites? What are you trying to accomplish?" I repeat my answer, "It's so important for Americans to learn about our past so we can clearly see our way forward in challenging times; so, we're bringing attention to our great nation's foundation." When that answer isn't what the reporters want to hear, we've asked them if they've ever visited these sites like the National Archives, Gettysburg, etc. When they confirm that they haven't, it's good to say, "Well, there you go. You'll learn a lot about America today."

It's probably also a good idea if you're going to launch a public bus tour of important historic sites to know the history you are "bringing attention to." I hope Palin learned a lot about American history from her trip. She obviously was good at making up her own stories about the nation's past.

I *have* visited the National Archives, Mount Vernon, the national monuments in Washington, Gettysburg, and Independence Hall. I have walked the Freedom Trail and visited Paul Revere's House, the Old North Church, and the Bunker Hill Monument as well as Lexington and Concord. Visiting those historic sites did fill me with enormous pride about the history of our nation, our diversity, and our great national heritage. And it deeply saddened me to see Sarah Palin use these sites for a publicity stunt. If there is one thing all these historic sites have in common, it is their essential role in the history of American democracy, a history that is not partisan but universal to all Americans.

That's why it's so disappointing that characters like Bachmann and Palin, who serve up searing rhetoric and distraction but little of substance to the national debate, are the darlings of television bookers who are chasing ratings and looking for heat rather than light. Cable television is continually staging conversations between people who represent the extreme ends of the political spectrum and hoping for a verbal slugfest. Public officials and supporters of the two parties, primarily at the extreme ends of the spectrum, are almost all we see on television and read quoted in print. The center is woefully underrepresented, if at all, in political coverage.

"Conflict, of course, is high in news value. Disagreement, division, polarization, battles, and war make good copy. Agreement, consensus, moderation, compromise and peace do not. Thus, the concept of a culture war fits well with the news sense of journalists who cover American politics," writes Fiorina.[28]

This coarsening of political debate has reached a dangerous level. Protesters on the Capitol grounds have shouted racial and sexual epithets at members of Congress, whose lives have even been threatened. They have been attacked, and their offices vandalized. On the floor of the House of Representatives, Republican members have called the President of the United States a liar and Democrats "baby killers," and a Democrat said Republican claims about the health care reform law were lies similar to Nazi propaganda.

A study released in 2011 by two professors from Stanford and Harvard found that more than 25 percent of all congressional press releases included "partisan taunts."[29]

The most horrific example of a culture gone haywire is the tragic shooting of Congresswoman Gabrielle Giffords in January 2011 outside a grocery store in her district in Tucson, Arizona. Giffords was holding a meet and greet for constituents when crazed gunman Jared Loughner opened fire, seriously wounding her and a dozen others and killing six of them, including a U.S. District Court judge and a nine-year-old girl. Loughner was obviously a mentally unstable individual who didn't get the help he needed and had far too ready access to high-powered weapons. But it is also likely that the highly charged political rhetoric in Arizona and around the country didn't help. At the time, Pima County Sheriff Clarence Dupnik, a friend of Gifford's, said, "The anger, the hatred, the bigotry that goes on in this country is getting to be outrageous . . . it's not without consequences."[30]

During the health care debate, when many members of Congress were harangued at town hall meetings, often by Tea Party members,

Democrats were advised by their leaders to stop holding such meetings. But despite being previously threatened and having just gone through a bruising reelection campaign in a swing district, Giffords, who was known for being a moderate who avoided inflammatory rhetoric and worked in a bipartisan way, refused to be intimidated. How terribly sad and ironic that at the very moment Giffords was trying to reach out to her constituents, she would be the victim of such a dreadful attack.

The night before she was shot, Giffords sent an email to Trey Grayson, congratulating him on being appointed to head the Institute of Politics at Harvard's Kennedy School of Government and talking about how they could work together to promote bipartisanship and civility, promising that she and her husband, Mark, would come visit him "after you get settled" and signing it "G."

"I would love to talk about what we can do to promote centrism and moderation. I am one of only 12 Dems left in a GOP district (the only woman) and think that we need to figure out how to tone our rhetoric and partisanship down," Giffords wrote to Grayson.

Giffords and Grayson had met about five years earlier at an Aspen Institute seminar for young political leaders and they had kept in touch. Giffords was in the Arizona state senate and Grayson, a Republican, had been elected in 2003 as Kentucky's secretary of state, at the age of thirty-one, the youngest secretary of state in the country. Grayson had sent an email out to friends and colleagues the day before the shooting, announcing his appointment at Harvard.

Giffords knew that Grayson was also no stranger to rough campaigns. Grayson ran for the U.S. Senate in 2010 but was beaten in the GOP primary by Tea Party poster boy Rand Paul, who handily won the general election. "It was a year in which being able to say you can work with the other side wasn't helpful," Grayson told me. A lot of voters who backed Tea Party candidates were angry but "anger doesn't necessarily result in good policy making. . . . We're all part of the problem. We all need to dial it back. . . . Civility is a problem. I get asked what do we do and I struggle with an answer to that."

. . .

A great many people are struggling with how to fix our broken system. There are a lot of good ideas out there, including demanding more civility from our officials and the media; reducing the power of money in politics and the influence of lobbyists and special interests; increasing the number of competitive congressional and state legislative districts, which would encourage more centrist candidates to run for office; and opening up the primary process in all fifty states to Independent voters. But unless Independent voters push for these reforms, they are unlikely to happen. The political parties, caught in a never-ending loop of finger pointing, blaming each other, and trading power don't seem willing or able to change things.

4

The NPR Republicans and the "Live Free or Die" State

New Hampshire

The New Englander is attached to his township because it is strong and independent; he has an interest in it because he shares in its management . . . he develops a taste for order, understands the harmony of powers, and in the end accumulates clear, practical ideas about the nature of his duties and the extent of his rights.

—Alexis de Tocqueville

WITH LICENSE PLATES THAT bear the phrase LIVE FREE OR DIE, New Hampshire is the epitome of an independent state. It has just a fraction of the nation's population and is not very ethnically diverse, but with its first-in-the-nation presidential primary, New Hampshire has for half a century held a unique place in American politics. The state's voters are accustomed to being the focus of a lot of political and media attention. They are well informed, take their politics seriously, and are known for their political savvy, unpredictability, and independence.

New Hampshire's strong libertarian tradition and "leave me alone" mentality are illustrated by the fact that it is the only state in the country where it's legal not to wear a seat belt and is one of only three states without a motorcycle helmet law. Residents of the Granite State are extremely mistrustful of big government and always have been. The small government, anti-tax message is nothing new here but is part of the state's DNA. The pride over having neither a sales nor income tax is almost a religion in New Hampshire, and woe be to any politician who threatens to change that.

But along with their penchant for government frugality, many New Hampshire residents also think government should stay out of people's personal lives. New Hampshire legalized gay marriage in 2009, and most of the state's voters, including Republicans, support the right of gays to marry as well as abortion rights.

New Hampshire is the home of many of what I call NPR Republicans—fiscal conservatives who are moderate or libertarian on social issues. The NPR Republicans are typically affluent and well educated and have been moving away from the GOP for years because of the party's alignment with the religious right. They believe strongly in the separation of church and state and do not wear their religion on their sleeve. According to Gallup polling, New Hampshire is one of the least religious states in the nation.[1]

The NPR Republicans are not an urban legend and do exist in significant numbers around the country. They were once the backbone of the Republican Party, but they have largely been driven out of a visible role in the party, out of elected office and party leadership by the right-wing takeover of the GOP. Now their chief role in the party, when they have one, is usually fund-raising.

These voters are strong fiscal conservatives who believe in controlling federal spending, using tax dollars wisely, and holding the line on tax increases. Many of them have become Independents over the past decade because of what they perceive to be the fiscal irresponsibility, general mismanagement, and incompetency of the presidency of George W. Bush and the Republican-controlled Congress, including the misguided war in Iraq. These voters are concentrated in the Northeast and in the suburbs of major cities, but they can be found all over the country.

NPR Republicans are horrified by politicians like Sarah Palin and

Michele Bachmann and believe they represent the worst elements in the Republican Party. These voters, who have also long been known as Country Club Republicans because of their affluence and lifestyle, consider themselves to be open minded. They read the *Wall Street Journal* and listen to NPR, whose federal funding they do not believe should be eliminated. They believe in government funding for the arts and consider themselves culturally sophisticated. They are comfortable not only on the golf course but also in an Indian restaurant or art gallery in a transitional urban neighborhood.

NPR Republicans are not exclusively WASPs, but if they aren't, they usually dress and talk like them. Because they are distinguished both by their education and their affluence, they support providing opportunity to others but they hate taxes and can't stand the idea of the government living beyond its means and bankrupting the next generation. They might be willing to pay more for Medicare through means testing, but they want to make sure if they do, that others have to sacrifice as well and there are additional federal spending cuts.

These voters either have a long family history with the Republican Party or adopted it after making their fortune. They are uncomfortable with excess, especially when it involves the government or political rhetoric, and are attracted by political candidates who appeal to intellect and reason and offer workable solutions to the nation's big problems. Many of them voted for Barack Obama, not only to show their annoyance at what they considered the recent wrongheadedness of the Republican Party but also to show how open minded they are. However, they are concerned about the explosive growth of government spending under the Democrats. That does not mean, however, that they would not consider voting for Barack Obama again in 2012 if there was no Republican candidate who appealed to them and they felt Obama had genuinely moved to the center and was seriously working on a plan to cut spending, reduce the federal debt, and deal with entitlement reform.

Cynthia Dokmo, Elizabeth Hager, and Paul Spiess are all NPR Republicans as well as former New Hampshire state legislators who lost reelection bids, largely because of their moderate views on social issues. Dokmo, sixty-four, explains it this way: "If you're not 100 percent Republican—what they believe a Republican is—they don't want you."

Dokmo describes herself as a "political junkie" who started out as an Independent and then became a Republican and served in the legislature for sixteen years representing Amherst, a small town not far from the Massachusetts border. "They primaried me for six of the last eight elections which I won and finally this time they not only had some in-state groups working against me but they had two national organizations send flyers out about me."

Conservative groups focused on Dokmo's stand on gay marriage. "I voted to support same-sex marriage. It was a difficult vote for me. I took a long time thinking about it. I knew I would be targeted, but you have to do what you think is the right thing.

"They portrayed me as someone who was out of touch but I don't think the people of New Hampshire believe the government should get involved in social issues." Dokmo says she is also pro-choice. "Abortion is a personal, moral, and religious choice. I don't think it should be a government choice.

"I've always thought it was rather odd that a party that believes in limited government wants government to dictate social behavior. It seems like a contradiction."

Dokmo lost her primary by six votes. She tried to run as a write-in candidate in the general election but found out "it's almost impossible" to win that way. "That's the way it goes—I always tried to vote the way I thought was right. I never wanted to be one of those politicians that voted certain ways to get reelected."

Independent voter Rita Lamy thinks that kind of attitude is much too rare in politics, and she appreciates Dokmo's vote and the legislature's decision to legalize civil unions and gay marriage. On January 1, 2008, on the steps of the New Hampshire State House on the day the state's civil union bill became law, Lamy and her sixty-two-year-old partner, Linda, got married in a civil ceremony with several dozen other gay couples. And a few years later when the legislature passed its gay marriage legislation, the couple's civil union officially became a marriage. "For me it was a validation of who I am. . . . It's symbolic—that's what any marriage is. . . . It's nice we can say we're married but does it really change anything—no."

Lamy, a fifty-nine-year-old nurse who lives in Manchester and works at a nursing home, decided to become an Independent voter in 2007. "I'm really jaded when it comes to the political system," says Lamy, who often writes in the names of other candidates when she doesn't like the Democratic or Republican choices. In 2008, Lamy wrote in Hillary Clinton for president.

Lamy, who lived in Canada for a while, said she thinks a multiparty parliamentary system makes more sense than our two-party system. She believes when someone wins the presidency, their vice president should automatically be the candidate from the other party, which could force politicians to actually be bipartisan and work together. But she admits something like that would probably never happen in this country.

Elizabeth Hager is also a Republican who is moderate on social issues and fiscally conservative. She lost her election to the state legislature in 2008 when she was targeted by GOP conservatives. She is from Concord, New Hampshire's state capital, where she is the executive vice president of United Way. Hager has had a long career in New Hampshire politics, serving on the city council and as mayor of Concord and in the state legislature three separate times for a total of twenty-six years.

"We moderates never have figured out how to have a serious rallying cry. We don't want to have too much government, but we don't want to destroy government either. We just want to be reasonable. Being reasonable is not too sexy."

Hager thinks Republican Party leaders should appreciate people who have served the party for so many years instead of trying to purge them. "It does make me really sad the amount of time they spend targeting the moderates."

Hager has thought about running as an Independent for governor because she knows she can't get the Republican nomination and she believes her views "completely represent the New Hampshire electorate—the average New Hampshire voter."

Because of the GOP's conservative swing, Hager thinks a lot of Republicans have become Independents. "They have driven so many people out of the party and I think they will continue to drive other people out."

Paul Spiess, sixty-one, a retired banker who served in the legislature for two terms, is one of those who was driven out of the Republican Party by what he considers to be extremists. "They have no tolerance for the big-tent theory. They became determined to oust from the ballot moderate Republicans."

In 2004, Spiess faced a conservative challenge and lost by two votes. Spiess believes the Republican Party is systematically trying to weed out moderate voices. "There is a faction in the state; it's a conservative coalition within the party, that have defined what they believe a Republican should be. They have a litmus test—how do you vote on marriage, gun rights, abortion, the budget—and if you don't grade above a certain level, you're on their hit list.

"What they represent is the far right extreme to which the Republican Party has gone at the expense of its moderate base. They've taken over the party for all intents and purposes," asserts Spiess. "And it's not just in New Hampshire. New Hampshire is representative of a much bigger problem. The result is that moderate Republicans have been driven out of both the state and national party."

Around the country, an ideological cleansing of the Republican Party is taking place. Moderate NPR Republicans like Dokmo, Hager, and Spiess are being driven out of the party, either by primary challenges or self-imposed exile because of their frustration over the direction the party has taken.

Throughout most of the nineteenth and twentieth centuries, New Hampshire was a solidly Republican state. In the thirty-four presidential elections between 1856 and 1988, the state voted Republican in all but six—only Democrats Woodrow Wilson, Franklin Roosevelt, and Lyndon Johnson managed to carry the state. New Hampshire didn't even vote for Massachusetts neighbor John F. Kennedy in 1960, instead giving the state to Richard Nixon.

There were always more registered Republicans in New Hampshire, and the state's main newspaper, the *Manchester Union Leader* was renowned for its political clout and its irascible, eccentric, ultraconservative owner William Loeb and his front-page editorial tirades.

But over the past twenty years, the paper has become more mainstream and the state more Democratic, reflecting significant demographic changes. New high-tech companies sprang up, and residents of New York, Massachusetts, and other New England states moved here seeking more affordable housing and lower taxes.

Even through the recession, the state maintained a relatively good economic climate. Census data shows New Hampshire is more affluent and better educated than the national average.[2] It is a center for financial services and has one of the highest growth rates and proportion of high-technology jobs as well as the highest percentage of citizens with Internet access in the country.

The state's shift in population and stronger Democratic presence became apparent in the change in its voting patterns over the past two decades, with Democrats winning the state in four of the last five presidential elections. Bill Clinton carried the state in 1992 and 1996. John Kerry won here in 2004, and Barack Obama carried the state with an impressive 54 to 45 percent victory. Al Gore lost to George W. Bush in 2000 by a razor-thin margin, Bush's only victory in New England, highlighting the fact that New Hampshire trends more conservative than its New England neighbors.

Andrew Smith, director of the University of New Hampshire Survey Center, predicts that because of demographic changes, the state could be Democratic in another decade. But for now, it is still a Republican-leaning swing state.

Many people from around the country know New Hampshire mostly for its beautiful fall foliage, maple syrup, and first-in-the-nation presidential primary status. Being the first primary state is both a source of political pride and an economic boon to New Hampshire, as every four years an influx of campaign workers, candidates, and media make the pilgrimage north. Most of the state's population lives within an hour of Manchester, its largest city, so campaigning here is relatively easy. Unlike much bigger states with large urban centers where national candidates campaign largely through buying expensive television time, New Hampshire requires retail politics of its presidential contenders. Shaking hands and meeting voters one on one is essential, along with the obligatory pancake breakfasts, Rotary luncheons, and visiting plenty of voters in their living rooms. New Hampshire voters don't feel like they know a candidate or can consider voting for them until they've met at least a couple of times.

State law requires that New Hampshire's primary remain first in the nation, and to preserve that status, the date of the primary has steadily been moved up over the past fifty years as other states have attempted to challenge its primacy. Traditionally, the primary was a solid determiner of who would win their party's nomination and ultimately the presidency, but that too has changed. The last three presidents (Bill Clinton, George W. Bush, and Barack Obama) all finished second in the New Hampshire primary.

The number of Independent voters in New Hampshire, or what the state calls "undeclared" voters, has been growing steadily and now significantly outnumbers both Republicans and Democrats. Smith said about 41 percent of the state's voters identified as unaffiliated voters, 29 percent said they were Republicans, and 24 percent Democrats according to a UNH Survey Center poll taken shortly after the 2010 election. In that election, Republican turnout was up about 4 percent, Democratic turnout was down by an equal amount, and Independent voters broke nearly two to one for the Republicans here, Smith explained.

Unlike many other states, New Hampshire permits Independent or unaffiliated voters to cast ballots in primary elections, and since they outnumber both Republicans and Democrats, they can have a serious impact on the outcome. All these voters have to do is show up at their polling place and ask for a Republican or Democratic ballot. If they want to maintain their Independent status, they just have to stop by the registration desk on their way out and change back to "Undeclared" immediately after voting, so they have to belong to a party for only the few minutes it takes to fill out and cast a ballot. They can switch back and forth between parties from election to election, which encourages Independent participation.

New Hampshire voters don't tend to like flashy or flamboyant politicians but instead prefer serious moderates of both parties who get down to business and don't make a lot of noise about it. Think taciturn Judd Gregg, the former governor and retired U.S. Senator, whom one New Hampshire political observer described as "hardly a colorful guy." Gregg epitomizes the kind of well-educated, strong fiscal conservative but socially moderate, or libertarian-leaning, politician that most New Hampshire voters like. "He's a flinty, curmudgeonly New Englander," observed New Hampshire's senior senator and also a former governor, moderate Democrat Jeanne Shaheen.

In his farewell address to the Senate, Gregg said, "We play politics in this city and in this country between the forty-yard lines. . . . We are not the government that ever moves too radically left or radically right. And that's the way it should be. In this institution, compromise is required. To govern you must reach agreement. We are 300 million people, obviously of diverse views. If we're going to govern 300 million people, we must listen to those who have legitimate views on both sides of the aisle."[3] It's a sentiment Shaheen says she shares.

When she ran for governor, she took a pledge not to support an income or sales tax and won overwhelmingly. When she defeated incumbent John Sununu to win her Senate seat in 2008, she became not only the first woman senator from New Hampshire but also the first Democrat to win a U.S. Senate seat from the state since 1974. Shaheen, not unlike Gregg, is a cautious, careful, almost boring moderate and also like Gregg has been extremely successful and popular in New Hampshire.

Shaheen, who calls herself a "pragmatist," faced a Republican-controlled legislature when she was governor and says it taught her some political lessons. "You have to work together or you're not going to get anything done . . . you make decisions and move forward." In the Senate, she frequently tries to work with Republicans on legislative efforts.

The current four-term governor of New Hampshire is in much the same mold. Centrist Democrat John Lynch, a former businessman who was elected to his first term as governor in 2004, is mild-mannered and cautious and doesn't get ahead on any issue. His political style and even his physical appearance somewhat resemble a turtle who keeps his head in his shell until he thinks it's safe to come out.

Like Shaheen, Lynch faced a Republican legislature when he took office and immediately stressed the need for bipartisanship, saying, "I was not elected to represent a party." He has the approachable, down-to-earth quality the state's voters appreciate and is almost like the mayor of New Hampshire, known for handing out laminated cards with his cell phone number printed on them. In such a small state, personal connections are important and New Hampshire's pragmatic voters generally select candidates who are electable, likable, and authentic.

Despite fiscal challenges, Lynch has kept New Hampshire's taxes among the lowest in the nation and is the kind of moderate, fiscally conservative Democrat that does well here. He is the only governor in the state's history to be elected to four consecutive two-year terms and has consistently had high approval ratings. He won reelection the first time with a margin of 74 to 26 percent—the largest victory ever for a gubernatorial candidate in New Hampshire history.

But in 2010, Lynch had to fight much harder for reelection. Lynch won about 53 percent of the vote but had to lend his campaign $850,000 of his own money to do it.[4] Even with a significantly smaller margin of victory, Lynch fared much better than other New Hampshire Democrats in a very bad year. The Republicans held on to Gregg's U.S. Senate seat, picked up both of the state's congressional districts, and won control of the state legislature.

Lynch's opponent was former New Hampshire Health Commissioner and business consultant John Stephen. Stephen's father was a Democratic state senator and Stephen told me, "New Hampshire voters are not about being a Republican or a Democrat, they're about being from New Hampshire."

There is an enormous pride of place in New Hampshire, and campaigns tend to be fairly genteel compared with many other parts of the country. "He's a nice person," the soft-spoken Stephen said of Lynch. "But nice is not the issue. You've got to lead."

Hurling what could be the ultimate insult here; Stephen said Lynch was governing more like a big spender from Massachusetts (which is where Lynch grew up) than a frugal son of New Hampshire. And reciting what might as well be the state motto, Stephen said, "We like limited government, less spending, and more freedom."

During the campaign, Lynch avoided any connection to the Obama Administration and declined to appear with Vice President Joe Biden when he visited New Hampshire. Lynch also did not campaign with other Democratic candidates or do much to help them. Lynch was willing to share the stage with former President Bill Clinton at a campaign rally in Nashua, forty-eight hours before Election Day, but stipulated that other Democrats couldn't be onstage with them at the same time.

Stephen is a pretty typical New Hampshire Republican and not a fire-breathing conservative. In the gubernatorial debate the week before the election, both he and Lynch said they would support the right of gay couples to adopt children. In June 2009, New Hampshire joined Vermont, Connecticut, Massachusetts, Iowa, and the District of Columbia in legalizing gay marriage.

Lynch, who originally said he would not sign the legislation, changed his mind on the state's gay marriage bill when it appeared a majority of New Hampshire voters favored it, and said he did not oppose it, because people in New Hampshire wanted marriage equality and "have a long history of opposing discrimination and supporting tolerance."

That history of tolerance may be challenged, however, by the overwhelmingly conservative state legislature that was elected in 2010. The New Hampshire General Court—its official name—is an enormous legislative body, especially given the state's small population. It has four hundred members in the House of Representatives, which along with the twenty-four-member state Senate, makes it the largest state legislature in the United States and the fourth-largest English-speaking legislative body in the world, behind only the English Parliament, the Parliament of India, and the U.S. Congress.

Members of the General Court earn just one hundred dollars a year plus expenses for their service, making it essentially a volunteer position and a true citizen legislature. Throughout the state's history, the legislature was traditionally dominated by Republicans, but in 2006 for the first time since the Civil War, Democrats won both houses of the legislature along with the governorship. That year, Democrats also won both of the state's congressional seats. Except for Lynch's reelection, all of that was reversed in 2010, when the legislature returned to Republican Party control and the GOP won back the state's two congressional seats. Republicans now have a 19–5 margin in the Senate and an overwhelming 298–104 margin in the House.

The legislature has traditionally included a significant number of moderate Republicans. But the Republicans elected to the state legislature in 2010 were extremely conservative, many Tea Party backed, and the number of moderate Republicans in the House was cut in half—to about twenty-five. In addition, mirroring what happened in congressional elections around the country, many of the moderate statehouse Democrats were defeated, significantly reducing the representation of the middle in the legislature. This made for a real sea change in the body's legislative approach, with a conservative legislative agenda pushed by the new members and GOP leadership in 2011.

Three of the NPR Republicans who remain in the state House are Ken Gould, Carolyn Gargasz, and David Kidder. They belong to what is known as the Main Street Republicans, a legislative caucus and support group for moderate Republicans whose members support fiscal responsibility, social moderation, and civility.

"I am frustrated with the extreme thinking in my own Republican Party. So much so that I will probably retire in 2012 and become an Independent voter," says Ken Gould, seventy-two. Gould has been a Republican since he first registered to vote fifty years ago. He was one of the Republicans who voted in favor of the measure to legalize gay marriage. "Issues like marriage and abortion is where I stray from the Republican line, I'd rather not be dictated to." Gould says he and the other moderate Republicans in the state legislature sometimes find it hard to coexist with the "very philosophical people to the right of us.

"Sometimes we vote with the Democrats and they don't like it. The leadership we have now in the Republican Party in New Hampshire is very conservative, and they don't like us much."

Like the other NPR Republicans, Gould thinks the hard conservative line is driving people out of the party. He was unhappy with the Bush Administration and especially the Iraq War and says in 2008 he didn't much care for any of the Republican candidates running for president. "I ended up voting for Ron Paul because of his position on the war. . . . I'm not particularly proud of that vote. I'm not sure I would want him to be president, but I just didn't think there were other choices."

Carolyn Gargasz, seventy-three, has been in the legislature since 2000, and represents the same seat her mother, Gladys Cox, held in the state House when she was in her seventies. Also like her mother, Gargasz has been a Republican her entire life.

Increasingly though, Gargasz finds herself voting for more Democrats, and she refuses to give any money to the Republican National Committee. "I don't feel that I fit in [to the national party]. I'm such a low-key person, I'm not an extremist. . . . I also don't agree with the way some Republicans are trashing Obama, questioning whether he was born in this country, or saying he's a Muslim. . . . I didn't vote for Obama, but I don't go for that kind of tactic."

She says the 2010 election was particularly rough on the legislature's moderate Republicans. "We lost some really good people—intelligent, thoughtful people who were really serious about the legislative process. They were there to do the business of the state. We lost them because of primary challenges."

David Kidder is a Realtor who has been in the legislature for six years. "I'm a hated moderate Republican," he says by way of introduction. Kidder is also following in the family footsteps—his father was a moderate Republican who served in the legislature for twenty years.

Kidder says the conservative wing of the state party has come after him every time he's run for reelection. "I have taken plenty of stands against the Republican Party. I take care of the people of my district and the state of New Hampshire, and the party comes third. A lot of people in Concord—the party comes first and that drives me nuts." Kidder spent a grand total of $297 on his campaign in 2010 for yard signs and a newspaper ad in the local paper, although his opponent and her supporters spent much more.

Kidder still considers himself a "true blue Rockefeller/Eisenhower Republican" and says "the party has moved away from me rather than me moving away from the party," and goes on to say, "I always thought that being a Republican was about individual rights and responsibilities. Stay the hell out of people's bedrooms and their private lives." Allowing gay marriage is promoting individual rights, he asserts. "How can you not be for that?" The Republican majority in the 2011 legislature said they hope to repeal the state's gay marriage rights, and Kidder thinks they are making a big mistake.

Polls show he is probably right. A University of New Hampshire Survey Center poll conducted in 2011 showed that New Hampshire residents, including Republicans, are much more pro-choice than the country as a whole and did not support repealing the state's same-sex marriage law. Only 29 percent of those polled supported repealing the law, while

62 percent opposed doing so. On abortion, only 9 percent of those polled believed abortion should be illegal in all circumstances, compared with 19 percent nationwide.[5]

"Each year it gets harder and harder to be a Republican, but I do think we've gotten to the point where there's going to be a backlash. I think people are going to start to get the picture that they're going too far," says Kidder.

When the Democrats took control of the legislature in 2006 for the first time in one hundred years, Kidder says, "They made a huge error in trying to get too many things the first year and what happened was they set themselves up for the Republicans to go after them. They overestimated revenues and had too much spending, and all of a sudden we're in a mess. Now the Republicans are making exactly the same mistake, they're going too far and I think it's going to come back and bite them in 2012."

The New Hampshire Republican legislature, like so many state legislatures elected around the country in 2010, didn't waste any time in asserting itself and acting as if it had a mandate to push a conservative agenda, whether or not it did. Legislation was quickly introduced to cut state funding for public kindergarten programs and many other state programs, limit abortion rights, and revoke the legalization of gay marriage in New Hampshire.

There were also a number of rather bizarre agenda items introduced. The first binding action the legislature took on a totally partisan vote was to allow guns on statehouse grounds and end a ban on guns in the House of Representatives chamber.

Another measure introduced early on would create a state militia or "permanent state defense force" separate from the New Hampshire National Guard, to assist with disaster relief and defend the state against "invasion, rebellion, disaster, insurrection, riot, breach of the peace or imminent danger."

You just can't make this stuff up. As the *Concord Monitor*, which took to calling the Republican-controlled state legislature "the asylum" wrote in an editorial opposing the measure, "Hand me down the squirrel gun, Ma, the Canadians are coming."

Not only was the proposal ridiculous on the face of it—but it would also cost the state money. At a time when New Hampshire, like other states, was forced to find hundreds of millions of dollars in cuts to erase a deficit, the cost of overseeing the proposed militia would add $450,000 a year to the state budget.[6]

Perhaps the most egregious proposal, an unconstitutional power grab aimed at disenfranchising largely Democratic voters, was legislation to prevent college students, as well as some members of the military temporarily stationed in the state, from voting in New Hampshire. As the *Nashua Telegraph* editorialized, "Every once in a while, a piece of legislation is introduced that is wrong at so many levels it's difficult to know where to begin."[7]

The Supreme Court has already decided this issue and ruled that college students are entitled to the same presumption of residency as any other citizen.[8] But apparently that's not good enough for the Republicans in the New Hampshire legislature. Their bill would require college students and military to vote in their home states by absentee ballot, even if they lived in New Hampshire twelve months a year. The legislation would also eliminate the state's same-day voter registration. The Speaker of the House said the college students were guilty of, gasp, "voting liberal."[9]

"They govern from the extreme, and if you're not on the bandwagon, they drive you out," says Paul Spiess of his party's leadership.

The pressure starts out insidiously and it winds up being pretty brutal. They tell you that you have to vote with them or your bills aren't going to get a vote or you don't get a good committee assignment. Those are pretty powerful tools to discourage people. If you vote against the party line, they're in your face. They pulled me aside and literally poked a finger in my chest and told me if I did any more of this, I could kiss my career good-bye.

Carolyn Gargasz says her role model for the kind of Republican and the kind of public servant she wants to be is the late Walter Peterson, an icon of New Hampshire politics. Peterson was a former governor and state legislator who also served as president of Franklin Pierce College for twenty years and then became a trustee of the state university system.

He was the quintessential bipartisan man who always enjoyed strong support from both Democrats and Republicans in the state. The grandfather of NPR Republicans in New Hampshire, he remained active in politics until his death in June 2011 at the age of 88. He served as honorary chairman of John McCain's New Hampshire campaign in 2008, but made campaign contributions to and supported both Democrats and Republicans for office.

"I don't think all of the wisdom is in one party. The Republican Party has changed and it's not the party I loved. The right wing has tried to take over the party here. I have disdain for the right wingers. The answer to that is getting more centrists to be involved," he told me when I talked to him at the New Hampshire State Capitol in the fall of 2010. Peterson was there to announce his support for Governor John Lynch's reelection and his role as chairman of "Republicans for Lynch."

The new conservative leaders of the state GOP obviously had no regard for Peterson and his brand of bipartisan politics. In May 2011, the Republican legislature passed an anti-union Right to Work bill that was vetoed by Democratic Governor Lynch. Although the Republicans did not appear to have the votes to override the veto, House Speaker William O'Brien threatened to call the override vote on the afternoon that Peterson's funeral was being held so that House members who wanted to attend the funeral were essentially held hostage at the legislature or risked missing the override vote.

In an email message sent to House Republicans, O'Brien said "the issue of a veto override is no longer just about Right to Work. Very simply, the issue is about whether the policy of the state of New Hampshire will be set by a Republican supermajority or by a Democrat[ic] governor."

Representative Marshall "Lee" Quandt of Exeter, New Hampshire, was one of those Republicans who planned to vote against the GOP leadership and to sustain Lynch's veto. He told the *Portsmouth Herald* the arm-twisting on the override vote was "maniacal" and said preventing lawmakers from attending Peterson's funeral was "the lowest thing I've ever seen and shows they want to win at any cost. They have no parameters of decency."[10]

There were a lot of people who knew Peterson and had tremendous respect for him who were prevented from going to the funeral, said Kidder. "I think it's absolutely horrible. We all should have had the chance to go to Walter's funeral. . . . It's not right. It's not the New Hampshire way. It's become incredibly partisan. The House in New Hampshire is basically out of control."

This drive to win at any cost, to even be willing to remove Republicans who opposed the Right to Work Bill from a committee in order to move the bill forward, did reflect a new level of partisan, hardball politics in New Hampshire. But to go so far as to show a fundamental lack of respect for a former Republican governor who had served the state for more than half a century was a low that seemed almost incomprehensible.

There was undoubtedly a struggle going on within the state GOP, similar to that taking place in a number of states, between the older more moderate Republicans and the new conservative firebrands and Tea Party–supported candidates. How it would all turn out remained to be seen. Republican Ken Gould said he hoped that in 2012, voters would reverse the trend and bring some rationality to the legislature by defeating some of the most extreme Republicans.

Republicans Kelly Ayotte, who won Judd Gregg's Senate seat, and Charlie Bass, who won the Second District congressional seat in 2010, represented the new and the old within the Republican Party.

Bass, who probably qualifies as an NPR Republican, was first elected to Congress from the Second Congressional District in 1994 as part of the Republican Revolution but differed from most of his classmates in his more moderate views and temperament. He is a member of several Republican pro-choice and environmental groups and after leaving Congress, served as the head of the national Republican Main Street Partnership, a centrist coalition that advocates "thoughtful leadership" and a "pragmatic approach to solving the nation's problems."

Although it was held by a Republican for ninety-two of the past one hundred years, the Second Congressional District, which includes Concord as well as the college towns of Keene and Hanover, home of Dartmouth College, is now the more liberal of the state's two districts. Barack Obama won it by a commanding 13 points.[11] In his first stint in Congress, which lasted twelve years, Bass called himself an "independent voice for New Hampshire" and departed from the Republican leadership on a number of votes, including opposing the same-sex marriage ban and drilling for oil in the Arctic National Wildlife Refuge. He also helped launch the petition drive that pushed controversial and scandal-plagued Majority Leader Tom DeLay out of his leadership position.

But in 2006, a bad year for Republicans, Bass lost his bid for reelection to Democrat Paul Hodes. When Hodes announced his run for the Senate in 2010, Bass was determined to win back his seat but faced a crowded field of primary candidates, including two Tea Party challengers to his right, and he barely won the GOP primary. Bass became a bit of a contortionist during the 2010 campaign, trying to portray himself as a true conservative to win the primary but also saying he was the only candidate who could win Independent and Democratic votes.

Like so many New Hampshire politicians with an old New England lineage, Bass's political career followed the family tradition. He holds the same congressional seat represented by his Republican father in the 1950s and 1960s, and his grandfather, Robert Bass, served as governor of New Hampshire in the early twentieth century, supported the Progressive Republican movement, and was a friend of President Teddy Roosevelt.

It's not clear whether it was just an attempt to match the Tea Party mood, or whether Bass really had become a much angrier man in the four years he spent out of office, but his campaign rhetoric seemed much more heated than in past elections. At a Republican Unity Breakfast held two days after the state's September primary in the ballroom of a Manchester country club, he told a crowd of more than four hundred loyal party members that Ann McLane Kuster, the opponent he faced in the general election, was "an extremist left-wing Democrat." The Democrats believed the stimulus wasn't big enough, that deficits don't matter, that health care reform didn't go far enough, and that government should be bigger, Bass thundered. "That's not New Hampshire and that's never been the state of New Hampshire."

The week before the 2010 general election, Bass and Kuster met at Saint Anselm College in Manchester for a televised debate where Bass looked fairly irritated most of the time and stressed the failure of the Democrats' economic plan and their affection for big government. For her part, Kuster tried to link Bass and his previous twelve years in Congress to the Bush Administration and the fiscal irresponsibility of that era and tie him to the Tea Party. Bass dodged questions about moving away from his moderate roots but did not shy away from support for the Tea Party agenda. "It's a grassroots movement of people that want change now. They want less spending and debt and smaller government," said Bass. "I support it." Perhaps Bass realized that he would need the energy and votes of Tea Party supporters to win what proved to be one of the closer congressional elections in the nation.

In a year that was disastrous for so many Democrats, Kuster ran what many political observers believed to be the state's best campaign in 2010 and lost to Bass by just a little more than 1 percent of the vote. Like Bass, Kuster also comes from an old New Hampshire Republican political family. Her father served as mayor of Concord and her mother, Susan McLane, was a state representative for twenty-five years and actually ran against Charlie Bass in 1980 for the very congressional seat he now holds. Judd Gregg launched his political career by defeating both Bass and McLane that year in the GOP primary.

A lawyer, consultant, and former state lobbyist for hospitals and drug manufacturers, Kuster is convinced the Republicans in the state legislature and Congress are going to overplay their hand. "They're going to do some things that are going to backfire. . . . New Hampshire voters are not flashy. They like the reliability factor. They drive reliable cars and wear reliable shoes," says Kuster, explaining a big part of the success of centrists like Governor Lynch and Senator Shaheen, who win support from Independents and moderate Republicans.

Kuster said she wasn't anywhere near through with politics and was eyeing a rematch with Bass. "I'm definitely running again," she told me in 2011.

Paul Hodes had no primary opponents, but trailed his Republican opponent Kelly Ayotte by double digits throughout the campaign and lost the Senate campaign by a whopping 23 percent. UNH's Smith said Hodes failed to build a strong grassroots campaign organization and the national party, realizing he had little chance of success, provided almost no support to his campaign.

Ayotte, a former state attorney general and establishment Republican candidate, faced a crowded primary field and only narrowly defeated conservative Ovide Lamontagne, a prominent lawyer and longtime fixture in New Hampshire politics, by just 1,600 votes, despite being the favorite of national and state GOP leaders. Ayotte was not only endorsed by Gregg but reportedly also handpicked by him to be his successor. One New Hampshire political observer said their views are extremely similar and called her "Judd Gregg in a skirt." She also enjoyed significant support from not only the national Republican political establishment but also from Sarah Palin, who used her Facebook page to endorse Ayotte, calling her a "Granite State mama grizzly."

However, Ayotte downplayed her conservative social positions after the primary, focusing on tax and spend issues and stressing Hodes's support of the Democratic agenda, calling him a "Nancy Pelosi puppet" who voted with the Democratic leadership 90 percent of the time. At forty-two, Ayotte became the youngest woman in the Senate and one of only five Republican women senators. Party leaders, who saw her as a powerful symbol, made sure to frequently include her in photo ops and news conferences to highlight the fact that they did have some younger women in the party.

Former Massachusetts Governor and presidential candidate Mitt Romney stayed neutral in the GOP Senate primary race, but in 2010 he gave more than seventy-five thousand dollars to the state party and Republican candidates. In early 2011, Romney was the favorite among New Hampshire Republican voters, far ahead of any other potential Republican candidates, although 79 percent of likely GOP presidential primary voters here said they didn't yet know whom they would support for president.

A few days before the 2010 primary election, Romney made an appearance at what has become a New Hampshire tradition—the Seacoast Republican Women's Chili Fest, where all the women bring a pot of chili, and hundreds of Republicans descend on the farm of Doug and Stella Scamman in Stratham. The décor for the fund-raiser featured pumpkins and hay bales, and the well-heeled crowd wore mostly khaki pants, oxford cloth shirts, and pearls and parked their BMWs, Jaguars, Mercedes, and Lincolns in an adjoining field.

"This really is a state that cares about politics," Romney said, acknowledging both the large number of GOP candidates running and the great turnout. He predicted big midterm losses for the Democrats because "people recognize our values are under assault" and said the Democrats are trying to "smother those quintessential American values" that have defined the nation. "Almost everything they [the Democrats] have done has had the exact opposite effect of what they had hoped. President Obama's agenda has failed, and that's why he'll be rejected in November," Romney predicted.

Former New Hampshire Governor and state Republican Party Chairman John Sununu, known for his colorful rhetoric, was more blunt in his criticism of Obama. "I've never seen anyone who could screw things up this bad," Sununu told me. "You understand how important this election is. It's probably the most important election of most of our lives."

In June 2011, when Romney made the official announcement of his presidential candidacy, it was also at the Scamman's Bittersweet Farm and chili was again served. What he had to say was quite similar to his message the previous fall. Romney, focusing on the economy and a lack of leadership on the part of Barack Obama, said the president "has failed America."

Romney made no mention of the other Republicans seeking the GOP nomination, instead warning that Americans' economic freedom and opportunity have been threatened by Democratic policies. "This country we love is in peril," Romney declared, blaming Obama and his administration for high unemployment, more foreclosures and falling home values, rising food and gasoline prices, and soaring national debt.

The seventy-year-old Scammans who hosted Romney and introduced him that day are moderate, pro-choice, NPR Republicans known for their service to the New Hampshire Republican Party and they are always willing to open their home for lobster bakes and barbecue fundraisers. They both retired in 2010 from the New Hampshire legislature. Stella served for three terms and Doug, who also held various positions in state government, was a former Speaker of the House.

Doug says he did not support legalizing gay marriage, but "socially I'm certainly a moderate. I think people should decide for themselves what they want to do and how they want to live. I don't believe in telling people how to live."

"I firmly believe a moderate is someone who listens to all sides. If you're not tolerant of other people's opinions and sit down and talk it over, you're not going to come up with the best answer," says Stella.

The Scammans remain loyal Republicans and still "think there's a place for us in the party," but they also regret what has happened to the GOP. "There's more division and it's that much harder to get people to work together," said Doug.

In January 2011, the state's Republicans selected a controversial and extremely conservative Tea Party activist, Jack Kimball, as their party chairman. The owner of an office-cleaning company and a man who said the Obama Administration and the Democrats were bringing communism and socialism to the United States, Kimball also said he considered conservative talk radio and former Fox TV host Glenn Beck to be "an American hero."

Kimball unsuccessfully ran for the Republican nomination for governor in 2010, and during that candidacy, he said he was "not a big-tent Republican." Kimball also said he felt New Hampshire, as the first-in-the-nation-primary state, had a responsibility to make sure the party nominated "a strong conservative presidential candidate." But after a number of Republican leaders expressed concern about those remarks and the impact they could have on the primary, Kimball recanted some of his more colorful pronouncements and promised to focus on party unity between "the new folks we've brought to the party and the old guard."

Kimball was not supported for the chairmanship by his predecessor John Sununu, who told party members he was worried about divisions within the GOP and warned its leaders not to alienate more moderate members and Independents. "We don't want to be seen as a party that's a sliver of a party. We want to be seen as a party that welcomes all views," said Sununu.[12]

Sarah Palin is probably exactly the kind of nominee Kimball would like to see heading the Republican ticket in 2012, but his views are not shared by a majority of New Hampshire Republicans. In a 2011 UNH poll, Palin was far behind Romney as the preferred choice of Republicans to be the party's presidential nominee. Only 6 percent of those polled said they preferred Palin, and her unfavorable ratings were among the highest, exceeded only by former House Speaker Newt Gingrich. Palin was viewed unfavorably by almost half the registered New Hampshire Republicans polled and by 56 percent of undeclared voters. And a stunning 62 percent of those between the ages of eighteen and thirty-four had an unfavorable view of Palin.[13]

Such results don't surprise David Kidder. "I think she's bad for the party because she becomes a focal point, and I think she's way to the right of what traditional Republicans are. I don't see her having a prayer in hell of having a chance at the nomination. She's just so over the top . . . a lot of Republicans that I know—she's just appalling to them."

"I just think she's a nincompoop," declared ninety-year-old Betty Hall. "Most New Hampshire voters see right through her."

Moderate NPR Republicans in New Hampshire, like Doug and Stella Scamman, may be disappearing from party leadership and elected positions, but they are far from a minority among voters here. However, more and more of them are becoming Independents as their disenchantment grows over the direction the GOP is headed.

The Republicans have gone from being ultraconservative to being reactionary, according to former legislator Cynthia Dokmo. "What bothers me is the intolerance toward other ideas and the lack of civility. The people who are now controlling the party believe that we are at war with the other side. They put the party loyalty before what's best for the people of the United States. To them, it's more important to gain and retain power than to achieve good public policy."

"Almost everybody I talk to who's not politically engaged is so disgusted with the behavior of both parties and the inability to govern. I think they'd like to see a new direction, but it's a daunting task. So many of them are exhausted by it and see no value in getting involved in politics," says Paul Spiess, who adds that if he ever did decide to run for office again, it would be as an Independent, "to draw some strength to the middle."

Many of these NPR Republicans don't believe they have left the party; rather they feel the GOP has become too extreme and has left them, giving them no choice but to become Independents. The focus on conservative social and religious issues over economic concerns, and the effort to weed out moderate voices through primary challenges, have left a much more narrow Republican Party in New Hampshire and in many other places around the country.

Kidder says he has thought about running as an Independent candidate, but figured if he was just one Independent in the legislature, he wouldn't have any impact and would be "a homeless waif." But now he's seriously thinking about trying to get a couple dozen of the centrist legislators who are fed up with things to try it in 2012, because if there were an Independent caucus in the legislature, they might actually have a chance to make an impact.

That's just the kind of Independent effort that could make a difference, and New Hampshire, with its large number of Independent voters, is just the kind of place to try it.

5

The Facebook Generation and
a Rocky Mountain High

Colorado

"Go West, young man, go West."
—ATTRIBUTED TO HORACE GREELEY

COLORADO IS SEEN AS a cool place to live by young people. Many of them move here to go to college or start a professional life and never leave. The state has one of the best educated and youngest populations in the country. The median state age is thirty-six, and a quarter of Colorado's residents are under the age of eighteen. More than 40 percent of the state's population is under the age of thirty.[1]

Nationally, the Millennials—those under thirty years old—outnumber all other generations. By 2012, it is estimated that Millennials will represent almost a quarter of the U.S. voting age population, which is a huge, largely untapped voting bloc. Historically, young people vote less reliably than any other demographic. They don't much like or trust either political party. They are highly ironic and detached. They do not consider themselves joiners of clubs or organizations and do not like party labels. They think the Republicans and Democrats have screwed things up. And as a demographic, more young people are Independents than any other age group. They are looking for something different and new from politics.

In Colorado, people under the age of thirty-five account for almost 30 percent of the state's 3.3 million registered voters. Among this group of young voters, 45 percent are registered as unaffiliated, or Independent, significantly more than any other age group. About 30 percent of the state's voters under thirty-five are registered as Democrats, and 24 percent are registered as Republicans, according to the Colorado Secretary of State's Office.

These young voters like the freedom and beauty of Colorado, with its many opportunities for outdoor activity. With its breathtaking mountain vistas, pro-environmental culture, and libertarian leanings, Colorado embodies the Western, pioneer mind-set. It is a state both of very modern cities and wide-open, glorious natural spaces. More than half the state's five million residents reside in the greater Denver area, and on Fridays you can find many of them on Interstate 70 West heading for the mountains and a weekend of skiing, snowboarding, hiking, biking, or mountain climbing.

Colorado is a state where the ultraliberal Boulder, Aspen, and Denver sharply contrast with extremely conservative areas like Colorado Springs, home to a number of Evangelical Christian organizations, including Focus on the Family and its leader, the Reverend James Dobson, influential in conservative circles. But as a whole, Colorado has always been relatively moderate on social issues, and that is probably due to its Western, pioneer heritage. In 1967, six years before the Supreme Court's *Roe v. Wade* decision, which legalized abortion, Colorado became the first state in the country to allow abortion in cases of rape, incest, or to protect the health of the mother.

The most conservative areas of the state are the two large western and eastern rural regions, which account for most of Colorado's geographic area but not much of its population. The Western Slope, which means everything in Colorado west of the Continental Divide, has a classically Western feel, and most residents there make their livelihood in ranching, mining, and tourism. There is a tension in the region between mining and logging interests who want to utilize and profit from the abundant natural resources and newer residents who want to limit growth and implement more stringent environmental regulations. The sparsely populated Eastern Plains is a farming, dairy, and livestock region, where corn, wheat, hay, oats, and soybeans are grown. The region, which comprises the westernmost portion of the Great Plains, feels almost Midwestern and borders Kansas and Nebraska. Both these regions are losing population while the urbanized part of the state is growing rapidly, thanks to new residents. Colorado's growth rate is almost double the U.S. average.

The eastern, urban area of the state, which contains all its largest cities, is known as the Front Range and stretches from Pueblo, south of Denver to Fort Collins to its north, all connected by I-25. Almost 80 percent of the state's residents live here, and this is where state elections are decided. Denver is the largest city and the capital. The rapidly expanding Denver suburbs, exurbs, and the I-25 corridor are home to many venture capital, high-tech, and biotech companies. Colorado is second only to California as the nation's biggest aerospace industry employer.

Colorado Springs, the second biggest city in the state, is a sharp contrast to Denver, located about sixty miles to the north. Situated at the base of Pikes Peak, Colorado Springs is a conservative, military community. In addition to Focus on the Family, the U.S. Air Force Academy and a number of army and air force bases are located here, along with many aerospace and defense contractors, including Boeing, General Dynamics, Lockheed Martin, and Northrop Grumman.

People often relocate to Colorado to take advantage of the climate, natural beauty, and lifestyle, and while there are plenty of native Coloradans, it is just as likely that someone you meet here—including many of the state's elected officials, such as Governor John Hickenlooper and both U.S. Senators Mark Udall and Michael Bennet—will be a transplant.

Being a relatively new resident is not an impediment to launching a political career in Colorado, since significantly more than half the state's residents were not born here. Transplants are not looked at skeptically but rather welcomed as part of the growth and constant renewal of the state.

Many of the state's newest residents are members of Generations X and Y—under thirty-five years old. I call the Independent voters among this group the Facebook Generation. They are more centrist in their views than many of their contemporaries.

The Facebook Generation lives much of its life online, including many of its social interactions. This age group doesn't really trust either political party and doesn't understand why it can't have more political choices. Young people are used to lots of options. The Independent Facebook Generation voters tend to be liberal on environmental and social issues. They are worried about the future of the planet and often volunteer in behalf of environmental or other causes. They don't understand the old battles over race and values. They take for granted that we have moved on from concerns about skin color or whom one sleeps with. But they are also worried about government spending and the deficit. They know they'll be footing the bill for the debt their parents and grandparents have racked up. Young voters doubt Social Security and Medicare will still be around for them and don't think their lives will be more secure than those of their parents. Even though the overall economy in Colorado fared better during the recession than most other parts of the country, young people here are still worried about their futures.

Since they are new voters, the positions of Facebook Generation voters are not well formed and their party alliances are very loose. They are trying to figure out where they fit in politically. According to a study done by Harvard's Institute of Politics, more than 50 percent of college freshmen consider themselves "middle of the road."[2]

When young voters are mobilized, as the Obama campaign was able to do in 2008, they can represent a significant voting bloc. They were captivated by the transformational nature of Barack Obama's candidacy and voted for him in large numbers, but since then have become disenchanted with the partisan gridlock in Washington and Obama's inability to bring about the fundamental changes to the political system that he promised in the campaign.

According to a poll conducted by Rock the Vote in Colorado a few months before the 2010 election, a significant majority of young voters said they were more cynical about politics than they were in 2008, and only about a quarter of those polled were pleased with Obama's performance.[3]

Many young voters tend to be liberal in their thinking and voted for Obama, but their allegiance could be fleeting, and it is possible the Democratic Party is merely renting but does not own their votes.

"They are much less likely to put a label on themselves. Neither party can claim that they own the demographic. They can't count on them for the rest of their life," says Steve Fenberg, the executive director and founder of a group called New Era Colorado. "Young people have a sense of being shortchanged. They feel like they graduated at the wrong time. . . . They think something needs to be done about the deficit because they know they're inheriting it," but they also want the government to fix the nation's problems. In that regard, they are like many of their baby boom parents, who want it all—they say they want the nation's budget balanced but also don't want cuts to their favorite government programs.

Elizabeth Wright, Richa Poudyal, and Ken Weber are Facebook Generation voters.

Elizabeth Wright is a twenty-one-year-old set to graduate from the University of Colorado in Boulder with an international affairs degree in 2011. She embodies the volunteer spirit that so many Facebook Generation voters have. She spent a semester studying in Ecuador in her junior year and decided to set up her own public service project in Puerto Cayo, a little town on the Ecuadoran coast. She planned to spend the summer after graduation there with eight friends teaching English, helping to organize an organic farming project, and launching an ecotour-ism venture for the town.

You might expect Wright to be a liberal Democrat. But you'd be wrong. She describes herself as a "very centrist" Independent. "I have conservative views on economics but liberal views on social issues and what we should use public policy for." She is very concerned about re-productive rights and opposes any infringement on them, and she sup-ports the right of gays to marry. But Wright says, "I do have a hard time when there is so much government involved in the economy. It feels like problems that occur later on happen because government is too involved. There are so many regulations.

"I took a test online—twenty questions—to figure out which party you fit in. I was a strange mix of Democrat, Green, and libertarian, and I think there's room for that." Wright says when she first got to college, she expected that CU Boulder would be a pretty liberal place, but as a volunteer for New Era Colorado helping to register voters, she saw that the majority of people registered as Independents. "It makes sense for our age group. We turn eighteen, and they ask you what you are. You have to check a box. But I think it takes a while to decide. We're all new to this game. In registering voters, I heard a lot of people say, 'I don't know what I am.' They'll walk up to the table and say, 'I don't know what I believe in. Do I have to say?' And I tell them, 'No, you can say you are unaffiliated.'"

Wright has a lot of friends who voted for Obama, as she did, and says she thinks it's because "young people like it when things get shaken up." But she also knows a lot of young women who were inspired by the can-didacy of Hillary Clinton and who wrote their college admission essays about that.

Wright says she is open to voting for a Republican but it would have to be a centrist Republican, and "it doesn't seem like the party is produc-ing any candidates like that." She would like to see candidates of both parties be more centrist and she's not sure what the answer is. "I don't think you're going to find a political party that has everything you want.

It's not just black-and-white and it can't just be red-and-blue. It fits me better to be an Independent because I can't totally agree with the blue side or the red side. I just wish I could vote in the primaries, but it seems like that should be something that would be easy to fix."

Wright has been an intern with New Era Colorado for two years. "It's just so fun. Everything we do is so hilarious. I remember at one event someone asked me what size shoe I wore and when I told her she said, 'Great, because we have these roller skates that are cowboy boots for you to wear while you register voters.'" Wright has also ridden the New Era bus known as *Tiny Dancer* to Fort Collins, Colorado Springs, and Denver to do voter registration. "We're making politics new. We're making it for ourselves."

Richa Poudyal is an eighteen-year-old high school student who lives in Boulder. She was born in the United States, but her parents are from Nepal. Her father is a software engineer. She registered to vote as soon as she could and chose to be an Independent.

> Since I live in Boulder everyone seems to be a Democrat, and I try not to get sucked into what everyone thinks. Registering as an Independent allows me to form my own opinions. I definitely lean left. If I were able to vote in the last election, I would have voted for Barack Obama, but I could also see myself voting for a Republican for president. I think it's good to register as an Independent because it forces me to pay more attention to the issues and understand things better and not just vote Democrat or Republican down the line.

Poudyal is still trying to figure out where she is on the ideological spectrum. For example, on fiscal issues—"I just feel like Democrats are not cutting anything and Republicans want to cut everything."

She is taking a politics class in high school that features discussions about issues and was kind of surprised at some of her classmates' opinions. For example, on affirmative action programs, most of them were opposed to affirmative action. Poudyal explains it this way. For them right now the most important thing is getting into college. "People think—what if I did better in school than that black guy—I deserve this—this is mine—I don't want anyone else taking my spot. Even people of color are against affirmative action. They say—I want to deserve my spot." Harvard's Institute of Politics voter survey found that young voters who considered themselves centrists are not particularly supportive of affirmative action.[4] Poudyal says some of her classmates are also wary of extending higher educational benefits to illegal immigrants. "A lot of kids are against it. They think—that takes away my spot."

Poudyal thinks people her age are mostly ignored by politicians or used as props. "People think high school kids don't care about politics, but there's no one asking them to care."

Steve Fenberg, twenty-seven, was an environmental policy major at the University of Colorado and describes himself as a "political junkie." He founded New Era Colorado when he graduated from college about five years ago. The nonpartisan, nonprofit organization's slogan is "Not Your Mama's Political Organization." The goal is to get young people more engaged in politics, not just voting but "playing more of an active role in the electoral and policy process. To be an engaged citizen, you need to do more than just vote," says Fenberg.

In two and a half years, the group has registered twenty-five thousand young voters—reaching out to them where they are at bars, festivals, concerts, and college campuses. Every year around Halloween, they throw a big party in Denver called "Trick or Vote" and knock on ten thousand doors, encouraging young people to register, ending the night with a concert.

That's the whole New Era strategy—combine social events and fun with politics. If you offer drinks and a band, they will come. New Era volunteers think nothing of dressing up in tutus and roller skates—and that's the men—and approaching young people to talk about local and state issues or encouraging them to register to vote. They manage to make politics fun as well as less intimidating. An Institute of Politics poll revealed that a majority of young people find the process of registering to vote or casting an absentee ballot confusing and difficult.[5]

On the first day of the Colorado legislative session, New Era gets a couple of hundred young people to turn out in a Denver bar to hear from state legislators. They also hold candidate debates that attract hundreds. It's hard to know how many come for the main event and how many come to mix and mingle with their peers, enjoy a cocktail, and listen to a band afterwards. But it doesn't matter. They get both. It's a great idea.

Fenberg also trains his staff and interns as lobbyists, and they've had some real legislative success. The group drafted a law to allow online voter registration in Colorado and got it passed in 2009. In just the first year, around 100,000 voters registered online—almost 10 percent of them were between the ages of seventeen and nineteen, and almost 60 percent were under forty years old.

During the 2011 legislative session, New Era lobbied in behalf of a bill to legalize gay civil unions. Ken Weber, a twenty-one-year-old junior at UC Boulder and a New Era intern, was one of those who testified in support of the bill before a state Senate committee. Weber supports gay rights and thinks if two people want to get married, they should be able to do so. A registered Independent, Weber describes his political views as being "right on the line between moderate and liberal."

He has voted mostly for Democrats so far. "I wouldn't be opposed to voting for a Republican, but in 2010 the Republican candidates were too extreme for my taste." Weber says he supports the right to gun ownership, but approves some limitations like background checks, a waiting period, and an assault weapons ban. He agrees with abortion rights, but thinks it's fine to put limits on them, like forbidding late-term abortions unless a health issue is involved.

He supports both the war in Afghanistan and the health reform passed by the Democrats. "We need a safety net, but the deficit is a concern.

We don't have to be running around cutting everything in sight. But you do need to cut some programs.

"What's right is right, and it doesn't matter what party it is," declares Weber. If the deficit is such a big concern, and he thinks it is, Weber wonders why the Republicans weren't talking about it when George Bush was in office. Similarly, he says the same politicians who criticized Barack Obama's decision to provide military support to the Libyan rebels and claimed the president didn't seek adequate congressional approval were the same ones who totally supported George Bush's military venture in Iraq. "If you support something, it should be because you believe it, not because of your party."

Weber, who is extremely articulate and well informed on political issues, says he gets his news from watching *The Daily Show*, looking at the websites of CNN and *The New York Times*, getting Yahoo AP News alerts on his phone, and checking out Rush Limbaugh and Glenn Beck's websites. He also used to watch Keith Olbermann on MSNBC because "I just want to see what all the sides are saying. Sometimes I think what they [Limbaugh and Beck] say is crazy, but sometimes they make some good points on issues. It's not all just crazy rambling, but that is a big part of it."

Growing up and living in Colorado Springs and going to college in Boulder, Weber gets exposure to both extremes of the political spectrum. With all the Evangelical Christian organizations based there and the military influence, Colorado Springs is conservative, and Boulder is a liberal college town.

The extremes of the two cities and the state are exemplified in their congressional representation. Colorado Springs is in the Fifth District and is represented in the House by Doug Lamborn, an extremely conservative three-term Republican who sponsored the 2011 legislation to take away National Public Radio's federal funding. Boulder, in the Second District, is represented by openly gay liberal Democrat Jared Polis, a multimillionaire Internet entrepreneur who spent $6 million of his own money to get elected in 2008. The extremes those two represent are a big part of the problem with politics, says Weber.

"The Fifth and Second Congressional Districts aren't competitive—a Republican is always going to win in the Fifth and a Democrat is always going to win in the Second District. No matter where I vote, at least for Congress, my vote is wasted. It's either going to be a conservative or a liberal. There's no moderate choice." Weber thinks the congressional districts should be more evenly balanced and more competitive but realizes when Democrats and Republicans are in charge of the system, you're not going to have much protection for Independents.

Weber's observation is smart and completely accurate. The extremes represented in Colorado's Second and Fifth Congressional Districts reflect the problems in our political system, and voters like Weber feel the deck is stacked against them.

The discovery of gold in Colorado in 1858 launched the Pikes Peak gold rush, and subsequent silver and gold strikes lured more prospectors to the state. Over the years, many arrived seeking their fortune. Colorado, which is known as the Centennial State because its admission to the union in 1876 was the same year as the hundredth anniversary of the signing of the Declaration of Independence, is still seen as a place to go for economic opportunity. And as each new wave of residents arrived, they changed the political balance of the state a little bit.

Colorado was considered solidly Republican over the past half century because the GOP usually controlled the state legislature and the Republican presidential candidate almost always won here. But Democrats held their own when it came to electing governors and U.S. Senators, so in some respects, Colorado has always been more of a swing state than it was given credit for. In the '70s and '80s, Colorado was represented by progressives in Congress like Gary Hart, Patricia Schroeder, and Tim Wirth, but in the 1990s the state's politics moved to the right. In the past few decades, with even more new residents arriving, the state has recently been trending more Democratic, and Democrats have won every gubernatorial and U.S. Senate race here in the past ten years.

A lot of this political change, which has made Colorado a swing state more hospitable to Democrats, is due to population changes. Similar transformations are also taking place in Nevada, Arizona, and New Mexico, where younger residents, transplants from other states, and especially Hispanics have significantly changed the states' demographics. Hispanics now account for more than 26 percent of the population in Nevada,[6] almost 30 percent in Arizona,[7] and 46 percent of all residents in New Mexico,[8] according to the latest U.S. Census. In Colorado, Hispanics now make up about 20 percent of the population.[9]

In 2002, Republicans held the governorship, both chambers of the state legislature, both U.S. Senate seats, and five of Colorado's seven House seats. Just two years later, Democrats won control of the state legislature, Democrat Ken Salazar was elected to the U.S. Senate, and they picked up the Third District congressional seat when Ken's brother John Salazar, a moderate Democrat, won the seat of retiring Republican Scott McInnis. In 2006, Democrat Bill Ritter won the governorship and Democrat Ed Perlmutter won the Seventh Congressional District seat when the incumbent Republican Bob Beauprez left it to unsuccessfully run for governor against Ritter. In 2008, Democrats picked up the other U.S. Senate seat with the victory of Mark Udall and another House seat when Betsy Markey defeated Fourth District GOP incumbent Marilyn Musgrave. So in the span of six years, Democrats managed to win the governorship, Democratic majorities in the legislature, both U.S. Senate seats, and five of seven House seats.

Barack Obama won 54 percent of the vote in Colorado in 2008, only the third Democratic presidential candidate to win the state since the 1940s. Bill Clinton carried Colorado in 1992, the year Ross Perot won almost a quarter of the state's vote. The only other Democrat to win Colorado during that time was Lyndon Johnson. According to CNN exit polling, Obama won Independent voters in Colorado by 10 points and self-described moderates, who made up about half the state's voters, by almost 30 percentage points. Obama won 61 percent of the Latino vote, and Udall won 63 percent of it in 2008.[10]

By 2011, the difference in party registration among Democrats, Republicans, and Independents here was razor thin, but Independent or unaffiliated voters outnumbered both of the two parties. Just over 34 percent of the state's voters registered as unaffiliated, 32.71 percent were Republican, and 32.37 percent were Democrats, according to the Secretary of State's Office. Undoubtedly, Colorado is a state where winning the Independent vote is essential to winning statewide elections.

In 2010, the Republican wave hit Colorado, reversing a few Democratic gains, but the outcome was not so bad here for the Democrats as it was in most of the rest of the country, partially because of Republican disarray. The Democrats lost two congressional seats with the defeat of John Salazar and Betsy Markey, leaving the delegation split in 2011 with four Republicans and three Democrats representing Colorado in the House of Representatives. In the state legislature, the Republicans managed to capture control of the House—but by just one vote—and the Democrats maintained their majority in the Senate. Former Denver Mayor John Hickenlooper, a Democrat, was elected to the governorship, and Democratic Senator Michael Bennet, who had been appointed by Ritter to fill Ken Salazar's Senate seat when Salazar was named Secretary of the Interior, was narrowly elected to a full term.

The story of how the Democrats managed to engineer their political turnaround in 2004 was the subject of a book called *The Blueprint: How the Democrats Won Colorado (and Why Republicans Everywhere Should Care)*, written by Colorado television journalist Adam Schrager and a former Republican state legislator Rob Witwer. The architects of the Democratic scheme were dubbed the "Gang of Four." Three of the four extremely wealthy individuals—Jared Polis, now a member of Congress; Rutt Bridges; and Tim Gill—made their money in the high-tech field. Pat Stryker inherited her wealth through her family's Stryker Corporation, a medical technology company. The Gang of Four decided to pool their resources and target certain state legislative seats, lavishing almost

$2.5 million on political groups that could legally funnel the money to Democratic candidates in four key Senate districts and ten House districts to facilitate a Democratic takeover of the state legislature.

Certainly vast sums of campaign cash always help win elections and there's no doubt the Gang of Four made a difference, but Democratic fund-raising prowess and organization are just part of the story of the changing political landscape in Colorado. Fielding good, moderate Democratic candidates who focused on local and fiscal rather than social issues, demographic changes that altered the political makeup of the state, a good national climate for Democrats, and the Republicans' insistence on running right-wing social conservative candidates who didn't appeal to the state's Independents and moderates are all equally important reasons for the rise in Democratic fortunes.

Moderates of both parties, but increasingly Democratic moderates, can do well in statewide elections here. In its turn to the right, the state GOP has alienated a lot of voters and nominated candidates who can't win. "The Democrats have had success largely because the Republicans have been lunatics," one Democratic consultant told me.

I heard that same sentiment expressed by many Coloradans, including, somewhat oddly, the former Chairman of the Colorado Republican Party, Dick Wadhams, a colorful and outspoken character. In announcing that he would not seek another term in 2011, he declared that he was "tired of the nuts" in the state party. In an e-mail to state central committee members, he urged them not to believe "uniting conservatives" was all they needed to do to win competitive races across the state, because that would mean "The ability of Colorado Republicans to win and retain the votes of hundreds of thousands of unaffiliated swing voters in 2012 will be severely undermined."[11]

The 2010 governor's race is an example of the kind of total Republican meltdown to which Wadhams was referring. Several months before the election, Wadhams admitted to me that the race was unwinnable for the Republicans, and John Hickenlooper would be the next governor, not the kind of thing you usually hear from a GOP state party chairman.

Former Congressman Scott McInnis was originally the front-runner for the GOP nomination until it was revealed that he plagiarized portions of an article on water policy for which he was paid $300,000 by a private foundation. Unknown candidate Dan Maes, who was backed by the Tea Party but had never held public office and was dogged by financial issues and campaign finance violations, narrowly defeated McInnis in the primary. Maes was urged to step aside in favor of a more viable candidate, but Maes would not get out of the race. Former Congressman Tom Tancredo declared that since Maes wasn't electable and wouldn't step down, Tancredo would run on the American Constitution Party ticket, focusing on the issue of illegal immigration.

In November, Maes, the official Republican candidate, wound up getting just 11 percent of the vote, the worst showing for a Republican candidate for governor in Colorado history and just barely over the 10 percent threshold required to retain the Republican Party's status as a major party in the state. Tancredo got 36 percent of the vote, and Democrat John Hickenlooper won with 51 percent.

Hickenlooper is an example of a pragmatic, centrist Democrat who is popular with business interests and can appeal to Colorado voters across the political spectrum. He is a fifty-nine-year-old former geologist who has described himself as a "geek." After he was laid off from his job, he became rich opening bars and restaurants—including Denver's first brewpub, the Wynkoop Brewing Company in 1988, in what was a run-down part of town known as LoDo that has since become a hip hangout. His first run for public office was for mayor of Denver in 2003, and he won by a 2 to 1 margin. He immediately reached out to the Republican governor to develop a partnership focusing on economic development in Denver and the state. He balanced the city budget by making cuts, and when he ran for reelection in 2007 he won 87 percent of the vote and was named one of the top five big city mayors in America by *Time* magazine.[12]

His campaign for governor focused on job creation and economic development. His campaign brochures called him "an entrepreneur on loan to the government" and highlighted his experience creating jobs, meeting a payroll, balancing budgets, and streamlining government. His campaign website boasted, "John has a track record of bringing people together to solve problems instead of stoking the same old partisan squabbles." Hickenlooper, who can be a bit aloof, has carefully cultivated an image that he is above politics and partisanship, and he capitalized on this during the gubernatorial campaign. One campaign ad showed him repeatedly getting in and out of the shower and rinsing off with his clothes on while he is heard to say, "I can't stand negative ads. Every time I see one, I feel like I need to take a shower" and vowing not to run any negative ads of his own.[13]

Hickenlooper is described by those who know him and have worked for him as more of a problem solver willing to look at all sides of an issue than someone who cares about partisan politics. On his first day in the mayor's office, he spent an hour in then Republican Governor Bill Owens's office to talk about how they could work together on problems affecting both the state and the city. "He turned out to be a very valuable mentor," Hickenlooper says of Owens, whom he still considers a friend.

In an interview with me before the election, Hickenlooper didn't sound much like a politician and he seems to relish being portrayed as a political amateur despite his obvious ambition. "I never wanted to be in politics. I didn't know anything about it," he declares. When asked why he decided to run for governor, Hickenlooper quipped, "I was too stupid to say no," but quickly adds, "the state is a much bigger canvas"—the implication being that it was obvious why he would want a promotion. Perhaps to show how hard he was working on the state's problems or what a man of the people he was, Hickenlooper announced shortly after taking office as governor that he planned to stop wearing ties.

Hickenlooper says his philosophy of government comes from his business experience and the single mother who raised him. "She felt that government should be smaller and more frugal but you needed government and too many Republicans were just anti-government."

Hickenlooper also mentioned his late mother in his gubernatorial inaugural address. "Even in adversity, she was an optimist. She was good at pinching a penny, and above all she believed that hard work could overcome almost anything."

But it's not at all clear that hard work alone will get the state of Colorado out of its current fiscal situation. Although Colorado's budget problems were not nearly so severe as those of many other states, Hickenlooper inherited a $1 billion state budget shortfall and was faced with a lot of tough choices when he took office. "We are Coloradans. We are not daunted by a little cold weather. We don't shrink from high passes or hard work," he said in that address. Hickenlooper vowed to "face our budget challenge squarely. We will make the hard choices necessary to balance Colorado's budget just like families do at their kitchen tables."

In early 2011, Hickenlooper unveiled a state budget that featured almost $600 million in cuts, including more than $300 million to K–12 education, which would force teacher layoffs and school closures and more than $30 million in reductions to higher education funding, a plan that drew more support from Republicans than from fellow Democrats. "We don't have a choice. For one year we're going to have to retrench," said Hickenlooper, who rejected the idea of using reserve funds or any revenue increases to make up the state shortfall.

When Hickenlooper first became mayor, he asked Michael Bennet, who like Hickenlooper had attended Wesleyan University in Connecticut, to be his chief of staff. Two years later, Bennet was appointed Denver Public Schools superintendent despite having no background in education. Bennet, who also has a law degree from Yale, had worked in Washington, including a brief stint in the Clinton Administration before moving to Denver. Before joining Hickenlooper's office, Bennet worked for an investment firm in Denver owned by billionaire Philip Anschutz.

During Barack Obama's campaign for president, Bennet served as one of his advisers on education policy, and after Ken Salazar was appointed Secretary of the Interior by Obama, Bennet was reportedly recommended by the White House as his replacement. Colorado Governor Bill Ritter, in a surprise move, selected Bennet, who had never run for or held political office, to fill the Senate seat. Although there were a number of Colorado politicians who were interested, including Hicken-looper, Ritter told me when he interviewed candidates for the job he was impressed with Bennet's private sector experience, competence, and thoughtful demeanor.

One of those who was especially disappointed in the decision was Andrew Romanoff, who also wanted the job. Romanoff, forty-five, had been a member of the state legislature and was the second youngest Speaker of the House in Colorado history. "Andrew was very upset with me," said Ritter. "He really believed he would be chosen. He didn't even think it was a contest. It was shocking to him when I didn't choose him," recalled Ritter, sitting in his office in the state capitol just a few hours before the polls closed on primary day 2010.

Romanoff decided to challenge Bennet in the Democratic primary and ran an aggressive and quite negative campaign, bringing up charges about Bennet's performance on financial deals during his time at the investment firm with a campaign ad called "Greed." Romanoff also ran an ad about a questionable financial decision Bennet made while head of the Denver school system. Bennet had supported a complicated financing deal involving pension certificates with a derivative attached and a fluctuating interest rate to pay for a shortfall in the system's pension fund, a deal that wound up costing the district more than $100 million dollars in interest and other fees.[14]

The primary split the state party, with Democrats forced to choose sides in a race between two bright, talented rising stars. Bennet had not only the governor's support but that of Senator Mark Udall and Barack Obama as well. Romanoff was endorsed by Bill Clinton and also had many state Democrats lined up behind him.

During the campaign, Romanoff went public with the fact that about a year before the primary election, he was contacted by an Obama aide about a possible administration job if he would not run against Bennet. Romanoff declined and said he planned to run despite Obama's intention to support Bennet. Romanoff, who refused to take PAC money and sold his house so he could put $325,000 of his own money into the campaign, was considered the better, more natural campaigner, and Bennet a bit stiff, not really a natural politician. But Bennet had the money. He spent more than $5 million on the primary campaign—more than twice as much as Romanoff—and won the primary with 54 percent of the vote to Romanoff's 46 percent.

In his victory speech on primary night, Bennet talked about the contentious and childish nature of the U.S. Senate and may also have been making a reference to the campaign he had just been through.

"I had no idea that being a parent would prepare me for the Senate most of all. . . . I think you all know exactly what I am talking about. Forty-five minutes into a long road trip, after the excitement wears off, the kids are in the backseat doing everything they can to bother one another. And every time you turn around, they immediately put on their best smile and point their finger at each other. Well, that backseat is a lot like the United States Senate. The bottom line is this: Washington needs a lot less finger-pointing and name-calling. And a lot more problem solving."

Meanwhile, the Republicans were having their own primary battle to settle who would run for the Senate seat, and while nasty in its own way, it also featured quite a bit of humor—thanks to the verbally undisciplined Ken Buck. Jane Norton, a former lieutenant governor, was the establishment candidate who was urged to get into the race by Senator John McCain and other national and state GOP leaders. Buck was the insurgent and Tea Party favorite.

Norton made reference to her sex during the campaign on more than one occasion and said she would be more electable because she was a woman. In a TV ad named "Backbone," she referred to the negative ads being run against her by independent groups and looking straight at the camera said, "You think Ken would be man enough to do it himself."[15]

That obviously got Buck's dander up. He had the chance to respond while attending an event sponsored by the Independence Institute, a conservative think tank based in Golden, Colorado. The event was billed as a party, to promote whiskey drinking, cigar smoking, and shooting "as a fundamental right . . . the most fun, most politically incorrect event of the year . . . a liberal's nightmare." It was the perfect place for Buck's sort of irreverence.

When a woman asked him why she should vote for him, he shot back, "Because I do not wear high heels." He added that he wore "cowboy boots, they have real bullshit on them."[16]

Later he would be asked by the media to explain the quip. "She has questioned my manhood, and I think it's fair to respond," he said in reference to Norton. Buck said he was trying to be humorous, but maybe it didn't come out that way. Norton turned the whole thing into another campaign ad.

Buck's plain-speaking, blunt style also got him in trouble when he was caught on tape saying of conservative supporters who were questioning him about Barack Obama's birth, "Will you tell those dumbasses at the Tea Party to stop asking questions about birth certificates." In an appearance on *Meet the Press*, he compared being gay to alcoholism when he was asked if being gay was a matter of heredity or choice.[17]

All the gaffes may have actually endeared Buck to the conservative base and helped propel him to victory over Norton. But it was a different story in the general election.

I caught up with Buck in the lobby of the Brown Palace Hotel in Denver a few days after the primary, and he was on top of the world. Asked why he won, he responded with a big smile, "I got more votes." When queried about where he grew up, he retorted, "I haven't grown up." That much seemed clear.

Born in New York, he attended Princeton and then law school in Wyoming and went to work for Dick Cheney while he was a congressman during the Iran–Contra hearings. Buck worked at the Justice Department and also served in the United States attorney's office in Colorado before being elected district attorney of Weld County, north of Denver. Buck's credentials were much more establishment than he tried to portray, and he had never worked in the private sector, but Buck still considered himself the "anti-establishment" candidate.

Buck admitted that, "I open my mouth a lot," but he believed the notoriety helped him. "There's no such thing as bad press," he told me. He called the Democrats charge "that Ken Buck is too extreme" utter "nonsense." But it wouldn't prove to be nonsense. The Bennet campaign and its supporters were very successful in portraying Buck as "too extreme for Colorado" in numerous campaign commercials. Buck's positions and words were used as evidence of this extremism in ads especially targeted at women voters. Buck was shown calling Social Security "a horrible policy" and saying that he opposed abortion even in cases of rape and incest. A rape case that Buck declined to prosecute in 2006 as district attorney because he said the victim knew her attacker and had previously had sex with him became an issue in the campaign. At the time, Buck said he did not think he could get a conviction in the case and a jury could decide the victim's claim of rape was "buyer's remorse."[18] The matter was raised at a Denver Metro Chamber of Commerce debate held a few weeks before the general election.

It was a much more sober and cautious Buck that I encountered after that debate. He seemed to be off his game, tentative, and on the defensive. The things that had been assets for him in the primary were turned against him in the general election. During the debate, in reference to all the negative ads Bennet was running, Buck said, "It's unfortunate that a sitting senator has to stoop that low to run away from his record."

But to a large extent, that was exactly the campaign Bennet was running. The Democrats were not popular nationally, many Americans, including Independent voters, were uneasy about the Democratic health reform plan, the deficit, growth in federal spending, and of course, the economy. So the Bennet campaign decided to take the focus off all of that and put it on Buck. In the months since the primary election, Bennet had gotten better and more natural at campaigning, but he still didn't reveal much. He came off as a bit distant on the campaign trail and more than a few Coloradans mentioned his accent to me. One Democrat told me, "He sounds like Thurston Howell" (the millionaire character on *Gilligan's Island*).

Bennet, forty-six, was largely seen by many Coloradans as a child of Eastern privilege. He was born in New Delhi, India, where his father, Douglas, was in the foreign service. His grandfather worked in the Roosevelt Administration and his father, who has a doctorate degree from Harvard, worked in the Carter and Clinton Administrations before becoming the head of National Public Radio and the president of Wesleyan University. His father's mother, Phoebe, is a direct *Mayflower* descendant, and Michael's brother James is the editor of *The Atlantic Monthly*.

On his mother's side of the family, though, the story is quite different. His maternal grandparents were Polish Jews who survived the Warsaw ghetto and came to the United States with his mother, Susanne Klejman, after World War II, having survived the Nazis but losing many family members in the Holocaust.

Growing up in Washington, Bennet attended St. Albans prep school and served as a page in Congress. At Yale Law, which his wife, Susan Daggett, also attended, Bennet was the editor of the *Yale Law Journal*. It is because of his wife that he moved to Colorado—she was taking a job as a lawyer with an environmental group.

They have three adorable daughters who were featured in his campaign ads, and some of the lessons of the campaign had obviously rubbed off on them. During one campaign event, Bennet mentioned that he had promised them a dog after the election, and when he asked his daughter Caroline what she would do if they didn't get a dog, without a missing a beat she said, "I'd run a negative ad against you."

Buck, with his cowboy boots and his "bullshit," may have connected with Tea Party, Western Slope, and Eastern Plains voters, but it was ultimately women and Independent and swing voters who decided this race. Even in such an overwhelmingly Republican year, Buck became more of an issue than federal spending, enabling Bennet to eke out a victory in one of the year's closest and hardest fought Senate races. At close to $50 million raised and spent, it was the most expensive Senate race in the country, with more than $30 million spent by outside interest groups and another —$16 million by the candidates and political parties.[19]

CNN exit polling showed that of the 38 percent of voters who considered themselves moderate, Bennet carried 60 percent. Bennet also carried the women's vote by more than 16 points.[20]

About a month after the election when I talked with him, Bennet told me he believed he owed his victory to Independent voters. "There is an independent spirit in the state. . . . I do think that Colorado is a swing state—it's a purple state. You have to win Independents to win." Bennet has no idea if he would have won against Norton, but says nominating an extreme candidate from either side is not a way to electoral success in Colorado.

> There's a strong sense that the way Washington does its work is out of touch with the way other people do their work. I think it's true to some extent . . . the hyperpartisanship of Washington is as bad as I thought when I came here and is disconnected from the problem solving people would like to see.
>
> I had a lot of friends who said to me, "Are you crazy, why do you want to go back to that place, it's so dysfunctional. . . ." This is the land of made-up facts. . . . There are a bunch of Washington special interests that are fighting with each other and masquerading as political parties.

Strong words for a child of Washington.

Ironically, for someone involved in the most expensive Senate race in the country, Bennet also says he thinks further campaign finance reform is one part of the solution. He has introduced lobbying reform that would place a lifetime ban on members of Congress becoming lobbyists; legislation to provide more transparency and accountability in the congressional earmarking process; and reforms to the Senate filibuster and other Senate rules.

His Senate colleague Mark Udall also introduced Senate reform legislation aimed at streamlining the legislative process and eliminating a lot of the delays bogging down the Senate while still respecting the rights of the minority. Any Senate rules changes would require sixty-seven votes—even more than the sixty votes required to break a filibuster—and Udall acknowledges getting significant reform passed will be extremely difficult. "My plan is to get these ideas circulating, continue the conversations, and work on this. The goal of these changes is to work better, more efficiently, and have more debate," Udall explained to me.

Udall has made it a point of trying to work with Republicans in Congress. "When I was elected to the Senate, I had a record of being independent and working together to solve problems. . . . I'm always looking to get something done, and that's what my constituents want—they want me to try and find solutions," he says. "I'm frustrated and worried as much as anybody about the system."

In his 2008 Senate race, Udall's opponent and the Republicans continually referred to him as a "Boulder liberal"—something Udall is a little touchy about, pointing out that he actually lives in a suburb of Boulder. Although he ran unopposed for the Democratic nomination, Udall spent almost $13 million on his Senate campaign—a Colorado record up to that point, but he won by the biggest margin for a Colorado Democrat in a Senate race since Gary Hart in 1974.[21]

When he decided to run for the Senate, Udall started to position himself as more of a centrist, stressing defense issues and moving to the right on things like gun control. Udall says he does think he is fairly representative of the state and the typical Coloradan, and he has moved even more toward the center since being elected to the Senate, although his past voting record has been pretty liberal—he had a 92 percent record of voting with the Democratic leadership in the last Congress.[22] Udall, who served in the House for ten years before being elected to the Senate, has a rich Western political lineage. His uncle Stewart was

Secretary of the Interior in the Kennedy and Johnson Administrations, and Stewart's son Tom—Mark's cousin, to whom he is close—also served in the House and was elected to the Senate in 2008 from New Mexico. Mark Udall's father, whom he physically resembles, was Morris "Mo" Udall, an eloquent, witty man with a wicked, dry sense of humor who served in the House for thirty years and made an unsuccessful run for president in 1976. He died in 1998, just a month after Mark was elected to the House.

The ruggedly handsome sixty-year-old Udall looks and acts the quintessential Coloradan. He headed Outward Bound there for ten years and has climbed a number of mountains, including Mount Everest. He was described to me by a Colorado journalist as someone who "perfectly looks the part of a Western senator." He is soft spoken, friendly, and extremely popular in Colorado.

After the 2010 election, Udall seemed to be making even more of an effort to be more moderate, especially on fiscal issues. He became co-chairman of a group of moderate Democratic senators that had previously been led by Evan Bayh and Blanche Lambert Lincoln before they left the Senate and whose membership included Virginia's Mark Warner and New Hampshire's Jeanne Shaheen.

He voted against President Obama's tax-cut package in December 2010, citing the cost and the increase to the federal deficit it would cause. He was the first Democrat to support a constitutional balanced budget amendment introduced by conservative Republican Richard Shelby of Alabama. And with Republican Orrin Hatch of Utah, Udall introduced legislation in 2011 calling for the creation of a committee that would target wasteful, redundant, and underperforming federal programs for elimination. Udall also said he would consider slowly raising the retirement age as a way to help ensure Social Security's solvency.

Udall calls Colorado "a pragmatic state," libertarian on issues like guns and who you choose to live with but fiscally conservative. The Western tradition is evident in the aversion by business leaders to regulation, but at the same time there is a desire to protect the environment. Udall believes if he were alive today, Teddy Roosevelt would be a Democrat.

Sitting in the governor's office with its magnificent view of the Rocky Mountains, former Governor Bill Ritter says Udall's voting record in the Senate has indeed been more moderate than it was when Udall was in the House, reflecting the fact that he is now representing the entire state.

Ritter, a district attorney in Denver and former U.S. prosecutor before he was elected governor, says he tried to work with Republican state legislators but got very little cooperation until he announced he wouldn't be seeking reelection.

The politics of Colorado are "right of center—it's a purple state," and the reason Democrats have had so much success is that they have fielded candidates who can appeal across the political spectrum, Ritter tells me. Although he is a Catholic who opposes abortion, Ritter believes it's a mistake for the Republicans to focus on issues like abortion and gay rights. "They are running on tired issues of the past. . . . The Republicans don't have their act together. . . . Here's the strategy for winning in Colorado, you've got to appeal to Independent voters. At some point, the Republicans are going to catch on to that."

Norma Anderson understands this. The first woman majority leader in both the state House and Senate, she is something of a grande dame of Colorado politics, one of the most pragmatic, moderate, and well respected Republican political figures in the state. Feisty and direct, she looks far younger than her seventy-nine years and is still involved in civic affairs and serves on various state boards and commissions. A lifelong Republican, she was a Goldwater girl who did volunteer work for the party until her first run for the legislature in 1982.

When she was majority leader, Anderson was known for her bipartisanship, and she says she never told her party members how to vote, unlike today. She says the Republicans and Democrats could work together to get things done back then, but toward the end of her time in the legislature, things were getting more contentious and partisan. Term-limited from running for reelection, Anderson says she decided to quit a year before her term was over because she got tired of all the fighting and not getting things accomplished.

I didn't want to be a lame duck, I decided I'm going to leave on my terms. I always believed in being fair to everyone. You don't always have to agree, but you have to be fair and listen. Sometimes the other side has some good ideas and you don't know unless you listen. Now the Republican Party is so divided that I don't know how they're going to win anything—it's the social issues, the religious issues, gays, guns, and abortion—and if you don't agree with them, they don't want you. That's what's happened to our party. It's been taken over.

Anderson says Coloradans care about education, transportation, health care, jobs, but her fellow Republicans wanted to focus on things like requiring a U.S. flag and a copy of the Ten Commandments in every classroom.

Another senior statesman of Colorado Republican politics is Hank Brown, who served for ten years in the U.S. House in the 1980s and one term in the U.S. Senate from 1991 to 1996. I met him at his home in the Cherry Creek neighborhood of Denver to talk for a few hours about Colorado politics. Brown had a record in Congress of being a staunch fiscal conservative, but also had a pro-environmental record, and he has always been pro-choice, which he thinks is in line with the way most Coloradans, especially Independents, think.

Brown says the Democrats in Colorado were simply smarter and better than the Republicans about recruiting candidates who would appeal to voters statewide. Brown had endorsed Jane Norton for Senate and thought she would have been a much better candidate. Of Bennet, he says, "It's not his style to show himself. You don't see inside with Bennet. People don't know him that well." Brown says Hickenlooper, "has a personality that fits Colorado. He's a real person. That makes a difference here."

Brown might just as well have been talking about himself. Soft spoken and thoughtful, Brown, seventy, who also served as president of the University of Colorado, had a reputation for being bipartisan when he was in Congress. "I never thought the way you proved how tough you were was to talk tough. I don't think I engaged in the kind of demagoguery that seems to happen these days on both sides.

"The best things we got done when I was in Congress were bipartisan." The kind of in-your-face politics that is standard today is not the style of the understated and gentlemanly Brown, who is a throwback to a different political era. Brown served with former GOP Majority Leader Tom DeLay and didn't like his take-no-prisoners style of politics. "He not only had to do it to you—he had to tell you he was going to do it to you.

"The electorate isn't as partisan as Congress is. The people are ashamed that Congress operates that way," says Brown. "There's no sense of fair play anymore."

Also representing Colorado in the U.S. Senate in the '90s was Ben Nighthorse Campbell, who had a very different style from Brown. Campbell, seventy-eight, a member of the Northern Cheyenne tribe, sold Native American jewelry and rode a Harley-Davidson motorcycle. He was larger than life. He wore bolo ties and his long hair in a ponytail.

Campbell says before he got into politics, he worked as a cop, truck driver, prison counselor at Folsom Prison, farmhand, and rancher. Colorful and direct, Campbell calls his political career "a blind-ass accident." He was living in rural Durango, Colorado, one of the more conservative areas of the state, when he was asked to run for the state legislature by the Democrats for a seat no one thought he could win. He won, served two terms, and then was asked to run for Congress in 1986.

He served in the House for three terms before being elected to the Senate in 1992. Three years later, after the Republicans had gained control of Congress, Campbell switched parties and became a Republican. He was reelected in 1998 but kept a pledge to serve only two terms and did not run again in 2004.

"Colorado voters like to measure you, and it is less important to them what party you are in than what you stand for."

Campbell explains his party switch by saying, "I got tired of the Democrats." He was getting more and more troubled about the Democrats' spending and found himself voting more often with the Republicans and "getting a lot of grief from party leaders and the left wing of the party" about it. At a public meeting back in Colorado, a voter told him, "You're nothing but a Republican in Democratic clothing," so that gave him the idea to become a Republican.

Campbell says he has never regretted the decision to switch parties. "I used to get pounded by the right wing just like I got pounded by the left wing. . . . I guess if you've got both ends mad at you—you must be doing something right."

"We've got what I call the 'wing nuts' deciding the party platforms and setting the agenda of the parties. And what they have is an intolerance of anybody else's ideas. The true believers are driving the train, and they don't want to let anyone else on board," asserts Campbell. "The party activists and interest groups are driving this. If you disagree with them one percent of the time, they trash you. What they want is rubber stamp subservience."

Campbell, who is pro-choice, recalls a Republican state convention where he had anti-abortion people screaming at him. "The Christian right elements like those in Colorado Springs for me ruined the party."

Colorado is full of quirky politicians who march to their own drummer. Another one of them is Richard "Dick" Lamm, who was governor from 1975 to 1987. In 1992, Campbell beat Lamm in the Democratic primary for the Senate campaign.

Critical of both political parties, saying they were controlled by special interests, Lamm in 1996 sought the presidential nomination of the Reform Party, which had developed out of Ross Perot's 1992 presidential run. Perot fought Lamm's effort and won the party's nomination. "I'm sorry that I did it now," admits Lamm. "The Democratic Party did a lot for me and this was an extreme act of disloyalty. It was all so useless, I definitely did burn some bridges, but I did it and that's me."

Now, Lamm says, "I really don't feel I have a political home. I think both parties are deeply flawed. I just think the Democratic Party is less flawed. The Republican Party is hopelessly controlled by their right wing, and the Democratic Party is hopelessly controlled by the unions and other special interests," Lamm, seventy-six, told me when I met him for coffee near his Denver home.

Lamm, who has always been rather pessimistic in his public pronouncements to the point where he earned the nickname "Governor Gloom," says, "There's a substantial question about whether democracy can make hard choices. I see substantial economic chaos ahead. . . . The country is in great peril and we are in danger of leaving a worse country to our children.

"I definitely feel America needs a third party. The fiscally responsible Democrats and socially liberal Republicans should form a new party that I'm sure would itself become corrupted in time. I don't think either political party has an agenda to keep America great or to address the magnitude of the problems we face." Lamm says he would call this new party the "grandchildren's party" and would focus on getting the nation's fiscal house in order. "We're having a very hard time downsizing expectations, but people have to understand what's at stake."

The Independents have to get motivated and make their voices heard, Lamm says, and he predicts "America is going to experience some sort of crisis that will scare people enough that they will take public policy seriously."

Two former Democrats who have become Independents and who are trying to build an Independent movement in Colorado are Joelle Riddle and Kathleen Curry. Riddle is from Durango, a town of about sixteen thousand in the southwestern corner of the state, three hours from Santa Fe and six hours from Denver. The famous scene in *Butch Cassidy and the Sundance Kid*, in which Butch and Sundance jump off a cliff into a roaring river, was filmed just north of Durango.

Riddle, forty-three, grew up here. Her father was in the oil and gas business. Her family was Mormon and her great-grandfather, John D. Lee, had nineteen wives. Riddle says she was raised to believe that it wasn't a woman's place to be involved in politics, and she never voted until she was thirty-three years old. But once she started to get interested, she says, "I jumped in all the way." Riddle got involved in local Democratic politics, and it didn't take long for her to become chairwoman of the La Plata County Democrats. In 2006, she decided to run for the three-member county commission and she won. Riddle says she thought she was elected to represent everyone in the county, to look at all sides of an issue, but, "The Democrats were not very pleased with that. They felt like they owned that seat and they wanted me to toe the party line."

She started getting pressure from party leaders and decided not to run for reelection. In 2009, she became an Independent. "I wasn't there to be a puppet or a pawn of the party. . . . I was tired of people getting after me for meeting with a Republican or trying to develop coalitions that were out of the norm—like meeting with farmers and ranchers to talk about environmental issues."

Riddle says the same partisanship and polarization that exists in Congress also takes place on the local level. "In a small community, it's even more difficult to buck the party system because you know these people and see them in the grocery store."

Riddle decided to get involved with the group IndependentVoting.org because she believes the political system is broken and fundamental change is required. "I think we need to start breaking down the ways the parties control the process."

She founded Independent Voters for Colorado to work on issues like equal ballot access for all candidates and opening up primaries to unaffiliated voters in the state. "I'm planning to take a shot at that. There's a great opportunity to organize Independents—not create another party but organize them in a way that's not happening now. I want to do something different. These partisan politics are damaging to our system at every level. We don't have democracy to the extent that we could, and this feeds voter apathy."

Kathleen Curry is also from rural, western Colorado, and her husband is a cattle rancher in Gunnison, a town of about five thousand where Wyatt Earp lived briefly after the gunfight at the O.K. Corral in Tombstone, Arizona. Curry served three terms in the state General Assembly and had numerous clashes with party leaders. She felt the Democrats were not fiscally conservative enough, and were too focused on raising revenue and not enough on cutting expenditures. At the end of 2009, she decided to leave the Democratic Party and officially become an Independent, the only one in the Colorado legislature.

The decision cost her dearly. Although she lost her committee chairmanship, Curry says she didn't regret the decision. Because the Democrats held such a narrow margin in the state House chamber and there were a lot of close votes, Curry says her colleagues called her "the wild card" because once she became Independent, she could vote whichever way she wanted and didn't have to follow the party leadership.

The constituents in her rural district—where more than 40 percent of the voters are Independents—supported her decision. Privately, some of her colleagues even admitted to being a bit jealous. She said both Republican and Democratic legislators told her they wished they could do the same thing, and she always told them, "You can."

"I don't in general like the two-party system. I'm not comfortable working within those constraints. I don't feel that is a good way to do business. It causes the parties not to be focused on the welfare of the state but on their own welfare—how to increase their numbers and hold the majority. For me, it's nonsense," declares Curry. "I want to find the middle ground. The parties are not focused on that, just on winning. "We need a different approach than the group-think approach."

Curry, who had run unopposed in her previous two elections, wanted to run as an Independent candidate in 2010 for another legislative term, but Colorado has some of the most restrictive ballot access laws in the country. Candidates who want to leave the Republican or Democratic parties and become unaffiliated and then run for office are required by state law to do it seventeen months before the election. Curry, who lost a legal challenge to the Colorado law, was forced to mount an uphill battle and run as a write-in candidate.

House District Sixty-one, which Curry represented, is a sprawling and extremely diverse district that includes the exclusive, liberal enclave of Aspen in the north along with tiny conservative towns with names like Silt, Basalt, and Rifle and more rural, ranching areas in the south like her hometown of Gunnison.

Although she was pretty well known in the district, Curry found trying to run a write-in campaign meant endless days and nights talking to voters one on one, trying to explain how and why they should cast a write-in ballot for her and answering the question, "How can you be elected if you're not in either party?"

One such stop during the 2010 campaign was at the Blue Bird Coffee Shop in Glenwood Springs, a city of about ten thousand that was originally known as Defiance in its earliest days when it was just a camp of tents, saloons, and brothels. President Teddy Roosevelt once spent an entire summer here, and Wild West legend Doc Holliday lived out the final months of his life in Glenwood Springs and is buried here. The Colorado and Roaring Fork Rivers converge here, making Glenwood Springs an extremely popular destination for fishing and rafting.

The Blue Bird is a Western amalgam of bookstore, outdoor clothing and equipment outfitter, and café featuring gourmet coffee, organic ice cream, gluten-free cupcakes, ceiling fans, and nineteenth-century saloon-style furnishings. Ultraliberal, politically correct bohemians and crunchy granola types coexist with conservative, "Don't tell me what to do" cowboys in Colorado towns like this one.

Bruce Christensen, the mayor of Glenwood Springs, is an Independent and a Curry supporter. He's lived here for more than thirty years, been an Independent for all of that time, and been mayor for the last five. "Partisan politics is a turn-off to the middle-of-the road people.

The way you govern is you build consensus. You meet in the middle and everybody gives a little and you get something done."

It sounds like just basic common sense, which Christensen says seems to be in short supply in Washington. "Especially when you live out here in the boondocks, what strikes you is the nastiness, which is not something the people want to see. . . . In both political parties there are people in the backrooms pulling the strings and telling the politicians what to do, and it's not what's best for the country . . . the people are being ignored."

A steady stream of people come in throughout the afternoon to meet and talk with Curry, like seventy-nine-year-old Joanne Clements, a retired teacher and a Democrat who has come to pick up a Curry campaign sign to put on her lawn. "Both parties suck," she tells me. "The parties aren't doing their jobs, they aren't listening to people. This is a ridiculous situation in Congress. I keep saying Ross [Perot], where are you now?"

The next morning, Curry holds an open house in a conference room on the second floor of the gleaming fire station in Aspen, but the only person who shows up is a local newspaper reporter. There are two giant plasma screen TVs in the meeting room and a Viking range in the extremely well-appointed stainless steel kitchen downstairs. Aspen, like Disneyland for the obscenely wealthy, makes Martha's Vineyard look like a rustic summer camp for the underprivileged.

Virtually any designer store you can find on Fifth Avenue has a branch here, from Dior and Prada to Gucci and Louis Vuitton. A restaurateur who was raised on New York's Upper East Side and attended prep school there tells me Aspen is every bit as sophisticated as New York. He said he has been in wine cellars in Aspen with hundreds of bottles worth thousands of dollars apiece that exceeds anything he has seen elsewhere. There are also Aspen art galleries that regularly have Monets and Picassos on view. What makes Aspen so special, he explains, is that it is a small town with all the big city pleasures.

And, of course, without all the inconveniences of having to deal with the less well heeled. It takes a lot of money even to visit Aspen for a few days, which tends to weed out the riffraff. It's almost impossible to get a hotel room for under two hundred dollars a night, and one local tells me "that would be a dump." It's pretty typical for a sandwich to cost twelve dollars and the most modest restaurant meal is upwards of fifty dollars.

The wealthy can come here to soak up a little culture, mix and mingle with the cultural and political elite who participate in the Aspen Institute's Ideas Festival every summer, and also rub shoulders with celebrities who own homes here and are relaxed about frequenting the town's boutiques and restaurants. Driving into Aspen past the airport, one has the jaw-dropping experience of seeing literally dozens and dozens of private jets the size of commercial airliners parked and waiting. This is wealth on a scale that most people can't even imagine.

The year-round population is only about five thousand, but the town swells when those who own second, third, and fourth homes here come for the ski season or the summer music festival. *The Wall Street Journal* calls Aspen "the most expensive town in America,"[23] more expensive than the Hamptons, Beverly Hills, and Palm Beach. The average home price here is $6 million, and someone who makes $100,000 qualifies for subsidized housing.

Obviously, trying to campaign in a place like this on a shoestring budget requires ingenuity, and Curry sometimes camps out in the homes of supporters. But that doesn't mean roughing it. A typical home in Aspen, fairly unassuming from the outside, features cathedral ceilings, slate floors throughout, sunken tubs, guest wings with their own kitchens, living rooms and massive stone fireplaces, and a doggy shower in the garage.

Curry mounted an aggressive campaign and out of some thirty thousand votes cast in her election, wound up losing by only about three hundred votes. She spent about fifty thousand dollars on the campaign and says the Democratic Party and its supporters spent about a quarter of a million dollars—more than any other state House race in Colorado—to beat her.

"I'm profoundly disappointed in the integrity of the system. What I learned is that money is a serious obstacle to change. Once they are elected, these officials owe everything to the parties and their supporters. I think there is a huge disconnect between the voters and the people who are getting elected," says Curry.

> What's sad is that as the voters get discouraged, they tend to walk away from the process. They tend to give up. I think the voters have shown their dissatisfaction with the two-party system by disaffiliating. But now they have to step up and support candidates who are Independent as well. That's the only way we're going to change anything. You cannot fix a party system from within. If the voters are really not happy with the two-party system, they're going to have to step up and support Independent candidates.

Facebook Generation Independent voter Ken Weber has a slightly different take but, like most of the Facebook Generation voters, expresses frustration with the political system. "People talk about having a third party. I don't think that's realistic. But I think there do need to be some reforms to the system. . . . I know a lot of young people are cynical and they don't think it matters whether you vote for a Republican or Democrat."

In order for the two parties to engage Facebook Generation voters like Weber, and win their support, political leaders will have to do things differently. They have to keep their promises, work together, and make some progress on big issues. These skeptical Facebook Generation voters are always on the lookout for a lack of authenticity and will stay home if they don't think politicians are delivering.

Just like many of the older Independent voters in Colorado, the

Linda Killian

Facebook Generation Independents care about personal freedom and environmental protection but are fiscally conservative. Voters here like moderate political leaders. There is a strong independent spirit in Colorado, driven by its Western, pioneer traditions, that is exemplified by its many quirky politicians. Coloradans, like so many Independents around the country, don't mind unpredictability, but they do want integrity.

6

The Old Dominion Is the New Virginia—
Home of the Starbucks Moms and Dads

Virginia

I like the dreams of the future better than the history of the past.
THOMAS JEFFERSON IN A LETTER TO JOHN ADAMS, 1816

No STATE HAS A longer and richer history, has undergone more significant transformation in recent decades, or better illustrates the demographic changes taking place in this country, especially in the South, than does the swing state of Virginia.

In 1607, the first permanent English colony in America was established here at Jamestown. The state was home to George Washington, Thomas Jefferson, and James Madison as well as patriots like Patrick Henry. The Virginia General Assembly is the oldest legislature in the western hemisphere. The Virginia Constitution, the first in the nation, was drafted in 1776 by Jefferson, Madison, and George Mason, and was used as a basis for Jefferson's Declaration of Independence and Madison's work on the U.S. Constitution.

Virginia is both deeply Southern and incredibly modern and diverse. Richmond, the state capital, served as the capital of the Confederacy during the Civil War, and its streets are dotted with statues of Jefferson Davis, Stonewall Jackson, and other Confederate figures. Many

131

Virginians still remain extremely proud of their Confederate history and like to celebrate it. More Civil War battles were fought here than anywhere else in the country, but the bucolic battlefields within a short drive of Washington are now surrounded by the exurban growth of condos, town houses, strip malls, and highways that has come to personify Northern Virginia.

Thirty percent of the state's population lives here, and the region is pivotal in deciding state elections. Its burgeoning immigrant population has significantly changed the character and political composition of the area. Almost 40 percent of the population growth in Virginia between 2000 and 2010 occurred in three Northern Virginia counties: Fairfax, Prince William, and Loudoun, and much of it was fueled by immigrants and minorities.[1]

Tom Davis, a moderate Republican and astute political observer, represented part of this area in the House of Representatives from 1994 to 2008. "Virginia is a diverse state," Davis explains. "Half of it is like New Jersey [the northern half], and half of it is like Alabama."

For much of its history, the state's rural economy was based on tobacco and agriculture, and one quarter of the state's land—more than eight million acres mostly in the southwestern part of the state—is still used for farming and is very rural. However, its economic center has shifted to the suburbs of Washington, D.C., where some of the richest counties in the nation are located and most residents make their living working for the federal government, defense and defense-related industries, government contractors, and high-tech firms. The Pentagon and CIA are here, and close to a million jobs in the state are related to defense. Virginia also has the highest concentration of technology workers in the country, and one third of the state's tech-company entrepreneurs are first-generation Americans. *Forbes* magazine calls Virginia one of the best states in the nation for business.[2]

The close-in suburbs of Alexandria, Falls Church, Arlington, and much of Fairfax County are Democratic areas, but the farther you get from Washington into Loudoun, Prince William, and even farther toward the Shenandoah Valley into Stafford and Fauquier Counties, the less Democratic the voters tend to be. Loudoun and Prince William Counties are true swing areas that have grown tremendously in the past few decades from rural enclaves dotted with horse farms and wineries to bedroom communities where open space is disappearing rapidly.

According to *Forbes*, Loudoun County, with a median income of $112,000, and Fairfax County, with a median income of $104,000, are the richest counties in the country.[3] That wealth is not comparable to the super rich one might find in Beverly Hills, Aspen, Palm Beach, or the suburbs of New York City but rather is due to the thousands of two-income professional families in suburban Washington.

More than a million people live in Fairfax County, and nearly a third of them are foreign born. There are sixty Starbucks, thirty-two golf courses, and half a dozen Fortune 500 companies here. The Tysons Corner area, dominated by mega-malls and office towers, is the largest suburban business district in the nation.

Hispanics now make up 8 percent of all Virginia residents, but the number is much higher in Northern Virginia, where jobs are plentiful. In Fairfax County, the Hispanic and Asian populations grew by more than 50 percent in the past decade according to the 2010 census, and whites now account for only about 55 percent of the residents in Fairfax County.[4] Asians are the biggest minority group, with large Vietnamese and Korean populations. The cultural, demographic, and lifestyle shift has been dramatic in areas that were extremely rural and to some extent dominated by horse farms and a white landed gentry not that long ago. In Prince William County, whites now make up less than half the county's population, which grew by 40 percent in the past decade, with the size of minority groups nearly tripling in that period.[5] Loudoun County was the fastest-growing county in Virginia in the past decade, largely due to the sizable increase in Hispanic, Asian, and black populations. Hispanics now constitute 20 percent of Loudoun County's residents.[6]

These changes in Northern Virginia mirror what has been going on in suburban and exurban areas around the country, especially in the

South. The suburbs used to be reliably Republican but now vote just as often for Democrats and tend to swing back and forth between the two parties. Nationally, the suburbs are far more diverse than they used to be, and one-third of suburban dwellers are now racial or ethnic minorities. Over the next decade, these demographic changes could significantly affect Republican support in states like Texas, Florida, North Carolina, and Virginia.[7]

More than half the nation's population lives in suburban and exurban areas on the outskirts of major cities, up from a third in 1980, and these voters are critically important. Half the 435 congressional districts are predominantly suburban and comprise most of the swing districts in the country.[8] Since rural areas remain solidly Republican and urban dwellers vote Democratic, the suburbs are where the action is.

In the 2006 midterm election, the suburban vote was very nearly split with 50 percent of suburban voters favoring Democrats and 48 percent supporting Republicans. In 2008, they voted for Barack Obama, but in 2010, only 42 percent of suburban voters cast their ballots for Democrats versus 55 percent for Republicans, according to CNN exit polling.[9]

Middle- and upper-middle-class suburban voters are a key swing group aggressively pursued by both parties—the Starbucks Moms and Dads who are the real power voters now—up for grabs and deciding elections in every region of the country, especially in swing states like Colorado, Ohio, and Virginia.

They are a fickle group who don't mind changing party allegiance every election cycle. They tend to be fiscally conservative and socially moderate, concerned about education, national security, and environmental issues. They are ethnically diverse, and many of them are young families with children still in school. Their children tend to be the obsession of the Starbucks Moms and Dads. They are so busy earning a living and driving their children from soccer to ballet to organized play dates, these parents have little time to focus on politics.

But they do worry about the future and tend to make political decisions based on individual candidates and issues of the moment, rather than a standing allegiance to one political party. Starbucks Moms and Dads are turned off by extremism in both parties and are concerned about the security of their own jobs and the state of the economy and the rising national debt.

Julia Pfaff is a Starbucks Mom. The forty-eight-year-old mother of two sons—ages fifteen and eighteen—lives in the Hayfield Farm neighborhood in Northern Virginia's Fairfax County. It's a pleasant, modest suburban subdivision of mainly Colonial-style, split-level, and two-story brick homes built in the late 1960s and early 1970s.

Pfaff's husband is in the military, and she is a former captain in the army who served in Saudi Arabia during Desert Storm. She is also the former executive director of the National Military Family Association.

An Independent voter, she is extremely concerned about what is happening in this country:

> I'm part of this huge group of Americans who feel disenfranchised. We don't like where we're headed. It's like we're riding on a bus, and the two parties are the drivers who are arguing over who gets to control the steering wheel. Meanwhile, there's a cliff in front of us and we're headed straight for it. The rest of us are stuck in the back of the bus, saying, "There's a cliff up there, do something."

Pfaff, intense, well informed, and very engaged in public affairs, has a master's degree in public policy from George Mason University. She calls herself "a moderate conservative" and is a classic Independent voter. The first time she voted for president, she recalls, was for Independent John Anderson in 1980. She also voted for Ronald Reagan, George W. Bush, and Barack Obama. "In 2008 I was on the fence, but as soon as John McCain picked Sarah Palin as his running mate that made the decision for me. I said, 'Okay, I'll vote for Obama.' I just couldn't see her as president if something happened to him."

In 2005, she voted for Democrat Tim Kaine for governor, but four years later supported Republican Bob McDonnell, although she voted for the Democratic candidates for lieutenant governor and state attorney general. She also likes Democrat Mark Warner and thinks he did a good job when he served as governor before being elected to the U.S. Senate.

In Virginia, voters do not have to register by party prior to the election, and Independent voters can vote in primaries if they want to do so. Pfaff says she votes in both Republican and Democratic primaries, depending on who is running. "The only place you really have a choice is in the primary. If one party goes to an extreme, then you're stuck in the general election."

She considers herself a deeply religious person and attends church regularly. She opposes abortion but she has no problem with gay civil unions or with gays serving openly in the military.

Pfaff doesn't necessarily support big government and does think federal spending needs to be controlled, but she also believes government has a role to play in helping people who need help. "I think it's an extreme position to say no tax increases at all, because you need taxes to pay for some government services."

She is critical of the anti-union activity going on in states like Wisconsin, Ohio, and Indiana and thinks

being so confrontational was not the way to solve the problem. That just makes the public more cynical. It's this extreme rhetoric of us versus them. I think the two parties are so institutionalized. It's not about governing. It's about each party getting power. We talk about governing as if it was a game with one side winning and one side losing. I find that to be very destructive. We're never going to solve the problems we're facing as long as we think governing is a football game. Governing is not a football game. Governing is governing. It requires compromise and consensus and making difficult choices and leadership.

Pfaff has decided she's going to try to do something and is attempting to help organize a Virginia chapter of the No Labels group, which is pushing for compromise and centrist solutions from political leaders. Sitting around her dining room table sharing sandwiches and cookies on a Saturday afternoon, some of Pfaff's neighbors and others interested in the No Labels and IndependentVoting.org movements gather to talk about their frustrations with the system and what they think should be done.

Steve Richardson, fifty-four, works as an analyst for the U.S. Labor Department and has been an Independent voter since he voted for Ross Perot. Richardson considers himself a libertarian who is very concerned about the nation's fiscal policies and doesn't really trust either political party. "It's gotten to the point where they think we're idiots. They're all playing to their base that's so off on one side or another . . . the center is sacrificed because they have to placate their base and demonize the other side."

Richardson doesn't believe that most people, especially Independent voters, are well represented and thinks the entire political system is driven by money. "They're playing us for fools, and that's insulting. . . . We have a ruling class and increasingly the divide is between that group and the voters. . . . I think the politicians in Washington are kind of contemptuous of the voters."

Pfaff and Richardson attended a national meeting of Independent Voting.org in New York City in February 2011 that brought together like-minded Independents to talk about issues like election reform that would open up the electoral system to them. "I just found it online," explains Pfaff about how she discovered the group. "I went because I was curious. If you say I don't want to be a Republican or a Democrat, but I want to be involved, I want to be part of the solution, what do I do? A lot of people are using the Internet to see what's out there."

Richardson, who has been attending IndependentVoting.org events for a few years, said the group has been trying to find its mission and discussed trying to form a third party several years ago but decided against it and instead to focus on election and political reform.

Pfaff's neighbor and friend Sally Frodge, fifty-four, has three children and is a single mother who also works for the federal government as an engineer at the FAA. She's been an Independent voter her entire life. Like most of the Starbucks Moms and Dads, Frodge says she's so busy with her job and her children that she doesn't have much time to follow politics or get involved. "My focus is on raising my kids. . . . I am a 'kiddist' . . . I tend to think if something is good for the next generation, it's probably good for the country."

Frodge is mostly turned off by what she hears from politicians. "They're so partisan. You listen to them and they're not saying anything of substance." But she is also extremely concerned about the nation's economic situation. "We do need a sense of urgency. We don't have as much time as we think to fix this."

Pfaff, Richardson, and Frodge are the kind of Independent Starbucks Moms and Dads who live in Northern Virginia and help decide which way Virginia will go in state and national elections.

Thanks in large part to minority voters and the votes of Northern Virginia, Barack Obama was the first Democratic candidate for president to win the state since Lyndon Johnson did it in 1964. In 2008, Obama won 60 percent of the vote in Fairfax County, and Mark Warner, who was running for the Senate, won a stunning 67 percent of the vote there.[10]

But Tom Davis thinks it's going to prove a bit more difficult for Obama to carry the state in 2012. "This state is a center right state—you've got to hold the center to win." Davis says Democrats can continue to win statewide if they stay centered, and that's something Republicans should keep in mind as well. "You cannot win statewide from the right—you have got to get those swing votes. That's where elections are decided."

Conservative Republican Bob McDonnell managed to do it, though, and win the governorship in 2009, carrying 51 percent of the vote in Fairfax County and almost 59 percent statewide. Independents account for close to 30 percent of the vote in Virginia, and McDonnell won

66 percent of the Independent ballots, a significantly better percentage than Obama got here in 2008.[11]

McDonnell, who served in the House of Delegates and as state attorney general before being elected governor, is a religious conservative who strongly opposes abortion and has supported a number of anti-abortion measures, including requiring parental consent before a minor could obtain an abortion. In its 2011 session, the Virginia General Assembly succeeded in passing several measures that could limit abortion rights.

Married with five children, McDonnell has views on social issues that became a flash point during the campaign over a thesis he wrote about 20 years ago while attending graduate school at Regent University, a Virginia Beach Christian school founded by televangelist Pat Robertson. In that paper, McDonnell wrote that "government policy should favor married couples over cohabitators, homosexuals or fornicators" and described working women and feminists as "detrimental" to the family. He also criticized a 1965 Supreme Court decision that legalized the use of contraceptives.[12]

Shortly after taking office as governor in 2010, McDonnell declared a Confederate History Month for Virginia that made no mention of slavery as a cause of the Civil War, explaining as his reason, "there were any number of aspects to that conflict between the states. Obviously, it involved slavery. It involved other issues. But I focused on the ones I thought were most significant for Virginia." Not long thereafter, in response to criticism, he apologized and amended the proclamation to include a mention of slavery.[13]

But despite his conservative views on social issues, McDonnell has managed to remain popular with many Independent Northern Virginia voters by working with the state legislature and supporting things that matter to them, like providing almost $3 billion in bond funding for road and highway improvement projects as well as additional aid for higher education.[14]

Virginia voters tend to be a bit contrarian. Since 1976, every time one party wins the presidency, the state has elected a governor of the opposite party the following year. Its governors, who by law can serve only one consecutive four-year term, are elected in odd-numbered years.

The part-time General Assembly meets for only forty-seven days during its regular session each year, one of the shortest state legislative sessions in the country. In 2011, Democrats held a narrow majority in the Senate and Republicans a majority in the House. While the state faced a $4 billion deficit in 2010, forcing significant budget cuts, Virginia was in a better position than many other states in 2011 and tax revenue was up, allowing some of the cuts to be reversed.

Virginia Delegate, Tom Rust is a moderate Republican from Herndon, a city of twenty-three thousand in Fairfax County. Rust has the deep Southern drawl, which I heard much more frequently as I traveled south and west in Virginia. Rust is a native born in the Shenandoah Valley. To say his roots go deep in the state would be more than an understatement—his family has been in Virginia since the mid-1600s.

Rust has served in the state legislature for ten years and before that was on the town council and mayor of Herndon for twenty years. Inside the Beltway, the highway that rings Washington and includes the inner suburbs, Rust says the voters are solidly Democratic, but in his district, there are about an equal number of Republicans, Democrats, and Independents. "I'm a centrist, I think I'm a fiscal conservative, but I also understand that in the area of infrastructure, roads, schools, you have to spend money. I think I am a Virginia centrist," said Rust. He understands that Northern Virginians, many of whom make their living from the government, don't have disdain for all government spending.

"I think unfortunately the Republican Party at least in the last ten years has been seen particularly in Northern Virginia as the party of no. They're not willing to invest in infrastructure and they are always stressing guns, God, and gays." Rust has not yet faced a primary challenge from the right, and the party may realize a more conservative Republican probably couldn't hold his seat, but Rust says he keeps expecting to get primaried. "The leadership of the party in Virginia is out of step with the mainstream Republicans," Rust believes. "That could drive folks like me out of office."

Moderate Republican John Warner, a former five-term U.S. Senator and the longest-serving Republican senator in Virginia history, was enormously popular with the state's voters, winning votes across party lines, especially in Northern Virginia. But he was not well liked by conservatives and state GOP leaders for his moderate stands on cultural issues. Warner was pro-choice, favored gun control, and refused to endorse the party's nominee and Iran–Contra figure Oliver North when he ran against incumbent U.S. Senator Chuck Robb in 1994. Warner was almost denied renomination by conservative Republicans in 1996, but because Virginia has an open primary system, he was able to win, thanks to Democrats and Independents who voted for him in the Republican primary. Rust calls Warner, who retired from the Senate in 2008, "a great Virginia statesman" but says Warner could never get nominated by the Republicans to run today.

Virginia has eleven congressional districts, and before the 2010 election, the House delegation had six Democrats and five Republicans—including fiercely partisan House Majority Leader Eric Cantor, who represents the solidly Republican Seventh District, which includes part of Richmond and its suburbs. The Republican wave hit Virginia hard and Tea Party activists were successful here in unseating three incumbent Democrats, including two Blue Dog moderates: freshman Glenn Nye, who represented the Virginia Beach/Norfolk area; and Rick Boucher, who was first elected to Congress in 1982, represented rural southwestern Virginia, and who did not even have a Republican challenger in 2008.

Now Democrats hold only three of Virginia's House seats, two of them in Northern Virginia and the other a black majority voting rights district that includes parts of Richmond, Norfolk, and Newport News. Bobby Scott, who represents the Third District, created in 1992, is the first African American to represent Virginia in Congress since Reconstruction. The two Northern Virginia House Democrats are Jim Moran, first elected in 1990 and representing the solidly Democratic Eighth District, which consists of Alexandria, Falls Church, Arlington County, and a piece of Fairfax County; and Gerry Connolly, who represents the Eleventh Congressional District. Connolly, former chairman of the Fairfax County Board of Supervisors, was first elected to Congress in 2008, taking the seat formerly held by Tom Davis. Connolly just narrowly eked out a reelection victory in one of the closest races in the country in 2010. The Eleventh District contains parts of Fairfax and Prince William Counties and, while recently trending more Democratic, is a swing district that went both for George W. Bush and Barack Obama.

Connolly grew up in Boston and has a clipped Massachusetts accent rather than a Southern drawl. He worked on Capitol Hill as a staffer and then for a defense contractor before beginning his political career. Connolly has a biting sense of humor, and when I ask him what it's like to be a member of Congress, he shoots back, "Every day's a holiday."

Connolly says it has become extremely difficult for Democrats and Republicans to work together in Congress and blames the punishing schedule, fund-raising pressures, and especially the leadership of both parties, who strictly enforce party discipline. "There are very bright lines beyond which you dare not cross." Especially on the Republican side, Connolly believes, "There's palpable fear. People have been told point-blank you will never move up or become a committee chair if you vote against us."

Everything now seems to be "a life and death struggle" focused on the next election. "If you're in the minority, you cannot let the majority succeed—ever. You must oppose every good idea I've got . . . both sides practice this. It's about control."

The other Virginia Democrat who battled hard for reelection but wasn't as lucky as Connolly was Tom Perriello, who represented the state's Fifth Congressional District. In 2008, Perriello first won the seat by a mere 727 votes.[15] The Fifth District in south-central Virginia is extremely diverse and includes the highly educated and relatively affluent Charlottesville, home of the University of Virginia and many wealthy retirees as well as extremely poor rural towns like Martinsville near the North Carolina border, a small city that has lost twelve thousand jobs over the past few decades and had a 20 percent unemployment rate in 2010. The district covers all or part of eighteen counties, making it the state's largest district, with an area of almost nine thousand square miles—larger than the state of New Jersey. John McCain carried this district over Obama 51 to 48 percent in 2008.[16]

This is the other Virginia, and Perriello styled himself as something of a populist to appeal to his district's more conservative, rural voters. "One of the great questions of our time is—will we save the middle class?" Perriello told me in the fall of 2010. "If we don't have manufacturing and construction and agriculture, we're going to start looking like a Central American economy of the 1980s." Perriello called himself "a Perot Democrat" and says Ross Perot "may have been nuts in the '90s, but he got a lot of things right. I'm not sure we would have had a balanced budget without his charts.

"He was also right about the great sucking sound" when it comes to jobs leaving the United States. Like all economic populists, including Perot, Perriello is extremely critical of NAFTA and other free trade agreements, which he says have cost U.S. jobs, including employment in his district.

As in many congressional districts around the country in 2010, jobs were the number one issue with most of Perriello's constituents, along with concern over the budget deficit and growth of government under the Obama Administration. "There are a lot of good people out there who want to support their family and don't have a job. Jobs tops everything, but the deficit is a serious second," he told me. Perriello also sensed a deep anxiety among his constituents about the country's future and the feeling that America may not be great anymore. "People are concerned we are past our prime—that we no longer make and build things—that we can't compete in the global economy."

Perriello was critical on the campaign trail of Obama Administration economic policy and called for Treasury Secretary Timothy Geithner and chief Obama economic adviser Lawrence Summers to be fired. "I have no confidence in them, and Geithner and Summers should go," Perriello told me in an interview, adding, "How fucking out of touch do you have to be as an economic team?"

Perriello, articulate, blunt, and somewhat combative, derided centrism in politics as "taking good ideas and watering them down." The Yale-educated—both for undergrad and law school—thirty-five-year-old loves to talk about big ideas, including trade, competitiveness, America's role in the world, and the future. *Washingtonian* magazine's "Best and Worst of Congress" poll of Democratic congressional staffers in 2010 ranked him as the number one "Surprise Standout" in the House.[17]

Obama didn't seem to take offense at Perriello's swipes and singled him out along with a handful of other Democratic freshmen around the country as being especially courageous for their support of health care and other Democratic agenda items despite the risk of losing their seats. Obama made a last-minute campaign visit to Charlottesville a few days before the election, and in a speech at the University of Virginia was effusive in his praise for Perriello.

> In this day and age, let's face it, political courage is hard to come by. The easiest thing to do, especially when you're a first-term congressman, the easiest thing to do is make your decisions based on the polls. You put your fingers up to the wind, you check which way the political wind is blowing before you cast every vote. That's how a lot of folks think they should do their jobs in Washington. And that's not who Tom is. He did not go to Washington to do what was easy, to do what was popular. He went to do what was right.[18]

Obama may also have been thinking of himself in the speech and the struggle to thread the needle between doing what he believes in and what will serve him best politically.

Unlike some of his Democratic colleagues, Perriello had no fear about going directly into the lion's den and defending his record. He had more town hall meetings in the summer and fall of 2010 than almost any member of Congress, many of them attended by Tea Party followers. In his quest for reelection, Perriello traveled his huge district nonstop and talked to just about anyone who would listen to him, including a Charlottesville Tea Party group meeting in an Arby's Restaurant, where I caught up with him that fall. Out of the hundred or so people gathered for the meeting, there might not have been five people willing to vote for him, and Perriello had to listen to people stand up and say they couldn't wait for him to be defeated—but he kept his cool and didn't back away from his support for the Democratic agenda.

Later, when I asked him what he thought might save him, he replied with one word—"conviction"—and said he intended to "fight like hell." "When I take a position, I don't hide. I make the case on what I think is right. I think people think this guy gets it—he fights for us."

But Perriello's support of Obama's stimulus spending, health care reform, and the cap and trade bill ultimately sealed his fate, despite the spirited campaign he waged. In a year when it was almost impossible even for much more moderate Democrats to hold swing seats like this one, Perriello simply may have been too liberal for the Fifth District. He lost to state Senator Robert Hurt, whose campaign slogan was "A Proven Conservative with Virginia Values."

Especially when it comes to Democrats, Virginia favors moderates and the state's two Democratic senators, Jim Webb and Mark Warner, both have appeal statewide with conservative and rural Democrats, moderate Republicans, and business interests. A Democrat cannot win the state without Northern Virginia, but also cannot win with those votes alone, something Warner particularly understands.

Early in 2011, Webb announced that he would not seek reelection and former Governor and Democratic National Committee Chairman Tim Kaine announced his plans to run for the seat. Kaine, a Richmond City Council member and mayor as well as Mark Warner's lieutenant governor before succeeding him as governor, has appealed to Independent centrist voters in the past, but as head of the DNC was much more partisan, becoming a cheerleader for Obama and Democratic politics. Obama, who considers Virginia crucial in his own reelection strategy, encouraged Kaine to run for the Senate seat.

The Republican field for the Senate seat was expected to be fairly crowded, including several Tea Party candidates, but the leading contender was former Governor George Allen, who lost the seat in 2006 to Webb. Allen's reelection was considered assured, and he was already eyeing a possible presidential run in 2008 when his candidacy was derailed over a racial epithet he used at a campaign appearance, referring to a Webb campaign worker of Indian descent as Macaca, a racial slur referring to the macaque monkey. "Welcome to America, and welcome to the real world of Virginia," Allen said to him. The video of the incident filmed by the campaign worker was quickly posted on YouTube and became a sensation and possibly the deciding factor in the race. Webb won 110,000 votes more than Allen in Northern Virginia, almost certainly what decided the election.[19]

The Macaca incident may not be much remembered or all that important in the 2012 race, but it still remains to be seen whether Allen can make a comeback. It is highly unlikely, with Northern Virginia's increasing diversity and its importance in winning state elections, that Allen will be particularly competitive there, not only as a result of his previous behavior but also because of his extremely conservative views.

With Webb's retirement, Mark Warner will become the senior senator from Virginia. Warner is an upbeat, energetic workaholic with considerable intellect who looks younger than his fifty-six years and who has cultivated an image as a "radical bipartisan centrist" as he likes to put it. He is a glass-half-full kind of guy. Essentially liberal on social issues, Warner is more pro-business and economically conservative than most congressional Democrats and has been extremely aggressive in trying to forge bipartisan compromises in the Senate on budget and economic issues.

Warner was mentioned as a potential presidential candidate before he decided to run for the Senate, and like Barack Obama before him in

2004, Warner was the keynote speaker at the Democratic National Convention in 2008, the year he was elected to the Senate. Warner, however, was somewhat overshadowed by having to give his speech on the same night that Hillary Clinton addressed the convention delegates. His speech, which focused on economic issues, didn't exactly bring down the house, but he won the Senate race against his predecessor as Virginia governor, James Gilmore, with a commanding 30-point margin.[20]

In the Senate, and before that as governor, Warner has always succeeded in establishing good working relationships with Republicans, sometimes to the dismay of his Democratic colleagues and leaders. And he is willing to put in hard, behind-the-scenes work with them, trying to address big national issues. "Neither political party has a monopoly on truth or patriotism," Warner told me.

Warner grew up in Connecticut, not Virginia, and attended George Washington University, where he was a political science major and valedictorian of the Class of 1977. While in college, he worked for former Connecticut Democratic Senator Abraham Ribicoff and later as a driver for Christopher Dodd, also a Democratic senator from Connecticut. Following his Senate victory some 25 years later, Warner, appointed to the Banking Committee, found himself working again with his old boss Chris Dodd, who was now the committee's chairman.

After college Warner attended Harvard Law School and, after receiving his degree, worked for the Democratic National Committee and later moved to Virginia and started a couple of businesses. His first effort failed in six weeks, the second in six months, but he found his stride in venture capital and, as he describes it, "got in on the ground floor of the cell phone industry." He was a cofounder of Nextel Communications, a cellular phone network that merged with rival Sprint, leaving Warner a very wealthy man. His current estimated net worth of $180 million makes him one of the richest members of Congress and one of the few whose wealth comes from being self-made rather than inheritance or a spouse. That endows him with significant business gravitas along with a certain freedom from having to toe the party line. Warner has always thought of himself as a dealmaker, a forger of agreements, and a problem solver because of not only his business background but also his experiences as governor. "I spent a career doing deals—I ended up often being the broker," he explains.

Warner, whose father was a real estate agent, was the first member of his family to attend college. He admits that he surprised himself by achieving the kind of wealth he has. "I didn't expect to become a Rockefeller." But the increasing wage inequality in this country over the past decade troubles him. The number of billionaires, the Wall Street financiers who don't really create jobs but just shuffle money, reminds Warner of the Gilded Age of the late nineteenth century and he tells me he thinks things have gotten "way out of whack."

As governor, Warner worked closely with the Republicans in the state legislature, and he believes Obama and the Democrats in Congress could have done more outreach with the Republicans in 2009 and 2010 but says the Democrats felt they "had the luxury of a big majority and picking up a big chunk of Republicans wasn't needed. . . . Maybe the Republican leadership was never going to come around, but there was a whole second tier of [GOP] members that could have come around," Warner believes.

But neither side saw much benefit in working with the other party. "There was a bit of—we won—we got a big mandate—and the progressive side was champing at the bit" to pass their agenda. However, Warner admits the Republicans were also extremely disciplined in holding their members in line and there was a sense of "just sticking it to you for the sake of sticking it to you. The pressure the moderate Republicans have been under, especially in the Senate, has been enormous" not to vote or work with the Democrats, Warner observed.

Warner never bought into this partisan balkanization. From his earliest days in the Senate, Warner made it a habit of walking over to the Republican side of the chamber and "chitchatting" when he was called to the floor for votes. That's how he began to develop a relationship with conservative Republican Senator Saxby Chambliss of Georgia in the summer of 2010. They began talking about the nation's deficit and debt crisis and what might be done about it. The two men started an informal bipartisan group to talk about fiscal issues and invited people like Federal Reserve Chairman Ben Bernanke to come talk to senators in small closed-door, off-the-record sessions. Eventually several dozen senators became interested in what they were doing. Warner and Chambliss focused on the work of the National Commission on Fiscal Responsibility and Reform, commonly known as the president's debt commission. After the commission issued its report in December 2010, and was essentially ignored by Barack Obama, who had created the commission, Warner and Chambliss started to talk about introducing the report as legislation in the Senate.

They asked four of the senators who were commission members and had voted in favor of the report to join their effort—conservative Republican deficit hawks Tom Coburn of Oklahoma and Mike Crapo of Idaho; and Democrats Kent Conrad of North Dakota, the chairman of the Budget Committee; and Richard Durbin of Illinois, the Senate's assistant majority leader. The group was dubbed the "Gang of Six" by the media.

Originally they met about once a week, but by the spring of 2011, as their work hammering out a deficit reduction plan grew more intense, the gatherings became more frequent until the senators were meeting almost every day for hours at a time, often over popcorn or a bottle of wine, or steaks at Warner's Alexandria home. They developed a centrist plan for deficit reduction that pointed a way forward between an early Obama proposal to raise taxes on the rich that offered little else in the way of specifics on spending cuts and entitlement reform, and House Budget Chairman Paul Ryan's plan for domestic spending cuts and privatizing Medicare that left defense spending untouched and would lower tax rates for the wealthy and corporations even further.

The Gang of Six plan was a politically difficult package that would have reduced the deficit by about $4 trillion over ten years and included a little bit of something for everyone to hate—tax code changes that included eliminating some tax breaks and deductions, Medicare reform, defense department cuts, scaling back agricultural subsidies and other domestic spending reductions.

Probably the hardest thing the group had to do, according to Warner, was developing trust among members of opposite parties. Republicans and Democrats not only were skeptical they could reach agreements on taxing and spending, they were also wary of getting too much out in front of their parties or being seen as too cozy with the enemy. "There are a lot of members that don't have much faith in the process. They start each sentence with—'That's so hard, let me tell you why it can't happen.'" One thing Warner realized about himself through the process was, "I don't want to be here so long that I start thinking that way."

The Gang of Six effort involved incredible heavy lifting and received almost no support either from congressional leaders or the White House. After basically ignoring the group's work for six months, Obama, in a surprise move in late July, gave them a lukewarm shout-out during a White House briefing on the debt ceiling negotiations when he was still pushing for a "grand bargain." Essentially, he was trying to co-opt the Gang's strategy without formally endorsing the plan and used typical Obama-speak, calling it "broadly consistent with the approach that I've urged."

What it says is we've got to be serious about reducing discretionary spending both in domestic spending and defense; we've got to be serious about tackling health care spending and entitlements in a serious way; and we've got to have some additional revenue so that we have an approach in which there is shared sacrifice and everybody is giving up something . . . . the framework that they put forward is broadly consistent with what we've been working on here in the White House and with the presentations that I've made to the leadership when they've come over here.

But there was no follow-up. Obama may have disagreed with some of the plan's details or perhaps he just didn't want the Gang to get the credit, but in any case he dropped his support for the plan as quickly as he had mentioned it. The White House had not informed Chambliss or Warner ahead of time that the president was going to talk about their deficit reduction blueprint. And the half-hearted Obama endorsement proved ineffectual and probably just made it harder for Republicans to endorse the Gang of Six plan.

Even though half the members of the Senate attended a briefing on the plan the day after Obama mentioned it, and 36 senators from both parties signed a letter endorsing its framework, the unveiling of the worthy Gang of Six plan came too late and got overtaken by events. Warner says he wished they could have gotten the plan out three months earlier, but it just didn't work out that way.

Still, Warner thinks all the time and effort, all the meetings and cajoling, were worth it. "If there was going to be any chance of a bipartisan plan, it was going to evolve out of this work." The indefatigable Warner saw his role as trying to keep the whole thing on track when it threatened to go off the rails—which happened a number of times. "I would bring discussions to a close on various issues when we got stuck and get everyone to move on. . . . Somebody's got to play a role to try to make the deal get done. . . . There have been more ups and downs than I care to recall. It's been an emotional roller coaster."

In May 2011, after months of negotiations, Republican Tom Coburn abruptly pulled out of the group, citing what he felt was an inability on the part of Democrat Durbin to consider adequate Medicare and entitlement reform, and leaving a Gang of Five. Coburn's move threatened to scuttle the entire deal and make it impossible for other Republicans to endorse it.

Warner knew that if the "grand bargain" ultimately succeeded he would be a hero and if it didn't he would have spent a year of his life in the Senate on an impossible quest. "I can't think of an issue that is more important or defining of our time than this one. If it doesn't work and we end up with a financial crisis—we would say why didn't we heed the warning signs?"

It's because of things like Warner's work with the Gang of Six and his business credentials that many Virginia Republicans refer to him as their favorite Democrat. When he ran for governor, a group called "Republicans for Warner" raised more than $1 million for his campaign, and his enormous bipartisan popularity in the state offers a model for how the Democrats can win elections by appealing to voters across the political spectrum. In Virginia, his name has become an adjective—being called a "Warner Democrat" defines a certain pro-business centrism and cross-party appeal.

Before being elected governor, Warner served as chairman of the state Democratic Party and made an unsuccessful run for the Senate against John Warner (no relation) in 1996 in which he had campaign bumper stickers that said "Mark not John." He lost Northern Virginia in that race, but won in the rural areas of the state, and afterwards spent a lot of time developing contacts and getting to know rural Virginia. "The Democrats had written it off for years, but I said I wouldn't forget those communities." Warner helped set up four venture capital funds for small business development around the state and still spends considerable time traveling to the state's rural areas.

During his gubernatorial campaign, Warner appealed to rural voters by sponsoring a NASCAR race truck, running campaign ads that featured pickup trucks and bluegrass music, and keeping the NRA from endorsing his opponent by opposing any new gun control laws in the state.

While serving as governor from 2002 to 2006, Warner successfully worked with Republicans in the state legislature to deal with a serious budget shortfall, which forced Warner to cut programs and lay off state workers. He managed to not only balance the budget but also get enough Republican state legislators to approve a tax increase to help pay for schools and transportation and still remain popular with the voters. Warner was named one of the best governors and Virginia one of the best managed states in the nation under his tenure.[21]

Warner, who is married with three daughters, lives in Alexandria not far from Washington and has a gentleman's farm and weekend retreat in

Virginia's King George County on the Rappahannock River. He never seems to tire of traveling the state and talking to voters and seems to have boundless energy for the meet and greets and endless speeches that are required of politicians.

Warner can be both earnest and a little geeky in these appearances. He seems genuinely interested in the people he meets and their concerns and is better in informal settings and give-and-take with voters than he is when making prepared remarks, when he can come off as a bit stiff and not particularly charismatic. He always has facts and figures about whatever subject he's talking about at his command, but no one has ever accused Warner of being slick or smooth, and perhaps his slight awkwardness is an advantage. It makes him seem more approachable.

One such day of travel around the state, before the 2010 election, began at seven thirty in the morning with a radio interview in Richmond, included seven speeches and appearances, and didn't end until well after 8 P.M. in Lynchburg in the south-central part of the state, about two hundred miles from Washington.

Both extremes of the current economy exist in Virginia—in Northern Virginia, there are millionaires, dealmakers, entrepreneurs. In the rural southern parts of the state, which has lost almost its entire manufacturing base, there are the perennial poor struggling to survive.

Warner's intense interest in economic development in Virginia and his business background mean he frequently visits factories, workplaces, and business groups like the Chesterfield Chamber of Commerce, just south of Richmond, where he stopped by at eight thirty to address about two dozen people at their regular breakfast meeting. His experiences so far in the Senate make him long for the days of working with the Virginia legislature, he confides. It's a conservative crowd, and a number of the questions center on the Democratic health reform legislation and the nation's fiscal situation. "I don't think there's a legitimate constitutional challenge to the health care bill—we'll see," says Warner in a reference to the lawsuit filed by Virginia's conservative

Republican Attorney General Ken Cuccinelli the very day the health care law was enacted. Half the states in the country have filed similar suits, claiming the health care law is unconstitutional because it forces Americans to buy health insurance.

Warner's next stop is DuPont's Spruance Plant on the outskirts of Richmond, along the James River. DuPont has had a facility on the five-hundred-acre site for more than eighty years, and the plant now manufactures a number of synthetic materials, including Kevlar used in body armor. The plant is DuPont's largest manufacturing facility, with more than three thousand employees. A tent has been set up on the lawn so Warner can talk to the workers and answer their questions. Warner tells them that the country has pulled back from "a financial abyss" but it's not out of the woods yet. What's needed is "a little more truth telling and a little less politicking," he says. Warner is asked about trade policy, China, how to stimulate the housing market. Warner thinks the Bush tax cuts for the wealthy should be allowed to expire but correctly predicts they will probably be renewed after the election. "Congress has a tendency to punt on any hard choices, but the federal government is going to have to spend less money. . . . We're in such a hole. We're going to have to cut spending and raise taxes."

His message is pretty much the same when he addresses a luncheon of about seventy elected officials and business leaders from eight South-side counties in Farmville, halfway between Richmond and Lynchburg. This is an area that used to grow tobacco and manufacture furniture and textiles, but it's been hit hard economically and almost all those businesses are gone now. Warner says a lot of manufacturing jobs that were eliminated in the past few decades "aren't coming back," and the United States needs to focus on exports and tax and trade policy that will stimulate job growth. "We haven't been very good at innovation . . . there are a billion Chinese and a billion Indians that ought to be buying our stuff. . . . We've got to have a level playing field. If there's a level playing field, we can compete with anyone."

Invariably when Warner is addressing a group, especially one like this, he refers to himself as "a business guy," never as a politician, and whenever a cell phone in the crowd rings, he likes to remind people that he was a cofounder of Nextel and doesn't mind the interruption at all. "I hear the sound of money when they go off . . . you hear an annoying sound, I hear *ca-ching*," he jokes.

People in Virginia still frequently refer to him as governor rather than senator, and almost every time he speaks to a group, he makes a reference to his time as governor. "There is no higher honor than being governor of Virginia," he tells me. It's clear he preferred that job and its executive responsibilities to being a junior member of the U.S. Senate, where things can move pretty slowly for a guy like Warner.

Since he didn't have time to eat at the luncheon, Warner has to wolf down a sandwich and chips in the car while returning some calls and checking his iPad about whom he will meet at the next appointment. He's now been going nonstop for more than seven hours, and when I ask if he's tired, he responds, "I love this. I love being in the smaller communities. . . . It's the best elixir for Washington blues."

As we drive, Warner points out to me the troubled racial past of this area and says that we are passing through Prince Edward County, which closed its entire school system in 1959 rather than be forced to integrate following the Supreme Court's *Brown v. Board of Education* decision. This was the only school district in the country that resorted to closing its public schools, and they were only reopened five years later when the Supreme Court ruled the district's action was unconstitutional and violated the Fourteenth Amendment.

In many ways, it doesn't seem possible that this happened less than fifty years ago. So much has changed in this region, and yet there are still many reminders of the past.

On the outskirts of Lynchburg, Warner's next visit is to a gleaming, high-security Babcock and Wilcox facility that makes commercial nu- clear plant components. Stationed at the checkpoint of the fortresslike complex are guards with machine guns. Lynchburg is a city of about seventy-five thousand on the banks of the James River in the foothills of the Blue Ridge Mountains. It was the only major city in Virginia that never fell to the Union during the Civil War, and following the war through the first half of the twentieth century, it became a tobacco and shoe manufacturing center and one of the wealthiest cities per capita in the country. In its heyday, the city's Craddock-Terry Shoe Corporation was the fifth largest shoe company in the world, but it went bankrupt about thirty years ago when shoes started to be made primarily overseas. Now the former shoe factory and a tobacco storage warehouse have been turned into a boutique hotel, part of an attempt to revitalize Lynchburg's downtown.[22]

Today one of the defining features of Lynchburg is Liberty University, a college founded by Minister Jerry Falwell, which is the largest Evangelical Christian university in the world.

On Main Street in Lynchburg is the White Hart, a café and used bookstore with wooden floors, a tin ceiling, and an impressive collection of volumes about the Civil War where Warner gathers with two dozen local business leaders to talk about the area's struggling economy. Most of the questions are about government regulations, why small banks in the area didn't get any of the TARP money and are not doing much lending and how they can get some federal support for their business enterprises. Warner has brought a representative of the government's Small Business Administration with him to field questions and take names. This area, like much of the country, is hurting. There are empty storefronts, retail businesses are in trouble, and in some nearby communities, unemployment tops 20 percent. People are scared, the area's housing market has collapsed, and they are afraid of what may come next. "We are on the edge," a local banker tells him.

Tom Capps is the owner of the local Capps Shoe Company, which employs about 175 people and primarily makes dress oxfords for the military. Capps tells Warner he is having trouble competing with companies that import their shoes and materials and can sell them for cheaper. Although he is a Republican, he says he voted for Warner for governor and Senate because of his business focus. Capps opposes the Democratic health care reform, which he thinks is going to significantly raise his costs and could force him to lay people off, but says in a deep Virginia drawl, "I have a good feeling about Warner. He's kind of moderate." Capps was born and raised in Lynchburg, and while he considers himself to be fiscally conservative and feels "the Democratic Party is totally on the wrong track," he also believes "government needs to help people that need help." He says he's turned off by extremism in both parties and can't stand Sarah Palin.

Warner doesn't like the partisan extremes either, but he is rarely openly critical and usually cautious and careful about his public comments. He is not the kind of guy who shoots from the hip. But after the 2010 election, it was in an interview with a Virginia reporter, that Warner's frustration about how Congress operates unleashed a backlash from the left, illustrating just how difficult it can be to talk honestly about our political system without attack from one extreme or the other.

> Both sides are going to have to be part of the solution. Democrats can't jam stuff through, which may be good, Republicans can't just say no, which is going to be good. There will be one of two routes. We're either going to let the extremes who say no negotiation under any terms rule the day or the folks who want to find some common ground in the middle are going to have to step up.

Warner equated members of MoveOn.org and the "super left" among Democratic Party supporters with "the Tea Party crowd in the other party" and said neither side was willing to compromise. "There were too many times I bit my lip in the first year or bit my tongue. I'm done," Warner said.[23]

The comments seemed like an accurate assessment of the way things work in Washington, but MoveOn.org and liberal bloggers immediately started attacking Warner in the blogosphere, and he was forced to walk back his remarks by calling them "in-artful."[24]

In fact, they were just honest.

"When you take on orthodoxy, you're going to get whacked," he told me a few weeks later. But Warner wasn't backing down from his criticism of the "dysfunctional" Senate and how things don't get done. In the Senate, there are "a lot of pressures trying to pull you to the left," he tells me.

"My patience runs a little thin when I hear some of my colleagues bemoan the loss of the glory days," Warner said. "If I hear one more time about the good old days when Ted Kennedy used to do things with Republicans . . . Why aren't they stepping up? Why not lead by example?" he asked about the senior senators.

The only way to get anything done is to put aside partisanship and find common ground, and that's exactly what Warner and the Gang of Six were trying to do.

That's what the Starbucks Moms and Dads want from their political leaders. They are willing to sacrifice, to see some of their favorite federal programs cut back or pay a bit more in taxes, but they want to make sure the sacrifices are shared across the board and fair to everyone. They don't want to see small businesses struggling and the middle class suffer while the wealthy and corporate America thrive. How the Starbucks Moms and Dads are feeling about their own economic situation usually determines how they vote.

Because of the explosion of growth in the suburbs and exurbs in recent decades, and the wide cross section of people who live in these areas, including many new minority groups, these voters are crucial to winning elections. The suburbs used to be more reliably Republican but now are very much swing areas in most regions of the country. Usually, as the suburbs go, so goes the nation and that will undoubtedly be true in 2012.

7

The Ultimate Swing State—
Home of the America First Democrats

Ohio

Capital is only the fruit of labor, and could never have existed if labor had not first existed. Labor is the superior of capital, and deserves much the higher consideration.

—ABRAHAM LINCOLN

OHIO IS THE SWINGIEST of swing states. No political party has a lock on the affections of Ohio voters. Politicians have to earn it here, election by election. A big part of the reason that Ohio is consistently a bellwether state is because it is so average. There is a little bit of everything here—big cities, manufacturing, suburbs, and farmland. Its income level, urban–rural balance, and ethnic mix are a microcosm of the country.

Ohio has been hit hard by the deindustrialization of America and has lost hundreds of thousands of jobs as manufacturing plants have closed and either moved South or overseas. The dismal economic situation of so many Ohioans was the issue that dwarfed all others during the 2010 midterm election, just as it was the primary concern of so many voters around the country. But in Ohio, the situation was magnified. Just as it has been for so many years and in so many national elections, Ohio was a bellwether—this time of the nation's economic misery. People were hurting, and they wanted to take it out on someone—the most likely targets were the Democrats and their incumbent governor. There's a reason the word *depression* means both an economic catastrophe and a mental state of deep despair.

It's not like Ohioans to complain, though, which just made it more obvious how bad the situation was. Ohio is decidedly Midwestern in feel and temperament. Most people you meet in Ohio have lived here all their lives and don't live too far from where they were born. Ohio is not the kind of place you move to—it's where you're from.

Ohio has been a closely divided swing state politically for a century. The state's governorship has been passed back and forth between the Democrats and Republicans with neither party holding it for more than eight years since 1899. Residents of the Buckeye State are extremely proud of their political history as kingmakers. For the past one hundred years, Ohio has voted for the winner in presidential contests in all but two elections, and since 1964, it hasn't missed once. No Republican has ever won the presidency without Ohio, and only two Democrats have done so since 1900, Franklin D. Roosevelt in 1944 and John F. Kennedy in 1960. It's no wonder presidential campaigns lavish so much attention on Ohio.

The largest city is Columbus, the state capital, located in the center of the state. It's also the home of Ohio State University, and the combination of state government and the college means a steady source of relatively high-paying jobs. Compared with the rest of the state, Columbus has been doing pretty well economically and been spared from the serious downturn that so much of the rest of the state has suffered in recent years.

Ohio's huge manufacturing base has been extremely hard hit over the past few decades. The state's other major cities—Cleveland, Cincinnati, Toledo, Akron, and Dayton—are all gritty manufacturing centers. Ohio is the largest producer in the country of plastics, rubber, fabricated metals, electrical equipment, and appliances. With about 630,000 workers employed in manufacturing,[1] Ohio's manufacturing sector is still the third-largest in the country behind just California and Texas, according to the National Association of Manufacturers[2] even though the state has lost thousands of manufacturing jobs in recent decades.

The overall unemployment rate in Ohio was almost 12 percent in January 2010 and remained above 10 percent for much of that year. A dozen counties had unemployment rates above 13 percent, and several in southwestern Ohio close to the Kentucky and West Virginia borders were above 15 percent and saw almost no improvement in 2011, remaining above 14 percent unemployment in the first half of the year.[3]

The lousy economy was the focus of the 2010 election here. So many voters were either already unemployed or concerned about losing their jobs that they were angry—and in a mood to take it out on Democrats. Voters do not register by party in Ohio, but the number of Democrats, Republicans, and Independents is estimated to be pretty close, with Democrats having an edge. However, many Democrats in Ohio are conservative to moderate in their views and swing back and forth, often voting for Republicans.

I call these voters the America First Democrats. They support a strong national defense, and because many of them work in manufacturing jobs, they tend to be populist and protectionist. They are also more traditional and conservative on social issues than they perceive the Democratic Party to be. There are large concentrations of America First Democrats in the Midwest and Rust Belt, but you can also find them in states like New Jersey and Massachusetts.

These are blue-collar and middle-class voters, and many are union members. While it doesn't really make economic sense for them to vote Republican, social issues and race largely convinced them to turn away from the Democrats. Economically, these voters have been the hardest hit group as the disparity in per capita income between the highest and lowest earners increased in the Bush years and manufacturing jobs were exported overseas or disappeared. Chances are the America First Democrats shop at Walmart, buying goods made in China, but oppose American trade policy and NAFTA, which they believe has cost U.S. jobs.

Previously, these kinds of voters have been known as Reagan Democrats. But that name mostly refers to blue-collar voters who voted for Ronald Reagan because they liked his muscular patriotism and social views. The America First Democrats also include middle-class voters who are too young to have voted for Reagan and probably should be Democrats but have become disaffected with the Democratic Party because of social issues and spending and have been moving away from the party for years. They liked Ronald Reagan because he was not embarrassed to talk about patriotism, kicking Commie butt, and the greatness of America, which they still believe in even if it hasn't worked out so well for them economically in recent decades. They perceive reluctance on the part of many Democrats to stand up for traditional American values both at home and abroad, and that is a big part of their discomfort with Barack Obama. They are moderate/conservative Independents and ticket splitters and are actively pursued by Republican strategists and candidates as well as by the Democrats.

These voters base their political decisions on whom they feel comfortable with and might like to have a beer with more than they do on which party could do them the most good. They liked Bill Clinton and voted for him. Many of them also voted for Hillary. The older America First Democrats first became disaffected with the Democratic Party in the 1960s and '70s over the issues of race, values, and national security. The civil rights legislation that brought African American voters into the Democratic tent also cost the party white voters, especially men. In addition to its support for civil rights, the party's opposition to the Vietnam War, identification with protest movements, and support for social rights including abortion rights, feminism, and gay rights chipped away at support for the party among working- and middle-class, middle-American voters around the country.

The Democratic Party came to be seen by them as a party of minorities and the well-educated elite but not ordinary people. The rift created between this group and the Democrats in the '68 and '72 elections has been exploited by the Republicans ever since. Why did "Joe the Plumber" become the McCain mascot of 2008? It wasn't an accident. The Republicans realized how important these voters would be to the outcome of the election. When Obama made his remark about small-town voters in Pennsylvania and the Midwest being bitter and clinging to "guns and religion," the McCain campaign jumped on the remark and wouldn't let voters forget it.

Many America First Democrats are mistrustful of Obama and the Democrats because they haven't seen any economic improvement in their communities, and their financial insecurity, fear about the future, and resentment of immigrants have been exploited by politicians who blame immigrants for many of our social and economic problems. America First Democrats have probably benefited from a government program in their lifetime, so many of them are less concerned about reducing the deficit and more tolerant of federal spending than Tea Party voters. While race may be a factor in their discomfort with Obama, their objection is more about his being a Harvard intellectual who doesn't really get the way they live.

Ohio is the home of many America First Democrats—including Keith Reisdorf, a fifty-four-year-old unemployed machinist, and Roy Gibson, also fifty-four, a receiving clerk. Both men participated in a focus group of Independent voters I conducted in Akron, Ohio, in the fall of 2010, a few weeks before the election. The bad economic conditions in Ohio were front and center for them, with other issues taking a backseat.

Reisdorf and Gibson expressed dissatisfaction with both parties and the system in general. Gibson had voted for Barack Obama, Reisdorf wrote in Ron Paul for president. Their mood was glum, and they didn't see much chance for change no matter who won the election. "We're not running the government, they're running us. They're pushing us around. It's not working," said Reisdorf.

"America should be the first and only priority to begin with. No-where else. Right here at home," said Gibson. Both men were extremely concerned about jobs and the economy. They were frustrated with the political process and dissatisfied with the direction the country was headed. They did not feel well represented by the political system and felt politicians were too partisan, cared mostly about their own reelections, and were controlled by special interests.

Chris Weigand is a thirty-seven-year-old industrial designer who creates store displays for American Greetings, an Ohio-based company. He lives in Sagamore Hills, halfway between Akron and Cleveland, is married, and has two young boys. His family has been trying to sell their house, but it has lost value and hasn't been easy to sell. Weigand voted for John McCain in 2008, but appreciated what he saw as Barack Obama's apparent willingness to come to the center after the 2010 election.

> Compared to the Republicans, he seems more rational. I think I've grown fonder of him, he seems more like a grown-up and willing to compromise. Somewhere there has to be compromise to balance our budget and reduce the debt. I'm not expecting to get Social Security—I can see the train coming down the tracks. . . . Because our political system has gotten so polarized, everything in our society is so black-and-white . . . both parties get hung up on their issues.

He likes and votes for his Republican Representative Steve LaTourette, who's been in Congress since 1994 and is more moderate than most of the other Republicans in the state's congressional delegation. But Weigand also voted for Democratic incumbent Governor Ted Strickland. "I liked our governor. I just think he was at the helm at the wrong time."

In 2006, Strickland campaigned for governor using the slogan "Turnaround Ohio" and carried seventy-two of eighty-eight counties and won the governorship with 61 percent of the vote.[4] But four years later, many Ohioans felt the state hadn't turned around and was worse off than when Strickland took office.

He worked at being bipartisan and held weekly meetings with Republican leaders in the state legislature. Faced with a tough state budget situation, he froze tuition increases at state colleges and universities, opposed tax increases, and reduced state spending. But it wasn't enough. The Republican Governors Association ran television ads during his reelection campaign saying 400,000 Ohio jobs were lost on Strickland's watch,[5] and right or wrong, many Ohioans thought the governor should be held accountable.

In one of the most closely watched elections in the country in 2010, Strickland's opponent was John Kasich, a boyish-looking fifty-eight-year-old conservative former congressman and fiscal hawk who was chairman of the House Budget Committee after the Republican takeover of Congress in 1994. Kasich had hosted a show on Fox News, flirted with a run for president in 2000, and run Lehman Brothers investment banking division in Columbus before that company failed. He's also the author of three books, including one on faith called *Every Other Monday*, which was on the *New York Times* bestseller list for a few weeks.

In 2008, Kasich earned more than half a million dollars in salary and bonus from Lehman, not long before the company collapsed, and his investment banking credentials were something Strickland hit hard on the campaign trail. He also blasted Kasich for calling for cuts in teacher salaries when from 2001 to 2009, Kasich received fifty thousand dollars a year from Ohio State University for his role as a presidential fellow, which Strickland said involved only about four hours a month of work.

Strickland, sixty-nine, is a former pastor and prison psychologist who ran for the U.S. House three times before being elected in 1992. He lost a bid for reelection in 1994 but won a rematch in 1996 and served in Congress for ten years before deciding to run for governor. He is a moderate Democrat, the kind Independent voters and America First Democrats, crucial in Ohio elections, generally like.

I spent several days with Strickland on the campaign trail in early September and again shortly before the 2010 election. He's an extremely likable man, very much in the Midwestern, don't make a fuss, down-to-earth mold. The first time I met him, it was Labor Day weekend and he was making campaign visits to county fairs in Canfield and Canton, south of Cleveland. Strickland knew he was facing an uphill battle, but no one was going to outwork him, even a challenger who was ten years younger. "I think quite frankly my opponent's kind of reckless in his ideas and extreme, and Ohio is not an extreme state. We're a moderate, middle-of-the-road state," Strickland told me. At the time, it wasn't exactly clear what Strickland meant, but Ohio voters would find out soon enough.

At the Stark County Fair in Canton, Strickland spent an hour or so, taking his time, stopping by the booths of local businesses and politicians, snatching a Tootsie Roll from a jar on the table of a candidate for judge. He was dressed practically and without any seeming desire to draw attention to himself, like any Ohio small businessman or insurance salesman might be, wearing khaki pants, a blue shirt, and a red tie. When I complimented the tie, he thanked me, saying, "I picked it out myself at T.J. Maxx." In one of the barns at the fairgrounds, a 4-H cattle auction was taking place, and the young steers raised by area children were going to the highest bidder. Strickland and his small entourage stopped for a while to watch the bidding. One young girl had even put glitter on her beautiful white steer in an effort to attract attention and the highest possible bid.

The next day, Sunday, at a union festival in Lorain, just east of Cleveland, Strickland was joined by about two dozen Democratic candidates for state and local office along with Richard Trumka, president of the national AFL-CIO, who did his best to fire up the hundreds of people gathered at a downtown park for the rally and get them energized for the final months of the campaign. "The future of our nation and our state is at risk . . . the Republican Party has been taken over by the radical right," Strickland told the crowd. The normally soft-spoken Strickland lashed out at Kasich, his voice continuing to rise throughout the speech until he concluded, "I am going to fight like hell to stop John Kasich from bringing Wall Street values into the office of the governor of the state of Ohio."

Labor Day dawned cold and drizzly in northwest Ohio, and Strickland was joined by Vice President Joe Biden for the annual Labor Day parade in downtown Toledo. Biden, who is more popular with union voters and America First Democrats than Obama, sprinted from one side of the street to the other—shaking hands, posing for pictures, and kissing babies along the mile-long route. There was no doubt that Biden was a more natural politician than Strickland, as well as being in very good shape for a sixty-eight-year-old.

Afterwards, I talked with some of the same union members who had marched in the parade, and it was clear that Strickland and the rest of the Democratic ticket did not have their wholehearted support. Two members of the International Brotherhood of Electrical Workers—America First Democrats—said they planned to vote Republican. They both declined to give their names because they said "this is a union town" and disloyalty to the Democrats is frowned upon.

One of the men had been out of work for almost a year and said 400 of the 1,800 members of his union—more than 20 percent—were unemployed. Referring to Obama's 2008 call for change, another man said: "The first change didn't work. Everything that was promised isn't happening. Something's got to be done."

A few weeks before the election, Strickland was at the Chevrolet/General Motors Lordstown plant with Mark Reuss, the president of General Motors North America, to celebrate the launch of the Chevy Cruze, an economy car with high fuel efficiency that both men hoped would boost the economic fortunes of both Ohio and GM. Referring to his critics and sounding as if he was talking as much about his campaign as the American auto industry, Strickland told a crowd of several hundred outside the plant, "They seem to see the cloud in every silver lining. They have long written off GM and manufacturing in Ohio." All the parts for the car are produced in Ohio. Employment at the plant was up to 4,500 since the company started preparing for the rollout of the Cruze, but it's still a long way from the 10,000 workers employed in the 1970s, when the Pontiac Firebird and Chevy Cavalier were built here.

Kasich didn't mention Strickland much on the campaign trail but instead focused on the economic problems facing Ohio and what he called the unfriendly business climate. At a meeting in economically depressed Steubenville with several dozen small business people who complained about overregulation and taxes, Kasich told them, "I'm just trying to determine what your problems are and what we can do about them. The government is not supposed to be your enemy."

Following the meeting, Kasich told me the state needed to be more "aggressive and business friendly" in recruiting companies to Ohio. "We don't have policies to create a good business environment and get the state focused," he said. "We've been drifting. We're doing worse than all of our neighbors except for Michigan."

Various polls had shown Kasich in the lead for months, often by double digits,[6] and while the gap shrank significantly in the last weeks of the campaign, largely due to the Democrats' organizational and grass-roots campaign efforts, it wasn't enough to hold the governorship. Kasich did well with Independent and conservative Democratic voters—the America First Democrats—and Strickland just couldn't overcome the depressed economy and high unemployment. While polls showed that Ohio voters saw him as likable,[7] he was blamed for job losses and for companies leaving the state.

Republicans swept the board in Ohio in 2010. Kasich wound up defeating Strickland by two points in the closest major race in the state. The GOP picked up all the statewide executive offices, including attorney general, secretary of state, auditor, and treasurer and took back control of the state House and held on to its majority in the state Senate. Five incumbent Democratic members of Congress were defeated, changing the balance of the state's representation in the House of Representatives to just five Democrats and thirteen Republicans.

The election also will affect Ohio and national politics for years to come, putting the Republicans in control of the once-in-a-decade re-districting process here and in many other states around the country. Ohio lost two congressional seats as a result of the 2010 census, and the five-member board in charge of drawing the new legislative districts included the governor, secretary of state, auditor, and a state legislator, all Republicans, and only one Democratic state legislator.

In the Senate race, Rob Portman handily defeated Democratic Lieutenant Governor Lee Fisher to fill the seat of retiring Republican Senator George V. Voinovich. Portman, fifty-four, from Cincinnati, served in the House of Representatives from 1993 to 2005 and followed that with stints as U.S. trade representative for George W. Bush and director of the federal Office of Management and Budget in the last days of the Bush Administration. Portman is a conservative but was not a Tea Party candidate. He comes off as a bland centrist, popular with GOP business leaders and wealthy donors. He makes no outlandish statements and ruffles no feathers—Portman is the kind of politician that Ohioans seem to like, very different from the fiery Kasich.

On election night, Kasich was jubilant, pumping both fists in the air as he took the stage at the GOP victory party to declare, "Guess what? I'm going to be governor of Ohio."

John Green, director of the Bliss Institute of Applied Politics at the University of Akron, does not believe there has been a fundamental shift of Ohio's America First Democrats toward the Republicans. "They move around a lot because they don't fit comfortably into either party's coalition. They're unhappy with everybody. They're hostile to free trade, and Republicans tend to be free traders—but if you take other issues, they're not that happy with the Democrats. It pretty much comes down to which party they dislike the least . . . they're trying to get the parties' attention, and that's one reason things can change rapidly."

Despite Ohio's $8 billion state budget shortfall, Kasich had predicted during the campaign that he would be able to turn the state's economic situation around in one year by cutting the budget and not raising taxes. He talked about making unpopular budget decisions and program cuts and privatizing some state functions, but he almost never discussed taking away the state unions' collective bargaining rights, which became a huge issue after the election.[8]

Across the country in 2010, Republicans made big gains in statehouses and governors' mansions. The Republican Governors Association targeted ten swing states where they wanted to win the governorship, including Ohio, Pennsylvania, and Wisconsin, and won in all of them except Colorado.

Republicans were now in charge of twenty-six legislatures and twenty-nine governorships, giving the GOP total control in twenty-one states where they held both the executive and legislative branches and significantly altering legislative agendas. The result was an onslaught of conservative legislation that would restrict abortions, expand school voucher and charter school programs, liberalize gun laws, and begin an assault on unions by weakening or eliminating their collective bargaining rights. This was characterized by Republicans as a necessary move to trim government expenses and balance state and local budgets. But many of the efforts went much further than trying to win economic concessions from the unions on pay, health care, and pension issues. These were an obvious attempt to seriously weaken the unions, perceived as a strong ally of the Democratic Party, and enemy of Republicans. According to the National Conference of State Legislatures, more than 750 bills on collective bargaining were introduced in state legislatures around the country, with more than 500 aimed at public sector unions.[9]

Wisconsin, Indiana, and nearly a dozen other states launched antiunion efforts, and the same thing was going on in Ohio, where a bill known as Senate Bill 5 was swiftly approved by the state legislature and signed by Kasich. The legislation limited collective bargaining rights for the state's 360,000 public sector employees, including police, firefighters, and teachers, made it illegal for them to strike, banned binding arbitration on contract disputes, and barred municipalities from collecting dues on behalf of unions.

SB 5 was whisked through the legislature, and several Republican members of committees considering the bill were removed from those committees because they opposed the legislation. Tim Grendell, a Republican senator from the Cleveland suburbs who was one of six from his party to vote against the bill told *The Washington Post* that Republicans were making a big mistake. "There's going to be a backlash in Ohio. People in the public believe that this collective-bargaining bill was a Republican overreach, and now you're going to see a sort of slap-back reaction."[10]

The Catholic Church in Ohio came out against SB 5, and polls showed more Ohio voters opposed it than supported the legislation. In the wake of its passage, Kasich's job approval was only 30 percent.[11] According to the U.S. Department of Labor, just under 14 percent of Ohio's laborers, about 700,000 people, are union members or covered by union contracts, several percentage points higher than the national average. But in just the last twenty years, the percentage of Ohio workers who are unionized has fallen by more than 6 percent.[12]

Many of the public sector employees affected by SB 5, especially police and firefighters, had a history of voting Republican and voted for Kasich for governor, a vote many were not willing to admit in the wake of SB 5.

"I woefully regret my vote now," Jerry Cupp, a fifty-four-year-old police sergeant in Columbus, told me. Cupp has been a cop for thirty years. He was born and raised in Ohio and went into the police force right after he got out of the army. He has consistently voted for Republicans, including John Kasich in 2010.

> I voted Republicans down the line. It was an emotional vote because of what I saw going on in Washington. Now we're all kicking ourselves in the ass because of what these guys have done to us . . . to try to put the debt of the state of Ohio on the backs of the police and firefighters and teachers. . . . It's not about the budget at all, and we know that. It's about payback time. They're trying to go after the unions because they give a lot of money to the Democrats. It feels

like a betrayal. We didn't see this coming. So many of my friends are lifelong Republicans who say they will never vote for a Republican again.

Cupp said he has finally realized that the Republicans don't have his best economic interests at heart. "I thought I was a Republican, but I'm not. I don't make the money of a Republican. What were we thinking that we thought we were Republicans? We're just middle class."

Independent voters Ryan Ayers and Allen Wells of Canton said they were bothered by what Kasich and the legislature were attempting to do to public employee unions. "I understand that some cuts need to be made in the unions' pensions and medical programs, but going right to eliminating collective bargaining seems to be overstepping their bounds. I just think they're getting a little too aggressive," said Wells of the Republican officials. "They're not talking about the pensions and health care benefits for the governor and legislators. . . . It's all political—if it wasn't, they would be negotiating with the unions and not just going after them. . . . I think it's going to come back to bite them. It looks like a power grab on their part."

"There's good things about unions and bad things about unions," said Ayers. "I think the Republicans are demonizing them so they can look like they're doing something. . . . It's easier for them to attack unions or a group of working people than it is to attack Wall Street."

Cupp, who has never been politically active before, vowed to help collect the more than 230,000 signatures needed to put a repeal of SB 5 on the November ballot, an effort being organized by the state's unions, which had also organized protests around the state, including several at the capitol, which drew thousands of participants.

"These Republicans have caused me grief in my life, so I guess I'm not a Republican anymore. I didn't say I was a Democrat, but I'm more of an Independent now."

Cupp also had bumper stickers made up that said, I VOTED FOR JOHN

KASICH SO THAT *DOES* MAKE ME AN IDIOT, a reference to a remark Kasich publicly made, referring to a police officer who pulled him over for a traffic infraction as an idiot. Kasich later apologized to the officer for the remark.

Kasich's blunt and controversial statements since taking over as governor had become somewhat legendary in Ohio. Just a few days after the election, the Ohio press reported that he met with a group of lobbyists representing medical, education, religious, and energy groups and told them they better get in line supporting his agenda. "We need you on the bus, and if you're not on the bus, we will run over you with the bus. And I'm not kidding," Kasich reportedly said to them.[13]

Kasich, obviously thin-skinned about criticism from his opponents, made reference to the many visits former President Bill Clinton, President Obama, the First Lady, and vice president had made to Ohio during the campaign. "We beat all of them. And if you think you're going to stop us, you're crazy. You will not stop us. We will beat you. And that's not arrogance."

In another meeting with an African American state senator about the lack of appointment of blacks to his cabinet, Kasich told her, "I don't need your people."[14] A Kasich spokesman did not deny the remark but said it was a reference to Democrats, not to blacks, although it was widely perceived in Ohio as an insensitive remark.

Kasich even took on the extremely popular Cleveland Browns football team, announcing at one appearance that he was a Pittsburgh Steelers fan, the team's chief rival—an unusual move by a governor to publicly support another state's team. "When you win a Super Bowl, let me know," he said to someone in the crowd,[15] a reference to the fact that the Browns have never won a Super Bowl but the Steelers have won six. It was exactly the kind of smarty-pants remark that Kasich became known for.

In April 2011, President Obama gave an interview to an Ohio television station in which he criticized the state's efforts against unions. "Let's certainly not blame public employees for a financial crisis that they had nothing to do with," Obama said. "And let's not use this as an excuse to erode their bargaining rights.

"And so whether it's Wisconsin or what we're seeing in Ohio, I strongly disapprove of an approach that basically says people who are doing their jobs, providing vital services to their communities, that somehow they are finding themselves not able to collectively bargain," said Obama.[16]

Kasich wasted no time in reacting. "The President of the United States has, I think, a $13 trillion debt. Why doesn't he do his job?" Kasich shot back. "When he gets our budget balanced and starts to prepare a future for our children, maybe he can have an opinion on what's going on in Ohio."[17]

There is no question that Obama pays close attention to what is happening in Ohio and considers the state very important to his own re-election. He carried it in 2008 but won only twenty-two of eighty-eight counties. He visited Ohio more than a dozen times in his first two years in office, including a number of campaign rallies close to the midterm elections. But those visits didn't seem to be helping his approval ratings in the state. A poll conducted in the fall of 2010 revealed a startlingly negative view of the Obama presidency. In answer to the question "Who would you rather have as president: George W. Bush or Barack Obama?" 50 percent of Ohioans said Bush as opposed to 42 percent for Obama.[18]

In September of 2010, Obama spoke at Cuyahoga Community College in a Cleveland suburb to unveil additional economic measures intended to spark the economy. In most of his campaign appearances, Obama was critical of Ohio Congressman John Boehner, who would become the next Speaker of the House. Some in the invited audience, handpicked by Democratic state officials, were unconvinced by Obama's pitch. Jackie Capasso, fifty, works in the accounting department of a manufacturing facility outside Cleveland that remains open but has downsized significantly and went through a closure scare. Capasso told me she had never voted for a Republican for president and normally votes for Democratic candidates. But not this year. She planned to vote for Kasich for governor. "We've lost way too many jobs, and whether it's right or wrong, he's going to take the fall for it," Capasso said of Strickland.

In addition to Strickland, a number of Democratic members of Congress were in trouble, including freshmen Mary Jo Kilroy of Columbus and Steve Driehaus of Cincinnati. Even Zack Space, a moderate Democrat who voted against health reform and tended to go his own way, even going so far as skipping the 2008 Democratic convention in Denver, was in trouble. All of them were ultimately defeated, along with Charlie Wilson, a Blue Dog moderate in his second term who had won his last election to the House with 62 percent of the vote and whose defeat was a surprise to many Ohio political observers and a testament to the size and power of the 2010 Republican wave in Ohio.

But the Ohio House member who got the most attention from Obama and the White House was John Boccieri, a freshman from Ohio's Sixteenth District, which had previously been represented in Congress for thirty-six years by moderate Republican Ralph Regula.

Appearing on *The Daily Show* before the election, Obama singled Boccieri out along with Virginia Representative Tom Perriello and Colorado's Betsy Markey as first-term House members willing to stand up and take some tough votes, including their support for the health care reform bill. "Folks took tough votes that they knew were bad politics because they knew it was the right thing to do," he said. "My hope is that those people are rewarded for taking those tough votes, and if they do [get credit], I think we'll be rewarded on Election Day."

The presidential endorsement didn't seem to help. All three, including Boccieri, lost their reelection bids.

Boccieri is a good-looking, articulate, forty-one-year-old former air force pilot and Iraq war veteran whose wife gave birth to their fifth child just a few days before the election. Former President Bill Clinton was speaking at a rally for Boccieri and Strickland in Canton, the biggest city in the Sixteenth District, about sixty miles south of Cleveland, when Boccieri had to rush offstage as word arrived that his wife had gone into labor. "The baby is now being born!" Clinton announced to the crowd. "I wish we could register that baby before it's too late."

Despite Obama's high praise, Boccieri was mindful of how unpopular the president and the Democratic congressional leaders were in Ohio that fall and didn't return the compliment when I asked him in an interview what he thought of the job the president was doing. "I think he passes," Boccieri said. But he wouldn't give Obama a letter grade, and joked that, as a former student athlete himself, he thought a C was a pretty good grade, an indication Boccieri thought that was all Obama deserved.

This was one of the country's highest-profile House races. Each candidate spent more than $2 million,[19] and independent interest groups spent another $2 million for campaign ads—almost all of them negative. About $650,000 was spent on ads targeting Boccieri, and almost $1.5 million against his GOP opponent James Renacci, most of it by unions, including the American Federation of State, County and Municipal Employees and the Service Employees International Union. Given what happened after the election, they probably should have been targeting state legislative races instead.

Obama got only 49 percent of the district's vote in 2008, but Boccieri won his race by a healthy 11 points that year.[20] The fifty-one-year-old Renacci is a businessman who owns nursing homes around Ohio and a financial consulting company. He is also general manager of the Arena Football League's Columbus Destroyers and served as mayor of suburban Wadsworth from 2004 to 2008.[21]

But his business background is not without controversy. Renacci has been involved in numerous lawsuits including those with former employees and a business partner. He was also assessed nearly $1.4 million for unpaid taxes, interest, and fees in 2006—a finding he fought vigorously but eventually paid.[22]

At a town hall meeting at the North Canton Community Center during the campaign attended by both Boccieri and Renacci as well as a number of angry Tea Party supporters, most of the questions focused on taxes, government spending, and jobs. A ninety-two-year-old woman stood up and asked Boccieri, "Why are you voting to destroy our country? I want my country back." Another man stood up and yelled, "We have the Democratic Party backing radical Muslims. . . . We thought Barack Obama was going to be middle of the road." Another asked what both men would do to "support the Christian values our nation was founded on." A different man in the crowd said the election of 2008 was about change, but the Democrats "went completely left" and he predicted if the Republicans won, they would go to the far right. "We need to meet in the middle," he said.

That was the mood of the electorate that fall. Angry, restless, and seeking the change they didn't feel they got after the 2008 election.

Not only Obama, but Ohio's senior Senator Sherrod Brown will be seeking reelection in 2012. It could be a tough year for Senate Democrats, who are expected to have to defend more than twenty seats, double the number Republicans have up for election.

Brown served in the U.S. House for fourteen years before his election to the Senate in 2006, when he defeated incumbent Republican Mike DeWine. Before his election to Congress, Brown was in the Ohio legislature and served as the secretary of state.

Brown has been a constant and vocal supporter of labor throughout his career in Congress and strongly opposed the North American and Central American Free Trade Agreements. He came out hard against SB 5, setting up a website on which he said, "Ohio Republicans are waging a full scale war on working families. They say these attacks on collective bargaining are about 'solving our state's budget crisis,' but the truth is much more alarming: by drowning out the voices of working people, their special interest friends will gain even more power and influence."[23]

On the Senate floor, he gave a speech in which he said "some of the worst governments that we've ever had, do you know one of the first things they did? They went after unions. Hitler didn't want unions, Stalin didn't want unions." The combative Brown later backed down slightly and said he was not comparing the Republicans to Hitler and Stalin.

One of the most liberal members of the Senate, Brown is an unapologetic populist, which in Ohio serves to counter his liberalism. He is also an incredibly hard worker and energetic, enthusiastic campaigner and is well liked around the state. Brown pulls no punches about where he stands on issues, he's honest and direct and voters seem to appreciate this even if they don't always agree with him.

In the first three months of 2011, Brown raised more than $1 million for his reelection campaign and held a fund-raiser in Ohio with Vice President Joe Biden. At that event, Biden said of Brown, "I've never met one who has more gumption. I've never met one who knows so clearly what he cares about and is willing to risk his career fighting for what he cares about."[24]

Biden, who visited Ohio fourteen times during the midterm campaign, will undoubtedly be coming back often through the 2012 election, along with Obama. It remains to be seen, though, whether that will help or hurt Brown's reelection chances. Brown's race could be both a referendum on the Obama Administration as well as the policies of Kasich and Ohio Republicans. The anti-Republican feeling among union members and their supporters expected to still be extremely high in 2012, following the vote on repealing SB5, should help Brown, who has always been a stalwart union supporter.

A few months after the 2010 election, I met with Ted Strickland again during a visit he made to Washington. He likened the result of that election to "lancing a boil . . . there was a lot of anxiety, pain, anger" on the part of voters. "It was almost cathartic. . . . It's true this was a tsunami."

Strickland compared it to 1994, an election he also experienced, losing his congressional seat that year. "That was a reaction to President Clinton, and this time it was a reaction to President Obama. . . . The middle class is under assault and the Democrats need to start talking in more populist terms. They need to clarify the issues, what's at stake and whose side the Democratic Party and the president are on. . . . We're in this mess because of unbridled greed and the actions of Wall Street," not because of what unions or the middle class have done, Strickland asserted.

He did not believe the election was an endorsement of the Kasich/ Republican agenda. "I do not think he has a mandate. . . . I don't think they voted to cut education or decimate unions or privatize large government operations. . . . Sometimes I think the attitudes on the part of Kasich and his administration don't reflect an understanding of what these decisions mean to real people."

At least one poll showed that Strickland was probably right. By March of 2011, Kasich's approval was only 35 percent, and 54 percent of those polled disapproved of his performance (according to a poll conducted by Public Policy Polling, a Democratic polling firm).[25]

The poll also showed if voters had the chance to do it over, Strickland would win the election by 15 points, and that Independents, who had heavily favored Kasich, would now vote for Strickland, 56 to 36 percent. In addition, 54 percent of those polled said they would vote to repeal SB 5, while only 31 percent would vote to keep it in place.

Independent voter Chris Weigand said he was concerned about how the Republicans had been behaving since the 2010 election. "A lot of Republicans that got elected think they have a blank check or a mandate, that it's their way or the highway. . . . I kind of shudder and cringe over how they're reading their mandate. . . . The Republicans seemed a little more smug than they needed to be."

It seemed clear that voters in Ohio, especially Independents, were not pleased with what the state's Republicans were doing. The election had been a reaction to the sour economy and reflected concern about jobs—voters were taking their anger out on the Democrats. But it was not a mandate for a conservative Republican agenda that included stripping unions of their collective bargaining rights. Most Independent voters thought that was going too far and was really beside the point. It was seen as an attempt to punish Republican enemies and divert attention from the state's real problems. How was that bringing more jobs to Ohio? It wasn't even saving the state money.

The America First Democrats, who had voted for Republicans, including for Kasich, now deeply regretted that vote. They seemed to have woken up to the fact that the Republicans didn't really have their best economic interests at heart, and they appeared ready to send that message to the GOP. But how they vote in 2012 could also depend on the economy and whether they have a job. Just as they punished Strickland for their economic pain in 2010, they could be prepared to do the same thing to Barack Obama in 2012. And without winning Ohio and its 18 electoral votes (down from 20 in 2008), it's pretty hard to see how Obama wins reelection.

8

Can Congress Be Fixed?

The debates of that great assembly are frequently vague and perplexed, seeming to be dragged rather than to march, to the intended goal.

—Alexis de Tocqueville

For a number of years, public approval of Congress has been at historic and somewhat shocking lows. People are disgusted with the partisanship, the stalemate, the lack of ability to tackle big national issues, the influence of lobbyists and special interest money and the amount of time and attention members of Congress spend on getting themselves reelected. The public just doesn't think Congress can get the job done anymore. In every focus group I conducted around the country, when I would bring up Congress, whether I would ask if people thought there was too much partisanship or not enough attention to important issues, my questions would inevitably be met with derisive laughter from the participants, as if the questions were so silly and obvious, they didn't even need to be asked. What does it say about our most important democratic institution and about the state of politics in America today that people think it is so broken, they barely take it seriously anymore?

There is very little you can count on from Congress except that the Republicans will ultimately oppose whatever the Democrats are trying to do and the Democrats will largely ignore the Republican position unless they have no choice. Also, that politicians will inexplicably change their positions on things if they think it is politically expedient. Those members of Congress who do try to work on bipartisan legislation with members of the opposite party get very little encouragement from their leaders and the national media, which prefers to highlight either the scandal du jour or the fireworks of partisan name-calling and conflict rather than focusing on the difficult work of compromising to reach accord on important and challenging issues. Even when fragile bipartisan agreements are worked out, they can crumble in a moment.

Independent voters are the most negative about Congress, probably because they are least represented by it. Although more Americans fall in the ideological center than at the left and right extremes, these moderates are woefully underrepresented in Congress. A Gallup poll taken at the end of 2010, after the Republican election victories, showed that only 13 percent of Americans approved of the job Congress was doing, the lowest rating in Gallup poll history.[1] And a Rasmussen poll in April 2011, taken after the near government shutdown, was even worse. It revealed that only 6 percent of Independent voters thought Congress was doing a good job.[2] In other words, 94 percent of Independents were dissatisfied with Congress. That unhappiness also spans party lines. Only 11 percent of both Republican and Democratic voters felt Congress was doing a good job.

A big part of the problem is the disappearance of the middle in Congress, especially among Republicans. When increasingly all you have are fierce partisans on the left and right, it makes it much more difficult to come to agreement and solve problems. When moderate Democrat Evan Bayh announced in 2010 that he would not seek a third Senate term, he declared, "I do not love Congress." Bayh, who also served two terms as governor of Indiana, cited concern about excessive partisanship and said there is "too much narrow ideology and not enough practical problem solving" in Congress. Bayh said as a result, the "people's business is not getting done."[3]

In the last Congress, Bayh voted with the leadership 72 percent of the time, the lowest percentage of any Senate Democrat, according to *The Washington Post*'s congressional vote database.[4] That record certainly did not endear him to Democratic leaders.

"Both sides really punish their moderates for any deviation from party orthodoxy," Bayh told me in 2011, a few months after he left the Senate. "They [party leaders] complain when you don't vote the party line, even when they don't need you—they don't like the optics of people voting against the party. . . . Being constantly pressured to vote for things—it gets old after a while. You go to Congress to vote your conscience and do what is right, but the leadership doesn't want you to deviate ever."

Leaders of both parties have a number of tools they can use to keep members in line. "They punish you by not raising money for you, not giving you committee assignments, not bringing your bills up," Bayh said. "You face this terrible dilemma—when you're there, you have an obligation to your constituents to get things done and you have to operate within the system and if you're just a renegade and iconoclast, you're not going to get anything done."

Bayh told me, "There are many forces that pull Congress apart but very few things that bring us together. In some ways, it's almost become tribal. The institution is structured in a way to maximize party solidarity rather than interparty cooperation. Any attempt to compromise is punished as heresy. Most Americans are pragmatists, but politicians take an all-or-nothing approach."

It's become all about winning and losing—which party is in control and what's going to happen in the next election—scoring points with their base and donors and getting media attention for their positions. Both Democratic and Republican congressional leaders tend to "tolerate" their moderate members but often treat them like second-class citizens, punishing them for voting independently and denying them committee chairmanships, leadership positions, and fund-raising help.

Ralph Regula, a moderate Republican from Ohio who served in

Congress for thirty-six years before retiring in 2008, says he experienced this firsthand. "I should have been chairman of the Appropriations Committee and I missed out because I wasn't conservative enough to suit my colleagues. . . . For a moderate who wants to govern, who wants to make the system work, it's a little challenging."

Regula says he understands the frustrations of moderate Democrats like Bayh and why they decide to leave Congress. "They don't feel comfortable with what they are called on to do by the Speaker and the leadership. We have the same thing on our side. The moderates are disappearing. The parties are so much one way or the other, the middle ground is not easy to occupy."

Although both parties engage in the quest for ideological uniformity and obedience to the party line, Republicans are more dogged about it. Privately, they refer to their more moderate members who are "soft" on social issues of importance to the GOP as "squishes" and will admit they are happy many of these moderate Republicans have lost their seats, even if a number of them were replaced by Democrats.

Mike Castle, the moderate from Delaware who lost the GOP primary for U.S. Senate in 2010 after serving in the House for eighteen years, said he voted against the Republican leadership so often, "they gave up on me after a while."

Speaking at a session held by the Bipartisan Policy Center in Washington about a month after the 2010 election, which featured three other members of Congress who had also been defeated either for re-election or seeking higher office, Castle said, "All of us go to caucuses—it happens in both parties—and we have our leadership stand up . . . and they will tell you how important it is to beat the hell out of the other side—to make them look bad. If you're a Republican, to make the president look bad."[5]

The 2012 GOP primaries could be even more brutal for Republican moderates, and among those expected to be targets are Dick Lugar of Indiana and Olympia Snowe of Maine, both enormously popular statewide and with high job approval ratings but deemed insufficiently conservative by Republican Party activists. Even conservative Orrin Hatch of Utah, after seeing what happened to his colleague Robert Bennett in 2010, was actively working to shore up support with the Tea Party and attempting to stave off a challenge. Senator John Cornyn of Texas, head of the National Republican Senatorial Committee, whose job is to get more Republicans elected to the Senate, warned GOP incumbents in early 2011 that they should expect primary challenges from the right and be prepared to fund their own primary campaigns.[6]

Accordingly, moderate members of Congress have to weigh party concerns against their own conscience and the will of their constituents when deciding how to vote, especially on high-profile issues. They are forced to make their party leaders happy and consider potential primary challenges. In the past, these moderates like Castle were the ones who helped craft bipartisan legislation. But with the disappearance from Congress of moderates like Castle, such compromise is becoming ever rarer, punished by party leaders and the system.

According to *Congressional Quarterly*, the average member of the House and Senate now sides with their party about 90 percent of the time, a level of lockstep agreement that reflects the most profound partisan polarization in Congress since World War I.

In the Senate, significantly more members are voting with their leadership and along straight party lines today than did so twenty years ago. In the 102nd Congress, which met from 1991 to 1992, 80 percent of the senators—a total of eighty-three—voted with their party less than 90 percent of the time. Over the past two decades, those numbers have reversed, and in the 111th Congress—which met in 2009–2010—80 percent of the senators voted with their party more than 90 percent of the time. On the Republican side, Maine Senators Olympia Snowe and Susan Collins were the most independent, voting with the GOP leadership only about 70 percent of the time.[7]

In the House, party members are even more in lockstep with their leadership. In the 111th Congress, only about forty members—fewer than 10 percent—voted with their party less than 90 percent of the time.[8] And many of them were moderate Democrats who were defeated in 2010, making the House even more partisan and polarized since the 2010 election.

Another way to track this trajectory of extreme partisanship is by the number of unanimous votes that take place in Congress. In 1960, there wasn't a single roll call vote in the House in which all Republicans and Democrats voted the same way, and there were only two such votes in the Senate, according to an analysis done by *Congressional Quarterly*. Over the next decade, the number of unanimous party votes was still in the single digits. In 1973, the year when a huge post-Watergate, reformist Democratic freshman class came to Congress, the number of partisan votes jumped, but that was temporary. Everything started to change, however, around 1992 when the number of unanimous votes on the Republican side more than doubled to about 50.

The extreme partisanship on the Republican side can be directly traced to one man—Newt Gingrich. Gingrich, who had been elected to Congress in 1978, had formed a group of GOP House members called the Conservative Opportunity Society and was advocating that Republicans become more partisan, negative, and less interested in compromise with the Democrats. In 1989, Gingrich managed to force the resignation of Democratic House Speaker Jim Wright, who had succeeded Tip O'Neill as Speaker in 1987, over an ethics charge.

Gingrich's success in toppling Wright was a major career boost, and he became minority whip the same year. Gingrich saw that directly attacking Democrats was the best way the Republicans could succeed politically, but it also meant the two parties would have a very difficult time working together. Gingrich laid out a plan for the Republicans to take over the House majority, and in 1992, despite Bill Clinton's presidential victory, Republicans picked up nine seats in the House. The Republican Revolution of 1994 and GOP takeover of the House that followed were a zenith of partisanship and discord in Congress. There were more than 150 unanimous GOP votes in the House in 1995, compared with only 17 unanimous House Democratic votes. In the Senate that year, there were more than 100 unanimous Republican votes versus about 60 for the Democrats.

The election of 1994 marked a major ideological shift. Many of the GOP freshmen elected that year were significantly more conservative than senior Republicans and in most cases, they had defeated moderate Democrats from swing districts—leaving mostly liberal Democrats remaining in the House. The 104th Congress of 1995–1996 was extremely polarized and partisan, and is perhaps most remembered for shutting down the government in a budget showdown with President Bill Clinton. Ever since, there has been increasing partisanship and lockstep party obedience in Congress, especially among House Republicans.

Another reason members of Congress find it hard to work together is a pretty simple one—many of them don't really know each other. With 435 representatives in the House, many members don't even know the names of many of their colleagues in the opposing party. Gone are the days when members would disagree about policy during the day but socialize and share a drink after hours in the mode of Ronald Reagan and Tip O'Neill. Increasingly, members of Congress spend their time in something of a bubble, surrounded by staff and people from their own party. Because of the perpetual campaign and constant fund-raising that begins virtually the day after an election is over, members of Congress are typically in Washington only from Tuesday through Thursday every week when Congress is in session. And in the evenings when they are in town, they are often attending fund-raisers. The minute their last vote is cast, most of them are in a car on the way to the airport trying to catch a flight back home, especially House members, who must run for office every two years and usually stay back in their districts until Monday night or Tuesday morning. If you don't know your colleagues and have no relationships on the other side of the aisle, it's much more difficult to develop trust and get something done together.

Even though congressional seats tend to be extremely safe for incumbents, members of Congress are always worried about their own reelection and raising piles of money to scare off challengers. The vast majority of House members represent ultra-safe gerrymandered districts that are either heavily Republican or Democratic. That's because the parties, through state legislatures and governor's offices, are in control of drawing the congressional districts in most states as well as the candidate selection and primary process. "Once nominated, there is no incentive for politicians to move to the center, either as candidates or legislators, because the only serious electoral challenge is likely to come from within their party's uncompromising base. Polarization is the inevitable result," explains former GOP Congressman Jim Leach.

Moderate Democrat John Tanner of Tennessee, who left Congress in 2010, repeatedly introduced legislation to reform the redistricting process and increase public input but couldn't get his colleagues to vote on his bill. Tanner was the cofounder of the moderate Democratic Blue Dog Coalition, created after the 1994 Republican takeover of Congress. Many of the House Democrats who lost in 2010 were Blue Dogs, and the size of the group was cut in half to about twenty-five members.[9]

Fewer than 20 percent of the 435 districts in the House are truly competitive, and Tanner, who served in Congress for twenty-two years, thinks the root cause is how members get elected.

> There's a real chilling effect against members going into the middle and sitting down and working together to get something done for America. There's no public good involved here—it's all about incumbent protection. The voters see a Congress that doesn't respond, and that's because Congress doesn't have to respond except to the base. If the Democrats say it's raining, the Republicans jump up and say it's sunny. There's no constructive cooperation between the parties. It's all a game of gotcha.

Because the moderates are a small minority within the more liberal Democratic House caucus and they occasionally vote with Republicans, they are often privately derided as a thorn in the side of Democratic leadership. Blue Dog members fought to scale back the scope of health care reform, reduce its costs, and limit some of its mandates, and were criticized heavily for their efforts by the progressive wing of the party. But the Democrats would have been wise to pay more attention to the concerns of the Blue Dogs.

The Democratic effort to reform the nation's health care system, the most expensive system in the world even though not all Americans have health insurance coverage, was a long and tortured process full of political pitfalls for President Obama and the Democrats, and ultimately they paid a high political price for their efforts.

The desire for universal health care coverage for all Americans is a deeply held belief among liberals, and the push for a plan that would accomplish this goal was strong among core Democratic supporters. In early 2009, Obama made it clear he wanted Congress to act on health care reform, but allowed members of Congress to take the lead on drafting the plan.

As congressional committees worked on health reform, Blue Dog Democrats pushed for more exemptions and tax breaks for businesses that would be required to offer their employees health care coverage, more cost controls and restrictions on abortion coverage in subsidized health plans.

House Democratic leaders largely ignored Republican input, but in the Senate, Democratic Finance Chairman Max Baucus attempted to work with Republicans on what he hoped would be a bipartisan plan. Ultimately, however, Republicans decided not to play, and all House and Senate Republicans opposed the scope and direction of the legislation and voted against it.

Republican leaders never offered their own comprehensive plan but did push for certain things to be included, such as more freedom for states to make their own decisions about how to handle health care; no new federal mandates; no employer requirements or Medicaid expansion; allowing sales of health insurance across state lines; helping small businesses band together and buy insurance; limiting damages in medical malpractice suits; and promoting the use of health savings accounts, in combination with high-deductible insurance policies.

During the congressional recess in August 2009, Democratic members of Congress faced constituents who were angry over their health reform proposal at town hall meetings, and they returned to Washington shaken over the depth of public opposition to what they were trying to do. Obama made an address to Congress and the nation on the plan that fall and rallied the Democratic troops. But the special election in Massachusetts in January 2010, in which Republican Scott Brown was elected to fill the seat of the late Ted Kennedy, changed everything. The Democrats no longer had sixty votes in the Senate to prevent a Republican filibuster, and the victory stiffened the spines of Republicans.

Obama called a televised summit of Republican and Democratic congressional leaders to talk about the reform and what the two sides could agree on. After the Massachusetts election and polling, which showed many Americans were uneasy with the Democratic approach, the Republicans weren't interested in cooperating and insisted the entire plan should be scrapped and they should start over.

In the end, the Democrats were forced to go it alone and use a parliamentary maneuver that would prevent the bill from being subject to a filibuster in the Senate, something the Republicans had used to pass both of the Bush tax cuts when they were in the majority. In March 2010, both the House and Senate passed the health care reform bill without a single Republican vote.

The provisions of the legislation, which will be phased in over a four-year period, include extending health insurance to an estimated 30 million people by expanding Medicaid eligibility; requiring that individuals purchase health insurance and providing subsidies for low- and middle-income families to do so; having a financial penalty or tax on those who do not; prohibiting insurance companies from denying coverage for people with preexisting conditions; allowing young people up to the age of twenty-six to stay on their parents' insurance policies; increasing

Medicare taxes for those in high income brackets; requiring states to create health insurance exchanges, where individuals and small businesses can buy insurance; requiring preventive procedures like immunizations, mammograms, and colonoscopies to be covered by insurance without copayments; creating a website called HealthCare.gov, where people can obtain information about insurance options in their states.

During the 2010 midterm election campaign, Republicans attacked the Democrats' health reform as an expensive and intrusive big government plan. Polls showed that the country was pretty evenly divided between those who opposed and those who supported the measure, and that was true among Independent voters as well.[10] Ultimately, health care was a big factor in the defeat of many Democrats from swing districts, giving Republicans control of the House of Representatives.

Dan Maffei, a freshman Democrat from upstate New York's Twenty-fifth District, decided only a few hours before the first House vote on health care reform, held in November 2009, a year before the 2010 election, that he would support the measure. His swing district had not been represented by a Democrat in thirty years, and he was mindful that what Congress did on health care would have a big impact on his reelection chances. As he was leaving the House chamber immediately after the vote, I asked him about this. "I think about [the election] every day," Maffei said, revealing what most lawmakers think but few are willing to admit publicly. Ultimately, Maffei lost his reelection campaign by just under seven hundred votes in one of the closest races in the nation.[11]

Despite heavy pressure on many junior, moderate Democratic members of the House from swing districts to vote in favor of health care reform, thirty-four Democrats, including Jason Altmire of western Pennsylvania, voted against final passage, risking the anger of President Obama and party leaders. Altmire, a member of the Blue Dog and New Democrat coalitions, struggled with his vote but ultimately decided the legislation did little to address the issue of spiraling health care costs. Altmire, from Western Pennsylvania's Fourth District, was reelected in 2010 and said a number of his colleagues who supported the House version of health reform deeply regretted their vote after hearing from constituents back home. "The debate started with reducing the cost for people who have insurance now—but it evolved into a social engineering initiative to cover everybody and raise taxes to do it."

Almost every House Democrat from a swing district who voted for health care reform lost in 2010. Of the twenty-two who voted yes, nineteen were defeated, including five members who originally voted against the measure when it first passed the House but then changed their votes to support the final legislation. Voters were so angry with the Democrats and what they were doing that even half the Democrats from swing districts who voted against health care reform were also defeated.

Six new Republicans were elected to the Senate, and more than fifty incumbent House Democrats were defeated in 2010, with eighty-seven new Republicans elected to the House. Including their open seat pick-ups, the Republicans had a net gain of sixty-three seats, the largest number of seats won by a party since 1948, giving them back control of the House of Representatives, which they had lost in 2006. Many of these gains were fueled by high Republican turnout and the energy supplied by Tea Party supporters, but the Tea Party was significantly more successful in House and state legislative races than it was in Senate races because it could target conservative constituencies. It was much tougher to run statewide and appeal to a large number of voters with extremely conservative candidates.

Democratic Senate incumbents Blanche Lambert Lincoln of Arkansas and Russ Feingold of Wisconsin were defeated, and Republicans won open seats in Illinois, Indiana, North Dakota, and Pennsylvania—a good showing for Republicans and the largest number of Senate gains for the GOP since the 1994 election. But Republicans lost high-profile contests in Colorado and Delaware as well as Nevada, where Senate Majority Leader Harry Reid, who was thought to be vulnerable, defeated challenger Sharron Angle. These defeats were largely considered to be because of the weak Tea Party candidates the GOP fielded who were too conservative, eccentric, and inexperienced to win.

The 2010 election did sweep in many Tea Party–supported conservative Republicans to the House who saw their election as a repudiation of Democratic policies and believed they had a mandate for severe budget cuts, extreme policy changes, and no compromise. A number of moderate Democrats were also swept out of office, making the polarization in Congress worse. Everyone went to their own corners and hunkered down.

There is no doubt the 2010 election was a protest vote. Independents, who had voted Democratic in 2006 and 2008, voted Republican in 2010. They were registering concern about the economy, their own lives, and the growth of government under the Democrats. But the vote was not a wholesale endorsement of the Republicans' approach, which promoted severe cuts in domestic spending and social programs, including defunding things like Planned Parenthood and public broadcasting, but little else in the way of a solution to the nation's problems.

Early in 2011, the new Republican House voted to repeal the health reform law. Unable to move such a repeal through the Democratic Senate, Republicans pledged to try to withhold money for implementing the law, something Obama vowed to fight.

In addition, more than twenty states have filed challenges to the law, mostly focusing on the individual mandate that requires insurance purchase, and it is expected that ultimately the Supreme Court will be forced to determine the constitutionality of the law.

It was all eerily similar to the election of 1994, the last time a Democratic president faced his first midterm election and the Republicans gained control of Congress and also a time when the Republicans misread a protest vote for change as a mandate for an extreme conservative agenda. In 1994, seventy-three new Republicans were elected to the House, and I wrote about their first two years in office in my book *The Freshmen: What Happened to the Republican Revolution?* It was the first time Republicans had been in control of the House since the Eisenhower Administration, and under the leadership of Newt Gingrich, they were eager to make their mark.

The Class of '95 called their election the "Republican Revolution," but there didn't seem to be as much swagger from the Class of 2010. It was a more serious time, with the country trying to emerge from the worst economic crisis since the Great Depression.

"We felt like we were Masters of the Universe," said Michael Forbes, a member of the GOP Class of '94 who represented New York's First District in Congress. Lack of self-confidence was never a problem for the raucous and colorful Class of '94, with members like Sonny Bono and Joe Scarborough. "We were rowdy," recalled John Shadegg of Arizona, who retired from the House in 2010. Many members of that class were willing to admit to me that back then they didn't really know what they didn't know and were often operating more on stubbornness than knowledge of the legislative process.

"I think there were a lot of things we got wrong or didn't understand. . . . We were not afraid to lose. We were prepared to fight," recalls J. C. Watts, who represented Oklahoma's Fourth District in Congress until 2002, when he decided not to seek reelection. Watts now has his own consulting firm in Washington.

They were more than willing to shut down the government in the fall of 1995 in a fight with President Clinton over the federal budget, a move that was not popular with much of the public. "People started running scared" after the government shutdown, recalls Senator Tom Coburn of Oklahoma, one of six members of that House class now serving in the Senate.

After the 1995 shutdown, the 104th Congress managed to balance the federal budget and pass welfare reform. But Representative Walter Jones of North Carolina, who is one of only a dozen of the Republican Class of '94 still serving in the House, said President George W. Bush and subsequent Republican Congresses "squandered the surplus."

"Everything has been going downhill since 2000," he said, adding, "We've got to figure out how to get this country out of the ditch and back on the right road.

"The Republican majority focused on power rather than principle", said Coburn.

Coburn's message was echoed by every member of the Class of '95 I talked with in early 2011 as they thought about what had happened since their historic election. "The system in time challenges your principles and integrity because of politics. . . . It becomes all about raising money for the next campaign," said Jones.

"Over time we became just like the people we replaced," said Shadegg. "We were going to change Washington and instead Washington changed us. . . . It begins to happen literally the day you arrive," Shadegg said. He said the Republicans are on probation because "the American people are losing faith in government completely" and if they don't deliver, they will be voted out in 2012.

The high number of scandals involving members of the Class of '95 has no doubt contributed to public mistrust of government. Some succumbed to the temptations of Washington almost immediately and lost their bids for reelection. Others flamed out later in more spectacular ways:

- Florida's Mark Foley engaged in unseemly behavior with Congressional pages, which cost him his seat and contributed to the Democrats winning back the House in 2006.

- Robert Ney of Ohio was caught up in the Abramoff scandal and served jail time.

- Mark Sanford, a member of the class before becoming governor of South Carolina, became the poster boy for the lovesick and the foolish.

- Mark Souder of Indiana admitted to having a relationship with a part-time staff member and announced his resignation from Congress in 2010.

- Nevada Senator John Ensign resigned over an affair with an aide and payments made to try to cover it up.

Watts said he well knows from his days playing college football that "the cheer of the crowd can be extremely intoxicating," noting, "I think

Republicans in general got swept up in a lot of the same things that we had hammered the Democrats on. . . . You come in thinking Washington is a cesspool, but if you stick around long enough, you start thinking it's a Jacuzzi."

The bad behavior is not confined to Republicans, or even members of Congress. There have been plenty of politicians from both parties who have engaged in illegal, immoral, and unseemly activities. The list of politicians involved in sex scandals is too long to recount but just a few of the top offenders include: former senator and Democratic presidential candidate John Edwards who fathered a child with his mistress, former New York governor and now CNN host Eliot Spitzer who enjoyed the services of call girls, former California governor and actor Arnold Schwarzenegger who fathered a child with a household employee, and former New York Congressman Anthony Weiner who had a thing for texting photos of his semi-naked body as well as his private parts. These are just some of the latest and most colorful examples.

When you are surrounded by staffers, lobbyists, and supporters who constantly tell you how great you are because they want something from you, it can warp your sense of reality. There are so many perks for politicians, and they live so much of their lives in a protected bubble, that it exaggerates their sense of self-importance and they come to believe they are above the rules.

All of this only increases public cynicism about our political leaders. Most voters, especially Independents, don't think these politicians are so special. In fact, as the polls show, they feel Congress is doing a lousy job.

House Speaker John Boehner, who was the Republican Conference chairman in the 104th Congress—the number four position in House GOP leadership—managed to outlast the rest of that leadership team—Speaker Newt Gingrich, Majority Leader Dick Armey, and Whip Tom DeLay—and he appeared to learn some valuable lessons from their experiences.

Boehner saw scandals, both personal and financial, take down a number of his Republican colleagues and clearly decided that sort of thing was not going to derail GOP efforts in the 112th Congress. Less than a month into the new Congress, when it was reported that married Republican Congressman Christopher Lee from upstate New York had sent a shirtless picture of himself to a woman on Craigslist, Lee resigned from the House just hours after the story broke. He was gone before many people even heard of the incident.

Boehner has proved to be a resilient and adaptable leader. In 1998, after two elections in which House Republicans lost seats, Newt Gingrich, highly unpopular among many House Republicans, including most of the Class of '94, resigned as speaker. In a secret ballot, Republicans also voted to replace Boehner in his leadership position with J. C. Watts. But Boehner bided his time and in 2006 engineered a return as House minority leader, the top House Republican. With the GOP victory in 2010, he was poised to become speaker.

After the election, Boehner avoided inflammatory rhetoric that would make him the issue, something Gingrich specialized in, and managed to hold his troops together despite attacks from the right.

In the spring of 2011, Boehner appeared wary of another government shutdown for which he probably thought the Republicans would be blamed. But his most conservative members, including many of the freshmen, believed they had been elected to effect major reductions in government spending and pressed for at least $60 billion in budget cuts. With less than two hours to spare, Republicans and Democrats on April 8, 2011, managed to agree to a plan that would cut $38 billion from the federal budget for the last six months of the fiscal year, far less than the Tea Party had called for, and prevent a government shutdown. When the House voted on final passage of the budget deal, 167 members voted against it, including some of the most liberal Democrats and 59 of the most conservative Republicans including, 27 freshmen.[12] A government shutdown was averted, just barely, and funding for the government continued. But the GOP budget hawks and Tea Party-backed freshmen led by Majority Leader Eric Cantor remained restive, hankering for a fight over the debt ceiling and eager to show they wouldn't compromise the next time.

Initially, Boehner seemed to be dealing with his new freshmen and right flank pretty deftly, keeping them in line while negotiating the budget deal with the Obama White House. But he faced criticism from the far right, and Tea Party supporters who didn't think he was going far enough and the budget clash also highlighted the GOP's emphasis on social issues like abortion. A Republican effort to defund Planned Parenthood was stripped from the final agreement, but the GOP did manage to win a provision that would restrict abortion funding in Washington, D.C.

That spring budget agreement was just the tip of the iceberg, though, when it came to dealing with the nation's fiscal problems. Still ahead were the fights over raising the debt ceiling, the 2012 budget, and how to put the nation's long-term fiscal house in order.

During the protracted debt ceiling negotiations Boehner became a captive of the GOP's Tea Party wing, unable to agree to any deal they didn't like. On July 15, in the midst of the negotiations, Boehner repeated the GOP mantra at a news conference. "There can be no tax hikes because tax hikes destroy jobs."

The Republicans may believe that but recent history has proven it to be false. In the first year of Bill Clinton's presidency the Democrats, without a single Republican vote, passed what was labeled the Deficit Reduction Act, which among other things raised taxes on the wealthiest one percent of taxpayers. Rather than slowing the economy, this country enjoyed the longest economic expansion in history during the Clinton presidency including a gain of around 22 million jobs. Unemployment was at its lowest level in 30 years, below five percent for 40 consecutive months. In addition, median family income increased by about $6,000 during those years. Despite Newt Gingrich's prediction that the measure would "kill jobs and lead to a recession" the economy took off. There was so much additional tax revenue to the federal treasury from rising incomes and stock-market gains, that the government was running record surpluses by the end of the Clinton Administration.

Conversely, George W. Bush and the Republican Congress lowered tax rates, including for the wealthiest Americans, and brought the rate on corporate stock dividends and long-term capital gains to fifteen percent, its lowest level since 1941, shifting the tax burden from the rich to the middle class, and further increasing income inequality and the federal deficit. And GDP growth, job creation, and financial-market performance were terrible during the Bush years.

Republicans have been saying since Ronald Reagan was president that all we have to do is cut taxes, especially the taxes of the wealthy, and the benefits will trickle down and our economic problems will be solved. But a decade of experience has proven that tax cuts, deregulation, and high federal debt don't create jobs or stimulate the economy. By 2011 tax revenue was less than 15 percent of GDP, a 60-year low, and yet the economy was arguably in its worst shape since the Great Depression.[13]

The Republicans only recipe for fixing the nation's economic woes is cutting taxes and reducing federal spending. Some spending reductions, especially those involving inefficient or duplicative government programs, along with entitlement reform are needed. But at a time of national economic crisis, they cannot be so severe that they further dampen growth and they must be combined with tax reform and revenue increases. A rollback of the Bush-era tax cuts for the wealthiest earners would produce almost one trillion dollars toward paying down the deficit.

As the summer unfolded and an August second deadline loomed for raising the federal debt ceiling, the two sides were unable to come to an agreement and many Republicans appeared unwilling to try. Many Tea Party freshmen even insisted it would be no big deal if the government defaulted on its debt.

Nothing better illustrates the problems with Congress, the two parties, and our political system than the fiasco over raising the debt ceiling. The drama which unfolded over the late spring and summer of 2011 was emblematic of everything that is wrong with Washington. The messy negotiations careened from stalemate to near-agreement to collapse several times in the space of a few weeks, while a default on the nation's debt hung in the balance.

All the while Americans looked on horrified as they witnessed their government in action. Numerous polls showed that more than 80 percent of the public disapproved of what they were watching and as one pundit put it – the other 20 percent just weren't paying attention. A Pew poll conducted in late July revealed that people used the words *ridiculous, disgusting, stupid, frustrating, terrible, disappointing, childish*, and *joke* most often to describe the debt ceiling negotiations. Only a miniscule two percent of those questioned, including Democrats, Republicans, and Independents had a positive view of the proceedings. Three out of four people who responded to a CNN poll said elected officials acted like "spoiled children" during the negotiations. At the conclusion of the debacle, various media and polling organizations reported that disapproval of Congress was at its highest level since they have kept track of it.

Raising the debt ceiling and agreeing to pay the federal government's financial obligations had always been a routine matter for Congress in the past. But the Republicans, seemingly controlled by their far-right Tea Party wing, made it clear they wanted major spending reductions and would consider no tax increases of any kind in exchange for their votes to raise the debt ceiling.

Although polls showed a majority of Americans and even a majority of Republicans believed members of both parties should compromise and the final deficit reduction deal should include both spending cuts and some revenue increases, the only voices that seemed to matter in the negotiations were those of the Tea Party supporters and other conservative, anti-tax leaders like Grover Norquist, the president of Americans for Tax Reform. Willing to hold the nation's creditworthiness as hostage, going almost to the edge of a financial cliff, they would brook no compromise. Senate Minority Leader Mitch McConnell, who along with Vice President Joe Biden finally engineered the agreement which ended the stalemate, admitted as much to *The Washington Post*. "I think some of our members may have thought the default issue was a hostage you might take a chance at shooting," he said. "Most of us didn't think that. What we did learn is this — it's a hostage that's worth ransoming."

As a result of their radical stance, these Tea Party freshmen got almost everything they wanted. House Speaker John Boehner confessed as much in an interview with CBS News the day the House passed the deal when he said, "I got 98 percent of what I wanted."

"We were dealing with people who were willing to allow the country to default—literally ready to cut the baby in half," Mark Warner told me the day after the Senate vote. "They were either great negotiators or just plain irresponsible."

Warner, tired and uncharacteristically down after the deal was struck, was pretty typical of most Democrats who took no joy in the outcome, even those who, like him, voted for it. All Warner could really say about the deal was, "At least we didn't default—it was a fix rather than a solution."

The agreement promised $2.1 trillion in non-specific domestic spending cuts over the next ten years, only about half of what was needed to really deal with our deficit problems, in exchange for presidential authority through 2012 to raise the debt ceiling. But it left open the question of how to make those cuts, ensuring that the fight over specifics would continue for at least the next year. "This is the way it is going to be until the election," one House member told *The New York Times* the day of the vote.

Despite the months of negotiation, Congress ultimately admitted it couldn't really do its job by including in the agreement a mechanism to create a Joint Select Committee on Deficit Reduction to be appointed by party leaders to come up with a recommendation for an additional $1.5 trillion in savings. Half of the committee's twelve members were from the House, half from the Senate, and they were equally divided by party, almost certainly ensuring more partisan gridlock. If the committee could not reach agreement on a non-amendable proposal within four months, the deal included a trigger mechanism that would institute $1.2 trillion in across-the-board cuts.

Warner, seemingly a glutton for punishment, offered his services but was not selected for the committee, although he did hope to continue talking with those who were appointed about the work already done by the Gang of Six. "There's going to be enormous pressure on both sides to pick people who are not going to rock the boat," said Warner. When I responded to him that probably meant people who wouldn't be willing to do anything serious about the deficit, he just gave a rueful laugh.

The House approved the debt limit measure by a 269-161 vote on August 1, 2011 with almost 100 Democrats voting against it. The Senate passed it 74-26 the next day. Warner and the other two Democratic members of the Senate's "Gang of Six" voted in favor but two of the group's Republicans, including leader Saxby Chambliss, voted against it. Tom Coburn, who also voted no, said he did so because the plan did not have adequate deficit reduction and was too non-specific and did not eliminate a single program, cut any tax earmarks or reform any entitlement programs.

The U.S. credit rating agencies acknowledged the deal was a halfway step. Moody's Investors Service and Fitch Ratings kept the government's AAA credit rating in place but added a "negative outlook" warning and said a future downgrade was possible. Standard and Poor's, however, in a controversial move, lowered the rating to AA, the first time it had been downgraded since 1941 when the firm began rating U.S. government debt. The rating agencies, in the explanations for their decisions, wrote not only about the size of the federal deficit but also the fractured and dysfunctional political process.

Citing the "political brinkmanship" in the debate over the debt, S&P wrote, "The downgrade reflects our view that the effectiveness, stability, and predictability of American policymaking and political institutions have weakened at a time of ongoing fiscal and economic challenge." S&P also said the deal fell short of what was needed and they doubted Congress would be able to come to any agreement and do what was necessary in the short-term. "Our opinion is that elected officials remain wary of tackling the structural issues required to effectively address the rising U.S. public debt burden."

Moody's, in assigning its negative outlook to the U.S. rating, said there was a risk they too could downgrade the rating if Congress did not adopt further fiscal constraints by 2013, which the rating agency said it considered unlikely since 2012 is an election year. "Wide political differences that have characterized the recent debt and fiscal debate, if they continue, could prevent effective policymaking."

The credit agencies actions, while not unexpected, were a douse of cold water in the face of investors and the American public. "The inability of Washington elected officials to make the tough but necessary choices to put our nation on a sustainable fiscal path has shaken the stock market, harmed our already fragile economy, and now resulted in the first credit rating downgrade in the U.S. government's history," said Dave Walker, a co-founder of the group No Labels, which had been pushing for a compromise and supporting the more comprehensive Gang of Six plan. "Enough. Listen to America. Start making the tough choices necessary to restore fiscal sanity by promoting progress over partisanship and the greater good over the special interests."

Many political pundits, both conservatives and liberals, assert that there is honor and purity in putting forth a distinct partisan vision of what government should be doing and letting the American people decide who is right. Republicans believe in less government and lower taxes, especially for the wealthy, and Democrats believe that government is often the answer to our problems rather than the problem itself. But those ideological perspectives oversimplify the debate. When 40 percent of Americans aren't on either side, but in the middle, a pretty persuasive argument can be made for a third way of looking at national issues. That doesn't mean you simply split the difference between the two and wind up in the "mushy middle." It means you work together to craft new solutions for dealing with our problems.

During Bill Clinton's presidency the nation saw both the height of partisan dysfunction with the 1995 government shutdown as well as bipartisan efforts between Clinton and the Republican Congress to balance the budget and pass welfare reform. But bipartisanship was also responsible for the 1999 legislation—lobbied for heavily by financial interests, written by Republican lawmakers and signed by Clinton—which deregulated the financial industry. The law allowed commercial banks, investment banks, securities firms, and insurance companies to consolidate, and many economists believe that deregulation cleared the way for the abuses that led to the subprime mortgage crisis and financial meltdown and the creation of institutions deemed "too big to fail."

What is needed now are thoughtful fiscal compromises like that proposed by the Gang of Six, balancing spending cuts with tax reform to deal with our deficit, and tax incentives that would reward companies that create jobs here in the United States and punish those who send them overseas. The only reason that hasn't happened already is because legislators fear the wrath of their supporters and don't want to jeopardize the campaign cash provided by the lobbyist/donors representing major corporations seeking ever more tax benefits, like the ability to write off their moving expenses when they open a plant overseas.

"The enemy isn't the president or the other party . . . we've all used borrowed money, but now there isn't any money to do more," Coburn told me. Coburn, one of the most conservative budget hawks in Congress, is a doctor who served in the House for six years, went home to Oklahoma to practice medicine for four years, and was elected to the Senate in 2004 and reelected in 2010. Coburn seemed willing to take on members of his own party and conservative anti-tax leaders in early

2011 in the effort to come up with a workable, bipartisan solution to the nation's debt crisis. A big part of the reason may have been that Coburn had decided he would not run for reelection and this would be his last term in the Senate.

The biggest mistake members of Congress can make is to worry too much about their own reelection and not about doing what is right, Coburn told me. "The Republican majority focused on power rather than principle. . . . It always starts breaking down when the allure of power overcomes your principles. . . . If we're going to solve the problems in front of us . . . you can't worry about getting reelected."

I have known Coburn since 1995 as the staunchest of conservative Republicans, but in an admission that truly surprised me for its candor and as a reflection of principle over party, Coburn said that he doesn't always vote for Republicans back home in Oklahoma, and he would vote for a Democrat over a career politician. "It's not about Republicans—it's about our republic."

Coburn was somewhat quixotic in his dealings with the Gang of Six. He dropped out of the bipartisan budget posse in May 2011—leaving a Gang of Five. But in July, at a closed-door meeting where the Gang presented its plan to about fifty members of the Senate, Coburn, in a surprise move, announced that he would rejoin the Gang even though just the day before he had introduced his own deficit reduction plan to cut $9 trillion out of the federal budget over the next ten years.

Mark Warner said the battles over the federal budget, debt ceiling and near government shutdown were a "validation that this place doesn't work very well. That hurts the country in a lot of ways. People think when you ask Congress to do something big, it can't."

"One thing you can say about Congress—if they can push off hard issues they will . . . The number of people who talk about change here versus the number of people who want to do it is very different," Warner says.

He observed that the Senate is a hidebound place whose members, and especially its leaders, don't appreciate change or any challenge to the established way of doing things. "The Gang of Six was a rump group and this institution doesn't like rump groups."

But Warner remains determined because he knows the key to the long-term prosperity of our country is some kind of significant plan that includes both entitlement and tax reform. Whether they will admit it publicly or not, "Both sides realize that has to be part of the final solution," Warner asserts.

The Senate office of Colorado's Michael Bennet is located next door to Warner's, and the two men are friends—they socialize together and their families took a joint ski trip out West during a congressional break. Bennet, who supported Warner's efforts to try to hammer out a deal, said he didn't know how members of Congress could possibly go back and face their constituents if they didn't fix the fiscal mess the country was facing.

"This place needs a couple of big wins on a bipartisan basis," said Warner. "We need a reemergence of a strong center."

The dysfunction of Congress, and especially the Senate, is widely acknowledged. Much of what is done in the Senate is designed to take advantage of arcane rules that raise obstructionism to a high art, slowing Senate action to a crawl or causing deadlock. Secret holds and threatened filibusters by the minority, which used to be rare, are now everyday occurrences. Almost nothing that takes place on the floor of the House and Senate could be described as actual debate. Instead, most of what goes on involves prepared speeches given by members to chambers where almost no one is listening.

The Senate Rules Committee, led by Chuck Schumer, held a series of hearings in 2010 to consider the Senate's filibuster rules and whether they should be revised to reduce the delay of Senate business and encourage more debate. Several members proposed changes, including legislation that would make it easier to break a filibuster and eliminating the "secret holds" that senators can put on appointments and legislation without identifying who they are or the cause of their opposition.

New Jersey Democrat Frank Lautenberg proposed the "Mr. Smith Bill," which would require any senator wanting to filibuster to actually show up on the floor and debate—à la Mr. Smith, the character played by Jimmy Stewart in the famous 1939 movie *Mr. Smith Goes to Washington*, about corruption in the U.S. Senate and one honest senator who stood up to the power brokers. Under Lautenberg's proposal, if a senator conducting a filibuster were to stop talking or leave the floor, the majority leader could move for an immediate vote.

Another more detailed proposal for dealing with Senate gridlock was introduced by Colorado's Mark Udall. He and his staff designed the legislation with the help of American Enterprise Institute scholar and congressional expert Norman Ornstein. Udall and Ornstein proposed reducing the number of votes necessary to cut off debate or stop a filibuster from sixty to three-fifths of the members present and voting on the floor. In other words, members would have to actually show up to block floor action, not threaten it over the telephone from hundreds of miles away. They also suggested making it easier for the minority to offer amendments to legislation and permitting only one filibuster per bill—or "one bite at the apple," as Ornstein described it, instead of allowing three or four filibusters on the same issue at different stages of the legislative process. The Udall bill was designed to streamline the process and eliminate a lot of the delays bogging down the Senate but still respect the rights of the minority.[14]

When the Senate began its new session in 2011, the Democrats and Republicans managed to reach a certain level of détente over filibusters and the way business is conducted in the Senate. They did not vote to officially change the rules but rather came to an informal agreement that Republicans would make fewer filibuster threats and not try to stop things from coming to the floor for a vote or force the reading of lengthy amendments to legislation in exchange for a promise by the Democrats to give them more chances to offer amendments to bills. The agreement was considered a modest improvement, but it was clear that reform advocates couldn't muster the sixty-seven votes needed to formally change the rules. The parties also agreed that senators wanting to place a hold on legislation would have to make public their position in the *Congressional Record*.

But no matter how you try to change the rules, you still need legislators who care more about working together to solve the nation's problems than about their own political advantage. That message was at the heart of most of the farewell addresses given by those who left the Senate in 2010.

The farewell address is a Senate tradition and typically is used to recount memorable moments or greatest hits of a legislative career and to thank staff and family members. But the latest round of farewell addresses by those leaving the Senate at the end of 2010 also sounded a warning about the dismal state of the nation's body politic.

Intense partisanship. The lost art of compromise. The vast sums of cash needed to run for office. Abuse of the filibuster. Repeatedly, senators said these things are crippling the political process, and that the country's future depends on changing that culture.

"I will begin by stating the sadly obvious. Our electoral system is a mess," said retiring Senator Christopher Dodd (D-Conn). At age fourteen, Dodd watched from the gallery as his father took the Senate oath of office. A few years later, he worked as a Senate page, and in 1980, after serving in the House for six years, Dodd was elected to the Senate and would become the longest-serving senator in Connecticut history.

His message to colleagues and successors was direct and stark. "Intense partisan polarization has raised the stakes in every debate and on every vote, making it difficult to lose with grace and nearly impossible to compromise without cost. Americans' distrust of politicians provides compelling incentives for senators to distrust each other, to disparage this very institution, and to disengage from the policy-making process." Obstructionism, delaying tactics, and the repeated "use and abuse of the filibuster have made bipartisanship almost impossible," Dodd said. "Politics today seemingly rewards only passion and independence, not deliberation and compromise."[15]

Dodd said that in his thirty years in the Senate, until the passage of the health care bill in 2010, he had never passed a significant piece of legislation without a Republican partner.

Republican Senator George Voinovich of Ohio, who retired after two terms, said the nation is in serious trouble. "We are on an unsustainable fiscal course caused by explosive and unchecked growth in spending and entitlement obligations without funding," said Voinovich. A big part of the reason is the partisan climate, he added. "When we are laser-focused on fighting, politicking, and messaging, [the American people's] concerns and plight are forgotten and nothing controversial gets done."

Voinovich warned the conservative wing of the Republican Party against virulent attacks on President Obama. "If we diminish the president in the eyes of the world, it is to the detriment of our nation's international influence and will impact our national security. We are on thin ice and we need the help of our allies and they need our help as well."

Both Dodd and Voinovich addressed the influence of lobbyists in Washington and the pressure on members to raise money. "Powerful financial interests, free to throw money about with little transparency, have corrupted, in my view, the basic principles underlying our representative democracy. As a result, our political system at the federal level is completely dysfunctional. Those who were elected to the Senate just a few weeks ago must already begin the unpleasant work of raising money for their reelection six years hence," said Dodd.

"An unacceptable amount of time is spent on fund-raising," concurred Voinovich, who estimated that senators spend 20 to 25 percent of their time on it. "The time spent raising money too often interferes with . . . doing the job the people elected us to do."

Voinovich said his last two years, after he decided to retire, were the most productive and enjoyable of his Senate career "because I have not had to chase money at home and around the country."[16]

"None of us like it, but nothing seems to get done about it," he said—in what could be the slogan of most of the farewell addresses.

Fighting tears throughout much of her speech, two-term Democratic

Senator, Blanche Lincoln of Arkansas, who was leaving in defeat, rather than voluntarily, encouraged her colleagues to put partisan differences aside. "Taking advantage of political gusts of wind is not what our constituents expect of us nor is it what they deserve. I urge you to have the courage to work across party lines. There is simply no other way to accomplish our nation's objectives. . . . Although you run the risk of being the center of attention for both political extremes, there is a far greater consequence to putting personal or political success ahead of our country, and I know firsthand. We must have the courage to come out of our foxholes . . . to the middle, where the rest of America is, and discuss our collective path forward.[17]"

Why is it that only former members of Congress or those who are about to be former members seem to be truly honest about the institution's problems, and what should be done to work together and address our big national issues?

Political scientists have found a strong relationship between party polarization and a lack of citizen trust in Congress. With approval ratings under 10 percent, you would think members of Congress would get the message. The American people, and especially Independent voters, don't think they're doing a good job.

The gerrymandered congressional districts, which have resulted in a disappearance of centrist members of both parties; the emphasis on party unity and the disincentives for working with members of the opposite party; the obsession of members to do everything they can to get reelected above all else; the incessant fund-raising, which crowds out time for actual legislative work; and the influence of lobbyists, which can be seen in every major piece of legislation, have resulted in an extremely dysfunctional Congress.

Ron Wyden, a Democratic senator from Oregon who is known for his seriousness and earnest attempts to work with Republicans on issues from health reform to rewriting the tax code, decried the "culture of procrastination" and "nonsense" that seems to define Congress. Unfortunately, many of Wyden's sensible proposals never seem to make it into legislation. One example, Wyden worked with Olympia Snowe of Maine to add a provision to the economic stimulus bill to prevent executives of financial companies that were receiving a federal bailout from getting exorbitant bonuses, but the measure was stripped from the final bill by Democratic leaders and the Obama White House.

Wyden, who was first elected to the Senate in 1996 and before that served in the House for sixteen years, told me, "There's no question you pay a political price for trying to work with people and come up with centrist, principled ways to solve problems.

"Part of what real and principled bipartisanship is about," explains Wyden, is getting broad support from both parties, not just convincing one or two members of the opposite party to sign on to a bill. It is genuinely working together to craft legislation that will solve a problem and garnering significant support from both sides. A very, very rare phenomenon in Congress these days.

"The Senate today, in the view of many, is not functioning as it can and should. I urge you to look around. This moment is difficult, not only for this body, but for the nation it serves," said Dodd in his farewell address.

> In the end, what matters most in America is not what happens within the walls of this chamber, but rather the consequences of our decisions across the nation and around the globe. Our economy is struggling, and many of our people are experiencing real hardship. By regaining its footing, the Senate can help this nation to regain confidence, and restore its sense of optimism. Maturity in a time of pettiness, calm in a time of anger, and leadership in a time of uncertainty—that is what the nation asks of the Senate, and that is what this office demands of us.

Unfortunately, Congress doesn't seem able to deliver on that promise. Most academics and politicians don't foresee any imminent change in the way Congress works, and until there is, it's unlikely there will be much progress on the nation's large, intractable, and increasingly serious problems. It could take a major crisis to force the two parties to work together. And if they fail to deal with the nation's fiscal problems, the fallout may very well provide just such a crisis.

9

A Question of Leadership

The Presidency of Barack Obama

A rule, wise and necessary for a legislative body, [does] not suit an executive one, which, being governed by events, must change their purposes as those change.

—Thomas Jefferson

Barack obama burst onto the national stage, literally, in 2004, when he gave the keynote address at the Democratic National Convention in Boston. He was an Illinois state senator and a candidate for the U.S. Senate who was unknown to most of the country at the time. Obama has given many great speeches over the course of his political career, his rhetorical skills in many ways defined him. But, perhaps because it was the first one that really mattered, his speech in 2004 was one of his greatest. If you watch the speech today, you will be struck by the now familiar poise and self-assurance of Barack Obama. It was all there in 2004. In that speech, he introduced himself and his unusual heritage and he tried out a few of the most important themes he would center his presidential candidacy upon, including the phrase "the audacity of hope." In retrospect, it seems clear that at that moment Obama was already running for president.[1]

The part of the speech that got the biggest reaction from the crowd, and the most important message Obama delivered that night, focused on the need for national unity:

> There's not a liberal America and a conservative America; there's the United States of America. There's not a black America and white America and Latino America and Asian America; there's the United States of America. The pundits, the pundits like to slice and dice our country into red states and blue States: red states for Republicans, blue States for Democrats. But I've got news for them, too. We worship an awesome God in the blue states, and we don't like federal agents poking around our libraries in the red states. We coach Little League in the blue states and, yes, we've got some gay friends in the red states. . . . We are one people, all of us pledging allegiance to the Stars and Stripes, all of us defending the United States of America. In the end, that's what this election is about. Do we participate in a politics of cynicism, or do we participate in a politics of hope?

It was a message that people wanted to hear, delivered by an appealing messenger. People were ready for a change, and after eight years of the Bush Administration, Obama offered something very different in 2008. He was offering his persona. Obama's very being reflected a different kind of politician, something the country had never seen. And while he didn't have much in the way of governing experience, he did offer hope and change.

But Obama was also a bit of an enigma, and during the 2008 campaign, which he started essentially as an unknown, people often saw in him what they wanted to see. He was the candidate against the war in Iraq with a reliably liberal voting record in his four years in the Senate—voting with the Democratic leadership 95 percent of the time in his first two years and 96 percent in the following Congress—a voting record pretty much the same as that of Hillary Clinton and Joe Biden.[2]

Not surprisingly for a junior senator, his legislative achievements were modest. He had, after all, announced his candidacy for president after serving in the Senate for only two years. He had never run a state or even a city. Prior to being elected to Congress he had been a law professor and a member of the Illinois state legislature. He had also written several books and been editor of the Harvard Law Review.

But despite his lack of experience and a track record, Democratic liberals thought he was the one and propelled him to victory over Hillary Clinton in the Democratic primaries. During the general election campaign, Obama managed to appeal not only to them but also to voters across the spectrum, especially Independents.

His acceptance speech at the Democratic convention in Denver was a historic moment but felt, for lack of a better word, a bit conventional. The speech just didn't feel as inspirational as the one he had given four years earlier. A big part of the speech focused on John McCain—whom he mentioned twenty-one times—and the failed Republican policies of the previous eight years. Only three sentences dealt with health care reform—the issue that in so many ways defined the first two years of Obama's presidency. He did talk about change toward the end of the speech:

All across America, something is stirring. What the naysayers don't understand is that this election has never been about me; it's about you . . . at defining moments like this one, the change we need doesn't come from Washington. Change comes to Washington. Change happens because the American people demand it, because they rise up and insist on new ideas and new leadership, a new politics for a new time.[3]

That message of change resonated with the American people, and for a time Obama's election seemed to vanquish the issues of race and values. On his historic election night, speaking in Chicago's Grant Park, Obama acknowledged the triumph as well as the struggles that lay ahead.

Our climb will be steep. We may not get there in one year or even in one term. But, America, I have never been more hopeful than I am tonight that we will get there. I promise you, we as a people will get there. This victory alone is not the change we seek. It is only the chance for us to make that change. And that cannot happen if we go back to the way things were. . . . Let's resist the temptation to fall back on the same partisanship and pettiness and immaturity that [have] poisoned our politics for so long. . . . And to those Americans whose support I have yet to earn, I may not have won your vote tonight, but I hear your voices. I need your help. And I will be your president, too.[4]

There is no doubt that Obama saw the 2008 election as a transformational moment in American history and himself as a transformational figure from the very beginning. Even before he had secured the Democratic nomination, he was making comparisons between himself and figures such as JFK and Ronald Reagan. To some extent, it seemed evident that he did believe he was "the One," as the McCain campaign liked to refer to him.

"I don't think there is anybody in this race who can inspire the American people better than I can," Obama immodestly told the editors of the *Reno Gazette-Journal* in an interview shortly after he lost the New Hampshire primary. He pointed out that the presidents who were able to move the country forward were those with a mandate for change. Obama saw his mandate as bringing people together. "I don't think that we're going to see significant changes in the political culture in Washington until the American people rise up and insist on it. And I think that's the opportunity in this election. The American people are not as divided as our politicians. . . . I think everybody shares a basic sense that government is not working."[5]

Obama compared the 2008 election to Reagan's victory in 1980 and to JFK's election in 1960. And, in a somewhat gratuitous swipe at Bill Clinton, Obama, who obviously harbored a grudge about Clinton's behavior during the primary campaign, said, "Ronald Reagan changed the trajectory of America in a way that . . . Bill Clinton did not. He [Reagan] put us on a fundamentally different path because the country was ready for it." Obama said Reagan understood what the American people felt at the time—that they wanted clarity, optimism, and "a return to that sense of dynamism and entrepreneurship that had been missing.

"I think it's fair to say the Republicans were the party of ideas for a pretty long chunk of time there over the last ten, fifteen years, in the sense that they were challenging conventional wisdom"[6]

In an interview with the CBS News program *60 Minutes*, two weeks after the election, Obama said he was looking for good ideas for how to govern from past presidents, no matter their political party. "If it comes from FDR or if it comes from Ronald Reagan, if the idea is right for the times, then we're going to apply it."[7]

It was the kind of rhetoric that appealed to the Independents and swing voters who wanted to see bipartisanship and problem solving from the new Obama Administration.

Obama's inauguration, on a bright, cold January day, was indeed a moment of transcendence. So many Americans, with so much hope, had descended on Washington to bear witness and experience the historic moment. Again, Obama pledged to eschew partisanship:

> On this day, we gather because we have chosen hope over fear, unity of purpose over conflict and discord. On this day, we come to proclaim an end to the petty grievances and false promises, the recriminations and worn-out dogmas that for far too long have strangled our politics. . . . What the cynics fail to understand is that the ground has shifted beneath them, that the stale political arguments that have consumed us for so long no longer apply.[8]

But the euphoria was not to last. There was a brief moment following the inauguration when it felt like true bipartisanship might have been possible, but it was squandered by Democratic hubris and Republican intransigence. The spirit of change seemed to get lost in the shuffle of attempting to govern at a very difficult time.

From the very beginning, there were problems. Liberals who controlled the congressional leadership and made up the Democratic base were champing at the bit to enact a big government agenda—the nation's largest stimulus package in history and health care reform that included universal coverage. The Democratic leadership knew they had the votes, and they intended to do what they wanted with them. For their part, Republicans were interested primarily in Democratic failure and obstruction. When the $800 billion stimulus bill, formally known as the American Recovery and Reinvestment Act, passed Congress, only three Republican senators and not a single Republican House member voted for it. That extreme polarization would in many ways shape the next two years of the legislative session and Obama's relationship with Congress.

Barack Obama didn't deliver on his grandiose pledge to shift the political paradigm and bring bipartisanship to Washington. He didn't even bring the change to Washington politics that he promised. Just one example: *The New York Times* reported that White House officials met hundreds of times with lobbyists in coffee shops near the White House to talk about everything from Wall Street regulation, health care reform, federal stimulus money to energy policy. The meetings took place outside the White House, so that they were "not subject to disclosure on the visitors' log that the White House releases as part of its pledge to be the 'most transparent presidential administration in history.' "[9]

Obama said his administration would be different, but in fact, it really wasn't. He was working within the same Washington power structure. Obama acknowledged his difficulty in trying to change the Washington political culture in a December 2010 interview with a local Denver television station. In response to a question about whether he felt he had succeeded in changing politics, Obama said,

No, I don't think there's a sense that I've been successful. I think people still feel that Washington is dysfunctional. . . . I think people still feel that overall Washington is about a lot of politics, a lot of special interests, big money, but that ordinary people's voices too often aren't represented. . . . Part of what I think frustrates people is also the constant partisanship and the constant looking at what's going to happen in the next election instead of trying to look out for the interests of the American people, and it's my responsibility as President of the United States to make sure that I'm rising above some of that and sending a message that we've got to do better than we're doing right now.[10]

Combine that with the dismal economic situation and the magnitude of the problems faced by the nation, and many Americans, especially Independent voters, were disappointed in Obama's presidential leadership.

Early in his presidency, Obama made it clear that he planned to be the kind of president who focused on big things in contrast to the last Democrat to occupy the White House. In his book *The Promise*, about Obama's first year in office, Jonathan Alter told the story of an Oval Office meeting in September 2009 in which Obama declared that he couldn't worry about the effect the passage of health care reform would have on the 2010 midterm elections, because what mattered was "whether we're going to get big things done." And taking a shot at Bill Clinton, said, "I wasn't sent here to do school uniforms."[11]

But just as Clinton discovered, fate and the electorate had something to say about Obama's ability to get big things done, especially things perceived as advancing a big government agenda.

The effort to pass health care reform came to dominate the first two years of the Obama Administration. Early on, when Obama's popularity was high and he had the support of Independent voters, he could have chosen a center-left path and focused on innovative solutions to address the nation's high unemployment and economic problems, like investing in infrastructure improvements, green and biotechnology innovation, and creating tax incentives for small businesses and companies to create new jobs in this country and disincentives for shipping them overseas. He and the Democrats did do some of those kinds of things, but not enough. And they didn't emphasize those efforts the way they did health reform. If Obama had taken that approach, it might not only have altered the 2010 election results but could even have insured the Democrats would retain control of Congress and the presidency for years to come.

Focusing so intently on whether or not health care reform would include universal coverage was missing the point as far as most Americans, especially Independents, were concerned. They weren't looking for a huge new government program. Instead, they wanted reform to address the spiraling increase in health care costs and include a couple of other things like guaranteeing insurance portability and the coverage of preexisting conditions. But Obama and the Democratic Congress pushed forward with their plan, despite the evidence that most of the American people wanted them to focus on the economy and jobs.

Virtually from the beginning, the two parties seemed incapable of working together on health care reform. Both conservative and liberal party activists derided the idea of cooperation and said their members should stay true to their ideological roots. Health reform is a terrific example of an issue that would have played out quite differently, perhaps with a better piece of final legislation that more effectively addressed the rise of health care costs, if there were more moderates in Congress, if they had more clout, and if compromise and bipartisanship were not considered selling out by their leaders and supporters.

Obama and some Democrats initially engaged key Senate Republicans like Olympia Snowe in the negotiations, but when it came time to put the final deal together, Republicans felt let down by the process and were pressured by their leaders not to vote for health care. Snowe complained of decisions made privately by Democratic leaders, sweetheart deals to win a few moderate Democratic senators' votes and refusing to allow the GOP to offer amendments to the legislation, which she said resulted in her decision to vote against the final bill. In the end, both parties deserved some of the blame for the failure to work together on health care reform and the process looked very much like business as usual to most of the American people—heavy lobbyist input, pork for individual members, and a process that was far from bipartisan.

When Obama met with Republican congressional leaders in February 2010 at Blair House for a bipartisan health care summit and made an effort to bring them into the discussion, the meeting came far too late. House Republicans had been essentially shut out of the process by Speaker Nancy Pelosi. Representative Peter Roskam, who had served with Obama in the Illinois legislature, told the president that the Republicans had been "stiff-armed" by Pelosi. Republicans maintained the health care reform bill had taken shape behind closed doors and the Democrats had a "go it alone—we're going to pass what we want—approach to legislating."[12]

But Obama blamed Republican politics for the failure to work together. "You've given yourselves very little room to work in a bipartisan fashion because what you've been telling your constituents is 'This guy's doing all kinds of crazy stuff that's going to destroy America.' . . . This is part of what happens in our politics where we demonize the other side so much that when it comes to actually getting things done, it becomes tough to do." But Obama's plea for a real discussion and not just the trading of talking points fell on deaf ears.

In his concluding remarks at the meeting, Obama acknowledged the obvious: The GOP base wasn't interested in the approach the Democrats were taking on health care reform, so politically speaking, there wasn't really any reason for the Republicans to support the measure. "I thought it was worthwhile to make this effort," he said with resignation. Making it clear the Democrats would go forward with or without the Republicans' help, Obama added, "And that's what elections are for." Exactly what the Republicans were counting on.

They were feeling pretty good after winning the Virginia and New Jersey governor's offices the previous fall as well as Ted Kennedy's Senate seat in Massachusetts in January 2010. The Republicans smelled blood in the water and saw little advantage in helping the Democrats with their health care reform dilemma.

During the campaign, Obama said the biggest mistake the Clintons made when they tried to tackle health care was, "They did it the wrong way because they went behind closed doors" and key Democratic players were shut out of the process, making it impossible to get the legislation through Congress. But Obama overlearned the lesson that he should allow Congress to take the lead on health care reform, and what resulted was a chaotic and leaderless process that featured many Democratic plans and a lack of Republican involvement.

The other lesson to be learned from the Clintons' experience, Obama felt, was that "The American people weren't enlisted and engaged in the argument. They didn't know what was going on."[13]

Obama had also failed to enlist and engage the American people in the Democrats' health reform effort. The problem this time around was not so much a lack of basic information as it was a failure to adequately explain to the public why and how the Democrats were doing health care reform. This failure to inform and persuade—to lead—would continue to be a problem for Obama, especially later in the debt ceiling fight.

Obama was largely perceived as abdicating leadership and allowing himself to be controlled by Congress. And for someone who had made persuasive rhetoric such a big part of his political career, he had failed to make the case for health care reform with the American people, convincing them why the Democratic approach was best and why this was really the right time to tackle the issue.

The power to lead along with the power to persuade, as scholar Richard Neustadt wrote in his landmark 1960 book *Presidential Power*, are the most important skills a president can possess.[14] Especially in working with Congress, the power of persuasion is critical. A president must persuade Congress to act in the way he believes is best for the country, and he must lead the American people by explaining why certain actions are necessary. In both these areas, Obama came up short in his first two years in office.

In an article in *The New Yorker* in May 2011 about the Obama Administration's foreign policy and the uprisings in the Middle East, Ryan Lizza quoted an administration official describing Obama's actions in relation to Libya as "leading from behind."[15]

The quotation referenced the effort by Obama and his foreign policy team not to get too far out in front or appear to act unilaterally and convince other nations to support the insurgents. But the phrase resonated beyond the specific instance and was a pretty good description of Obama's overall governing style. Whether the issue was health care reform, tax cuts for the wealthy, balancing the budget or coming up with a deficit reduction plan, Obama did indeed appear to lead from behind throughout much of his first term.

Again, in relation to his foreign policy approach, Lizza wrote that Obama talks like an idealist while acting like a realist. "Obama's aides often insist that he is an anti-ideological politician interested only in what actually works. He is, one said, a 'consequentialist.'"

That pragmatic approach became more pronounced after the "shellacking," as Obama described it, that he and the Democrats took in the 2010 election and a realization of the limits of ideology and the necessity of compromise forced by a divided nation and a divided government. In a news conference shortly after the election, Obama said he believed the message from the voters was "work harder to arrive at consensus, focus completely on jobs and the economy."

"This is a growth process and an evolution," Obama said in describing his relationship with the American public, one that peaked with his election and had "gotten rockier and tougher" in his first two years in office. "It underscores for me that I've got to do a better job."[16]

That kind of admission was well received by Independent voters who had perceived Obama as aloof, overly intellectual, and arrogant. Jeanna Grasso, the twenty-nine-year-old Independent voter from Denver, said she didn't vote in the 2008 presidential election, because, "I did not believe in the candidates." Grasso felt Obama was too elitist and did not really get working-class and middle-class people. Although she's not old enough to have voted for former President Bill Clinton, she says she would have if she had the chance. "I like Clinton. He understood and could relate to the poor. I grew up kind of poor and around minorities and I felt [referring to Obama] this guy is not one of us."

In addition to the qualities of leadership and persuasion, presidents also need to have a bond with the American people, including the ability to relate to and understand them—to feel their pain. Americans have to believe the president is one of them. The role of emoter-in-chief did not come naturally to the cool, restrained Obama, and after the election he turned to the master—Bill Clinton. Whether or not there were any lingering ill feelings from the primary campaign, Obama knew enough to take advantage of Clinton's experience and advice. Despite his previous disavowal of wanting similarities to the Clinton presidency, it appeared that Obama was ready to take a page from the Clinton playbook.

Clinton, after all, had weathered a similar midterm defeat, successfully outmaneuvered a Republican Congress, turned their deficit-cutting, government-reducing message and government shutdown to his advantage, claimed the political center, balanced the budget, passed welfare reform, and gotten himself reelected. In spite of any taint that lingered over his involvement with Monica Lewinsky and the impeachment battle in his second term, Clinton still remained an extremely popular figure with much of the American public. A few months before the 2010 election, a Gallup poll showed that 61 percent of Americans and 60 percent of Independents had a favorable view of Clinton, compared with 52 percent overall and 50 percent of Independents who had a favorable view of Obama, still higher than George W. Bush's 45 percent favorability rating and 37 percent approval with Independents.[17]

The lame duck congressional session held after the 2010 election showed a willingness on Obama's part to work directly with the Republicans, even if it resulted in questionable policy that would significantly increase the deficit. In announcing the deal he had struck, Obama acknowledged, "Economists from all across the political spectrum agree that giving tax cuts to millionaires and billionaires does very little to actually grow our economy." The agreement involved massive tax cuts. It extended for two years the Bush tax cuts to the wealthiest Americans in exchange for middle-class tax cuts. It also included a one-year payroll tax reduction; an extension of unemployment benefits; a deal on reducing the estate tax; a huge investment tax credit for American businesses; tuition tax credits; and an expansion of the Earned Income Tax Credit. In other words—tax cuts for all—bound to be popular, but not necessarily right. Obama said because the Republicans refused to go along with any deal that didn't include the billionaire tax cuts, he had no choice. But after all of the talk about the deficit in the election, the package added more than $900 billion to the debt and was not linked in any way to deficit reduction.[18]

Just six months later, Obama and the congressional Republicans would be in a deadlock over how to reduce a deficit they had made considerably worse with this tax cut deal, and the president would be saying much the same thing—he didn't have a choice—he had to give in to them. If Obama had linked authority to raise the debt ceiling with the tax cut agreement when he had a much more reasonable Congress to work with before the Tea Party freshmen were sworn in, a great deal of trouble could have been avoided. Senator Mark Warner told me White House negotiators "said they tried."

But apparently not hard enough.

After spending more than an hour in the Oval Office talking with Bill Clinton about the election and the tax package, Obama brought him to the briefing room to endorse the tax cut deal. Handing out a rare compliment to Clinton, Obama told the press, "I thought, given the fact that he presided over as good an economy as we've seen in our lifetimes, that it might be useful for him to share some of his thoughts."

Clinton called the deal "the best bipartisan agreement we can reach to help the largest number of Americans, and to maximize the chances that the economic recovery will accelerate and create more jobs." Looking pretty happy to be back in the briefing room, Clinton then continued to take questions. After a few minutes, when Clinton made no move to cut things off, Obama excused himself, saying his wife, Michelle, was waiting for him to attend a White House Christmas party, leaving Clinton to face the media by himself for another twenty minutes. The whole thing had a slightly *Home Alone* quality to it.

Clinton was asked a number of questions about comparisons to the 1994 election, what advice he had given Obama, triangulation, and likely opposition to the deal from liberal Democrats.

"I think it is an enormous relief for America to think that both parties might vote for something, anything that they could both agree on. And there is no way you can have a compromise without having something in the bill that you don't like," Clinton said.

> Yes, I think the one thing that always happens when you have divided government is that people no longer see principled compromise as weakness. This system was set up to promote principled compromise. It is an ethical thing to do. In a democracy where no one is a dictator, we would all be at each other's throats all the time, and we would be in a state of constant paralysis if once power is divided, there is no compromise.[19]

The deal *was* a bipartisan moment, but it also confirmed many of our worst fears about government—that bipartisanship can be achieved only on things that are incredibly easy and popular, like tax cuts, not on things that are difficult, like reducing the deficit and entitlement reform.

"I'm surprised how fast everybody has forgotten what Bill Clinton did—he addressed the deficit and the economy took off. . . . He handed George Bush a surplus and Bush squandered it with tax cuts for the wealthy and spending," Rhode Island's Independent Governor Lincoln Chafee told me. Chafee did not believe Obama and the Democrats were persuasively making their case to the American people and called the tax deal "another classic fold" on their part.

Chafee, who had endorsed Barack Obama for president in 2008, wrote a *New York Times* op-ed in February 2010 in which he expressed disappointment with Obama's performance as president. "Barack Obama stood in as a kind of third-party candidate in 2008, with an attractive message of hope, change and a post-partisan approach. He captured that popular, centrist energy for the Democrats," Chafee wrote. "So far, I'm sorry to say, he's proving my assertion that Republicans lead in the wrong direction and Democrats are unable to lead in any direction at all."[20]

Chafee wrote that Obama's "failure to devise a stimulus bill that could win a single Republican vote in the House" was a "crucial first test that set the tone for the stalemate on health care reform." Some months later, Chafee told me he thought both fights killed any chance Obama had to build on the "post-partisan momentum" he had won in his election.

In the months that followed the 2010 election and well into 2011, the Republicans dominated the national debate on how to deal with the deficit and debt crisis at the same time Obama and his team were also forced to deal with uprisings in the Middle East and other major world events.

Obama's 2010 State of the Union speech in January had been a call for Congress to finish the job and pass health care reform. Obama delivered it in the same smooth, effortless way he might have played a pickup basketball game with members of Congress—a little humor, a little self-deprecation, some spine-stiffening encouragement for his teammates, and some taunting of his opponents thrown in for good measure.[21]

The 2011 State of the Union address, in the wake not only of the fall election defeat but also coming just a few weeks after the tragic Tucson shooting of Arizona Congresswoman Gabrielle Giffords, her constituents and aides, and a federal judge, had a more somber, conciliatory tone, not only from Obama but also from the members of Congress who were sitting together in the House chamber as proposed by Mark Udall and the Third Way group.

A few days after the shooting, Obama had delivered a moving tribute at the memorial service held at the University of Arizona for those killed in which he called for national unity.

> At a time when our discourse has become so sharply polarized—at a time when we are far too eager to lay the blame for all that ails the world at the feet of those who happen to think differently than we do—it's important for us to pause for a moment and make sure that we're talking with each other in a way that heals, not in a way that wounds. . . . What we cannot do is use this tragedy as one more occasion to turn on each other. That we cannot do.[22]

Obama's restrained, calm appeal for Americans, and especially politicians of both parties, to do better, to be more mature and thoughtful in dealing with one another as a way to honor the fallen was pitch-perfect for the moment—a sharp contrast to the odd, self-absorbed remarks of Sarah Palin, who released an eight-minute video on Facebook in which she said the politicians and media who were criticizing her for her past actions and statements which might have contributed to the toxic political environment were engaging in a "blood libel."[23]

In his State of the Union speech, Obama repeated the call for the two parties to work together:

> Amid all the noise and passions and rancor of our public debate, Tucson reminded us that no matter who we are or where we come from, each of us is a part of something greater—something more consequential than party or political preference. . . . That's what the people who sent us here expect of us. With their votes, they've determined that governing will now be a shared responsibility between parties. New laws will only pass with support from Democrats and Republicans. We will move forward together, or not at all—for the challenges we face are bigger than party, and bigger than politics.[24]

The moment of unity, however, was short lived. It would continue to prove difficult for Republicans and Democrats to transcend party politics and work together, and the near government shutdown over the federal budget in early April was one more example. The reserve and restraint that had served Obama so well in the wake of the Tucson shooting were not what was needed in dealing with congressional leaders over the budget impasse. Preferring not to take the lead in the negotiations, but rather to stay at arm's length from them, Obama let House Speaker John Boehner and Senate Majority Leader Harry Reid and their lieutenants hash it out to the brink of shutdown, while he cajoled from the sidelines. "Like any worthwhile compromise, both sides had to make tough decisions and give ground on issues that were important to them," Obama said after the eleventh-hour deal for $38 billion in spending cuts was announced.[25]

With the 2011 federal budget finally resolved, halfway into the fiscal year, attention turned to the nation's larger debt and deficit issues, and Republicans, focused entirely on cutting government spending and taxes, were driving the discussion. Obama acknowledged as much when he said "the debate isn't about whether we reduce our deficit. The debate is about how we reduce our deficit."

The president's bipartisan National Commission on Fiscal Responsibility and Reform had delivered its report at the end of 2010, and as with so many other issues, Obama remained somewhat sphinxlike, not really embracing the commission's recommendations but not rejecting them either.[26] This turned out to be a huge mistake and a missed opportunity. Had Obama endorsed the commission's report, even if there were details he wanted changed, it would have provided a framework for the later debt ceiling negotiations and he wouldn't have been criticized for having no plan, being wishy-washy and unclear, changing his terms in the middle of the negotiations—etc. There were numerous opportunities to do so, including during his State of the Union speech a month after the report was released.

Polls in April 2011 showed that Independents agreed with Obama's position on tax hikes for the rich and Medicare at the same time they disapproved of his handling of the economy and the deficit issue as well as his overall performance. A significant 63 percent of Independents supported raising taxes on those earning over $250,000, and 75 percent opposed cuts to Medicare. But only 28 percent of Independents approved of Obama's handling of the deficit, and only 42 percent approved of his overall performance.[27]

New York Times columnist David Brooks called the Republican position on taxes "a sacred fixation." He wrote that "the Republican Party may no longer be a normal party. Over the past few years, it has been infected by a faction that is more of a psychological protest than a practical, governing alternative. The members of this movement do not accept the logic of compromise, no matter how sweet the terms. If you ask them to raise taxes by an inch in order to cut government by a foot, they will say no. If you ask them to raise taxes by an inch to cut government by a yard, they will still say no."[28]

According to a Quinnipiac Poll released in mid-July, voters believed the Republicans would be to blame if the debt ceiling was not raised, they also felt an agreement to address the nation's fiscal problems should include closing tax loopholes and increasing taxes for the wealthy as well as spending cuts.[29]

Obama was obviously aware that more of the public seemed to be siding with him and that next to the Republicans he looked like the adult-in-chief but he failed to press that advantage. Acting more like a mediator than a tough negotiator who was willing to knock heads and force an agreement, he was far too willing to tip his hand too early in terms of his bottom line, which he ultimately caved on.

Obama's message, which he repeated in a dozen different ways at news conferences, was that dealing with the debt and the nation's financial problems was difficult, but was also the right thing to do and everyone had to give a little to solve this problem for the nation. "It is hard to persuade people to do hard stuff that entails trimming benefits and increasing revenues. But the reason we've got a problem right now is people keep on avoiding hard things, and I think now is the time for us to go ahead and take it on . . . We don't need more studies. We don't need a balanced budget amendment. We simply need to make these tough choices and be willing to take on our bases. And everybody knows it."

It was what the country wanted and needed, Obama argued.

This is not a matter of the American people knowing what the right thing to do is. This is a matter of Congress doing the right thing and reflecting the will of the American people . . . Every so often there are issues that are urgent, that have to be attended to, and require us to do things we don't like to do that run contrary to our base, that gets some constituency that helped elect us agitated because they're looking at it from a narrow prism. We're supposed to be stepping back and looking at it from the perspective of what's good for the country. And if we are able to remind ourselves of that, then there's no reason why we shouldn't be able to get things done.[30]

But the Republicans were having none of it. On July 19th House Republicans passed what they called the "Cut, Cap and Balance" bill that included a balanced budget amendment and severe cuts in domestic spending. Republican Congressman Walter Jones of North Carolina was one of nine Republicans who voted against the measure. Jones considered the vote "a political show." Like so many others, he felt there would be catastrophic economic consequences for failing to raise the debt ceiling. "To me this is bigger than politics. A default would be devastating."

Jones was not afraid to be critical of the GOP leadership or to vote against them and had been punished as a result. Although he had been in Congress since 1995, he said the leadership refused to give him a committee or subcommittee chairmanship.

Jones told me it wasn't clear who in the Republican leadership was driving the train and making decisions about strategy—Boehner, Cantor or the Tea Party and other outside right-wing interest groups—but said, "I think they're losing touch with a majority of the people . . . The longer this goes on, the more exasperated people become." Jones thought the public would blame Republicans for the mess.

As a member of the House Class of '94 Jones had been through something like this before when the government shut down in 1995. "The American people, when we closed down the government, that thing turned on us real quick. If we default there would be a real good chance they would take it out on the Republicans."

"This is a very strange time up here, the strangest I've ever seen. Everything is dysfunctional," Jones said.

Solving a problem of the magnitude of our nation's debt and fiscal future will require a combination of painful spending cuts, reforms in Medicare and Medicaid and tax increases. And it can be accomplished only by using a bipartisan approach like that put forth by the Gang of Six.

There was a phrase in the air in Washington that was repeated so often in regard to this problem that it became almost ridiculous. I heard it over and over in virtually every interview I did with members of Congress on the nation's fiscal problems. They kept using the phrase "kicking the can down the road" to refer to Congress's inability to deal with the deficit and debt problems head-on. They all told me they wanted to find a solution and didn't want to continue to kick the can. But it remained to be seen who had the courage to actually put the can in the garbage.

Clearly Obama thought most of the American people wanted a balanced and fair plan for putting the nation's fiscal house in order and to see him try to work with the Republicans to get it done. It was a message designed to solidify Obama's brand—immediately and for the 2012 election—"I tried to be reasonable but the Republicans just wouldn't put aside petty partisan concerns and do what was best for the country."

But Obama and the Democrats wound up doing all the compromising and what resulted wasn't a very good deal for them or the nation. In a statement in the Rose Garden shortly after the Senate passed the measure, Obama said, "Voters may have chosen divided government, but they sure didn't vote for dysfunctional government."

But that is exactly what we have.

The debt ceiling legislation was signed without fanfare and in private, almost as if Obama and Congress were ashamed of the deal, which at least did manage to avoid a default and a second vote on the debt limit before the end of 2012. But it all felt like just another botched missed opportunity.

"From the president on down, political leaders didn't do a good job of explaining what was at stake," says Warner. "You have to sell the problem before you sell the solutions." As far as many Democrats were concerned, Obama had blown it.

From the ineffectual stimulus early in his term—which either did not go far enough or did not adequately target things that would create private sector jobs—to the health reform legislation, to the tax cuts to the debt ceiling fight, it's hard to know exactly what Obama really believes. He hangs back until a deal of some sort is inevitable even if it's not the deal he said he wanted. Either he is so afraid of conflict he will do whatever it takes to get to yes or he is taking the positions he thinks will most lead to his own reelection. In either case, it doesn't make him a leader.

Even though Obama came into office saying that he didn't care if he was reelected and planned to do what he thought was right regardless of the political consequences, his behavior showed he was very much concerned about reelection. In early April, the Obama reelection effort, based in Chicago, was formally launched, with former Deputy Chief of Staff Jim Messina leaving the White House to manage the reelection campaign and White House Social Secretary Julianna Smoot, who was the campaign's finance director in 2008, becoming deputy campaign manager. Obama began fund-raising in earnest all over the country, and because he had rejected federal funding of his 2008 campaign so that he could exceed federal spending limits and raise a record $745 million for the campaign,[31] it was considered likely that the 2012 Obama effort would do the same and be the first presidential campaign in history to hit the billion-dollar mark. In the second quarter of 2011 alone, the Obama campaign, combined with the Democratic National Committee, raised more $85 million.[32]

There were plenty of visits to key swing states, and Obama began inviting television reporters from cities in Colorado, Indiana, North Carolina, Ohio, Texas, Pennsylvania, and Virginia for one-on-one interviews with him at the White House.

Just as the Democrats had picked Denver, Colorado, for their 2008 convention to shore up support in a key swing state, the party announced that the 2012 convention would be in Charlotte, North Carolina, a swing state Obama badly wants to win again.

It was obvious the Obama team knew how important Independent voters in swing states would be to their reelection campaign, and his midcourse correction after the 2010 election seemed designed to reflect the understanding that the Democratic expansion of government programs was not what the Independent voters around the country wanted.

John Nemmers, a forty-year-old Colorado Independent voter and former Republican, said he felt "a little bit of balance had been restored" by the election results. Like so many voters, he was disappointed that Obama focused so much on the passage of health care reform instead of on job creation. "Overall I would give him passing marks."

Nemmers didn't know whether he would vote for Obama in 2012. "I'll be looking for the economy to be moving in the right direction—is unemployment going down, are programs being created to foster small business and innovation and job creation."

Nemmers believed it would take real economic sacrifice on the part of all Americans to tackle our debt and deficit problems and get things going in the right direction. He didn't think things could get much worse financially for the country, and the time for dealing with the problem had definitely arrived. "It's almost like an alcoholic having to hit rock bottom before things can change."

Steven Borne, a forty-seven-year-old New Hampshire Independent voter who does sales for a high-tech company, voted for Obama in 2008. "I had the hope that he was going to pull the country together and get us going in the same direction—but he didn't really do that and I've been hugely disappointed in Obama."

As Thomas Jefferson observed, presidents are governed by events and "must change their purposes as those change." So much of what a president faces is what is thrown at him, and he needs to inspire confidence in the American people that he can handle it. Something that went a long way toward proving Obama was up to the task was his decision to approve the mission that led to the discovery and killing of Osama bin Laden in May 2010. The daring and success of the effort showed that Obama could make the tough decisions when it came to defense and foreign policy issues—the 3 A.M. phone call—as the Hillary Clinton primary campaign ad had put it.

Almost overnight, the event significantly improved Obama's poll numbers, with 57 percent of Americans in a *New York Times*/CBS poll saying they approved of Obama's performance versus 46 percent the previous month. Among Independents, Obama's approval jumped 11 points to 52 percent.[33]

But it was clear that Obama, and the nation, still had a long way to go. There remained the sense that he was too cautious, holding himself at arm's length from the American people and to a certain extent from the governing process—unwilling to commit too much or throw himself completely into the fray. Obama's sense of cool detachment, undoubtedly helpful in decision making and analyzing problems, kept him at a distance from the public. At a time when so many people were struggling economically, they wanted to know their president was fighting for them. But to many of the Independent voters, it felt like they were on their own.

Speaking at a fiscal summit in Washington in May 2011, Bill Clinton said, "People hire the president and Congress to win for them and to win for America." That was a big part of the Democrats' problem in the midterm election, he said. "People want to feel fixed . . . in 2010 people didn't feel fixed yet." A huge challenge for the nation, Clinton said, is that many Americans have begun to doubt that this country's greatest days still lie ahead. "We can't allow ourselves to be so paralyzed by the present that we can't look to the future."[34]

Since the early 1950s, consumer confidence indexes have only been as low as they were in 2011 twice—in 1980 and 1992—the only two times when an elected presidential incumbent was defeated.

In late July Obama's public approval fell to 40 percent, its lowest level since he took office, and Obama's numbers with swing voters were even worse. In presidential polling done by Gallup over the past 35 years, public disapproval has always been linked to the state of the economy. Whenever the country is experiencing a recession or economic slow-down, the president is held responsible. In the summer of 1979, Jimmy Carter's approval was at a dismal 29 percent and three months before his defeat in the 1980 election it stood at 32 percent. In the early 1980's when the economy was in recession, Ronald Reagan's approval fell to 35 percent, the lowest of his presidency. In the early 1990's the country was again in a recession and George H.W. Bush had an approval rating of only 32 percent and did not win reelection. His successor Bill Clinton had an approval rating of 39 percent early in his presidency but as the country's economic picture improved so did his ratings and even at the height of the impeachment battle in late 1998 and early 1999, Clinton's approval ratings were 64 and 69 percent. In early 2006, George W. Bush's approval fell to 39 percent and didn't get any higher for the rest of his term, falling as low as 27 percent in September 2008.

In his 2011 State of the Union speech, Obama repeatedly used the phrase "winning the future" and called this our generation's "Sputnik moment," in reference to the Soviet launch of a space satellite in 1957, ahead of the Americans. The U.S. responded by creating NASA and going to the moon, and Obama said a similar effort is needed now to address the nation's challenges. "That's what Americans have done for over two hundred years: reinvented ourselves."[35]

But there seems to be a fundamental loss of faith that we *can* reinvent ourselves this time around and that Obama can help us do it. Despite his rhetorical talents, Obama doesn't have Clinton's political skills, and to win back a majority of the American people and the votes of Independents, he will need to do better.

Obama clearly understands the enormity of the problems we face and has ideas about how to deal with them. But he hasn't successfully communicated that or convinced most Independent voters that the approach his administration has taken is the best one. And he has not put forth a comprehensive economic plan to put Americans back to work and deal with the housing crisis.

Obama ended his inaugural address with this quote from Thomas Paine. "Let it be told to the future world that in the depth of winter, when nothing but hope and virtue could survive, that the city and the country, alarmed at one common danger, came forth to meet [and to repulse it]."

In our time, much of the danger faced by the nation is unfortunately of our own making, and it's not clear if our political leaders have the will and ability to work together to deal with our challenges.

Solving these serious fiscal and political problems will take not only hope but also presidential leadership, as well as the cooperation and involvement of all our political leaders and citizens.

10

Trying to Restore Sanity

*Reflection, . . . with information, is all which our countrymen need,
to bring themselves and their affairs to rights.*

—THOMAS JEFFERSON

I T IS AN APT commentary on the state of American politics and media that one of the most trusted sources for political news, especially
with young people, is *The Daily Show with Jon Stewart*. Stewart, who has
been hosting the Emmy-award winning show on Comedy Central for
the past twelve years, always disavows any political clout on the part of
what he calls just a comedy show. And yet, when he decided to hold a
quasi-political rally on the National Mall a few days before the 2010
election, several hundred thousand people showed up.

Stewart's show averages about 1.5 million viewers and is the most
watched late night show with people under thirty-five,[1] many of whom
say they get a lot of their news and political information from it. *The Daily
Show* may feature segments on things like Gaylaxicon, a gay science fic-
tion convention, and its male correspondents may dress up like Batman, a
slutty nurse in a platinum wig, or a Na'vi from *Avatar* complete with
blueface, but the show has also won two prestigious Peabody broadcasting awards for its coverage of the 2000 and 2004 elections. Stewart
likes to skewer political hypocrisy and also frequently takes aim at the

mainstream news media. There's no doubt people watch *The Daily Show* for a laugh, but they also feel they are getting a certain perspective from it that they aren't getting elsewhere.

And that's the mission of the show as Stewart sees it, served with a generous helping of silliness. That's why so many people showed up at Stewart's Rally to Restore Sanity in Washington, which was broadcast live on Comedy Central as well as CNN. With the Capitol dome as a backdrop, Stewart and fellow Comedy Central host Stephen Colbert lampooned politics and indirectly the Glenn Beck rally at the Lincoln Memorial, which had taken place a few months earlier and attracted a crowd about half the size of Stewart's.

The extremist rhetoric and divisive politics practiced by politicians and pundits reflect the United States in "a funhouse mirror" and makes solving problems much harder, Stewart told those attending the rally. "The image of Americans that is reflected back to us by our political and media process is false," Stewart declared. "Most Americans don't live their lives just as Democrats or Republicans, liberals or conservatives."[2]

That is also the way Virginia Independent voter and Starbucks Mom Julia Pfaff sees it and why she went to the Stewart rally.

You know when you are irresistibly drawn to something and you're not sure why. To be part of that event meant something to me. . . . The whole notion of a rally to restore sanity made perfect sense to me. The sense that I got from a lot of people that were there that day was that they are disillusioned with what is happening in the country. . . . These two extremes that are out there don't represent us, and we need a way to express that. . . . What the rally did was give me hope that we could change and provided energy to that hope.

Four months later, Pfaff attended a much smaller rally but one with a similar purpose. The group No Labels had gathered a couple hundred people on a sunny, breezy March day on the lawn of the Capitol's east front to talk about how to promote bipartisanship, further a centrist agenda, and announce support for the Gang of Six deficit reduction efforts. Retired moderate Republican Sherwood Boehlert, who represented upstate New York for twenty-four years and left Congress in 2006, said, "I have never seen partisanship at a higher level or the lack of tolerance for other points of view at a lower level." Boehlert, who frequently faced primaries from the right when he was running for reelection, said invariably his challengers would level the shocking charge against him that, "He actually has friends who are Democrats and on occasion he votes with them." But Boehlert said he believes the "overwhelming majority of people are not partisan . . . they're more centrist."

And that's the principal belief of No Labels, whose founders are a politically well connected and experienced bunch. Nancy Jacobson is a longtime Democratic fund-raiser who worked for Gary Hart, Al Gore, Evan Bayh, the Democratic National Committee, and on Bill Clinton's campaigns. She is married to Mark Penn, chief strategist for Hillary Clinton's presidential campaign. Other founders include Mark McKinnon, a senior adviser to former President George W. Bush and to Senator John McCain during his 2008 presidential run and John Avlon, a columnist, television commentator, and author of *Wingnuts: How the Lunatic Fringe is Hijacking America.*

The group raised $1 million in seed money and hopes to recruit a million members and organize volunteers in all the congressional districts in the country by the end of 2012, set up 150 chapters on college campuses, establish a rating system to hold elected officials accountable for their actions and monitor them for bipartisan behavior. No Labels also plans to create a political action committee to support centrist candidates who are in line with the No Labels bipartisan mission, like Maine's moderate Republican Senator Olympia Snowe. After its well-publicized launch in New York City in December 2010, No Labels took some hits from political pundits at both ends of the political spectrum, including Rush Limbaugh and *The New York Times*' Frank Rich, who wrote "the notion that civility and nominal bipartisanship would accomplish any of the heavy lifting required to rebuild America is childish magical thinking, and, worse, a mindless distraction from the real work before the nation."[3]

In response, Joe Scarborough, former GOP congressman and host of MSNBC's *Morning Joe*, who attended the No Labels kickoff, said commentators like Rich and Limbaugh "have the luxury of never actually governing."

"Frank Rich and the left have had a year of magical thinking . . . they believed they could get absolutely everything they wanted, and when they didn't, they became petulant and went off in a corner and pouted," said Scarborough.[4]

Conservative columnist George Will called the No Labels message "mush" and said that politics *is* partisanship. "When people label themselves conservatives or liberals we can reasonably surmise where they stand concerning important matters," Will wrote.[5]

But not everyone in this country is a liberal like Rich or a conservative like Will, and they don't make their living as members of the "political-media industrial complex." There are more people in the middle than on either side. And right now, they are not being well served by the system. No Labels is trying to help with that—but it will undoubtedly be a hard slog.

Using Facebook, emails, the web, telephone town halls, and visits around the country meeting with like-minded supporters, No Labels has been reaching out directly to voters in the center.[6] "We know the majority of Americans are in this space that we're talking about," Jacobson told me. "The last time these people were organized was when they supported Ross Perot."

Another No Labels supporter is Jonathan Cowan, who is also one of the founders of the D.C.-based center-left think tank Third Way. Cowan and Matt Bennett, who both served in the Clinton Administration, founded Third Way in 2005 with Jim Kessler, who previously worked for New York's Democratic Senator Chuck Schumer. The organization's mission is to provide policy ideas and support, primarily to moderate Democrats, and try to influence national issues.[7] Third Way, which now has about forty employees and an annual budget of more than $7 million, is officially nonpartisan, but Bennett says since moderate Republicans have been basically driven out of Congress and "silenced" by their leadership, Third Way tends mostly to work with moderate Democrats.

There are an estimated four hundred think tanks in Washington, more than any other city in the world. Among the most prominent are the conservative Heritage Foundation, the liberal Brookings Institution and Center for American Progress, the libertarian Cato Institute, and the pro-business American Enterprise Institute. Third Way has helped to fill the policy vacuum created by the demise of the moderate Democratic Leadership Council, founded in 1985 by Al From and a group of moderate Democratic governors and members of Congress including Bill Clinton, who headed the group for two years before he was elected president in 1992.[8] The DLC's pro-business, centrist approach to policy included support for welfare reform and the North American Free Trade Agreement. The DLC formally folded up shop in early 2011, but it had been limping along for a few years. Its former CEO Bruce Reed, who also served in the Clinton Administration, where he helped to write the welfare reform law, took a leave of absence in 2010 to become executive director of President Obama's debt commission. It was shortly after the announcement that Reed would become chief of staff to Vice President Joe Biden that the DLC announced its closure.

Third Way was responsible for suggesting that members of Congress sit together at the 2011 State of the Union address rather than segregated by party as had been the custom. Partisan seating first started in Congress in the middle of the nineteenth century. In 1913, President Woodrow Wilson became the first president since Thomas Jefferson to deliver the State of the Union personally before a joint session of Congress, and members sat segregated by party and have done so ever since, until 2011.

In the wake of the shooting of Congresswoman Gabrielle Giffords and others in Tucson by deranged gunman Jared Loughner, Third Way's idea was championed by Democratic Senator Mark Udall of Colorado in a letter to the other members of Congress that was derided by some bloggers as the "kumbaya letter." However, many members quickly picked up on the idea, and the media did a raft of stories on the prom date–quality of the whole thing as members scrambled to find someone from the opposite party to sit with. Udall's partner in the effort was Alaska Republican Senator Lisa Murkowski, and the two held a press conference on the morning of the speech to talk about how the idea had taken off. "We want to change the tone," said Udall, from that of a "high school pep rally" to a more serious, respectful atmosphere. Murkowski acknowledged it was a symbolic gesture, but important nonetheless.

Why not start with a symbolic gesture . . . to try to come together if only for a couple of hours. Oftentimes at the State of the Union, it becomes more a situation where the attention is not focused on the president's words, but who's standing up, who's sitting down, who's sitting there with their arms across their chest. That's not what the State of the Union should be about. So let's come together for an hour or two. And if for nothing else, sit together with a colleague that perhaps we don't know as well and be part of a process that I think is good for all of us.

It was a pretty successful experiment, and most members did seek someone from the opposite party to sit with or gathered with their state delegations. But the camaraderie and good feelings were extremely short lived. It will be interesting to see whether the bipartisan seating was a one time thing or will happen again.

Even though Third Way promotes solutions to national problems that are not left or right but represent "the voices of millions of Americans in the forgotten middle," Bennett admitted that he is skeptical about the chances for large-scale bipartisanship. "After 9/11, the bipartisanship lasted for a few months, but if a real change can't happen after something like that, I don't know that it can happen."

The Bipartisan Policy Center, created in 2007 by four former Senate majority leaders—Democrats Tom Daschle and George Mitchell and Republicans Howard Baker and Bob Dole—promotes bipartisan solutions to national problems through forums, panels, and policy research.[9] Because of its high-profile founders, the group has an impressive array of former members of Congress and governors involved in its efforts, including senior fellow and former Democratic congressman Dan Glickman. "The goal here [at the Bipartisan Policy Center] is to find those issues where you try to develop common ground. There's too much gamesmanship in politics—too much power for power's sake," Glickman told me.

Glickman is also the executive director of the Aspen Institute's Congressional Program. As the name suggests, the Aspen Institute was launched in Aspen, Colorado, in 1950, where it still holds seminars, policy programs, and public conferences, but it is now based in Washington, D.C., and headed by Walter Isaacson, the former chairman and CEO of CNN and editor of *Time* magazine. In addition to its public programming, Aspen brings national leaders together to talk about critical issues and "foster enlightened leadership and open-minded dialogue."[10]

Elliot Gerson, who is Aspen's Executive Vice President for Policy and Public Programs, says the organization is "religiously nonpartisan," and bringing all sides together to have a civil and open dialogue on important national issues is "at the heart of what we do."

Aspen is a place "that convenes people from all parts of the political spectrum," and "sometimes we do find common ground. . . . We think a lot is accomplished by bringing people together. . . . Instead of dueling, spitting sound bites at a hundred paces at least we can have a civil discussion. If you've had lunch, dinner, sat around a table with someone, it's harder to denounce them in a personal way," explains Gerson.

But he admits that mission is getting harder, as fewer current politicians are willing to "sit down and talk openly and exchange ideas and listen. They often don't get beyond the talking points they use on TV."

And yet, there is an ever greater demand for what Aspen does because of the obvious lack of cooperation and civility in politics. "It is very hard for people in the middle to be involved in a meaningful way, and they're very frustrated and tuning out," Gerson says.

"Their tuned-outness is a commentary on the political system," according to Jackie Salit, the founder and president of IndependentVoting.org, a group that is trying to address the problem by pushing for election reform to open up the process.[11]

IndependentVoting.org evolved out of a group called the Committee for a Unified Independent Party, which supported the presidential candidacy of Ross Perot as well as the idea of creating a third political party out of the Perot movement and the Reform Party. The members of IndependentVoting.org, who meet once a year in New York to discuss the group's mission and goals, no longer believe the best way to accomplish reform is through the creation of a third party, according to Salit, who thinks most Independent voters feel the same way. Instead, they are fighting for an end to extreme partisanship and special interest politics by pushing for structural reforms to the political system, like opening up all primaries to Independent voters, making it easier for Independent candidates to run for office, and pushing for reforms to the way legislative redistricting is done.

"We're trying to be the engine for reform by opening up the political process to Independents and voters in general and chipping away at the control that the parties have over the political process," Salit explains.

She is convinced that Independent voters were instrumental in Barack Obama's primary victories in states like New Hampshire, Iowa, and South Carolina, where they were able to participate in the primary process, as well as his general election victory. She says exit polling indicates that about 19 million Independent voters cast their ballots for Obama, about the same number that supported Perot in 1992.

"Independents will tell you all the time—I vote for the candidate not the party. They see the parties as institutions that are more concerned with their own self-preservation than doing what's right for the country," says Salit. "I think the power dynamics are shifting. Politicians are not pro-Independent, but they are aware that Independents are determining the outcomes of major elections and that they're turned off by partisanship."

A group called Americans Elect 2012 is betting it can capitalize on that frustration and the desire for something beyond what the two parties are offering by setting up an online process Americans can use to nominate an independent presidential ticket.

The group raised an impressive $20 million in 2010-2011, mostly from deep pocket donors, to pay for signature gathering efforts to win ballot access in all fifty states. One of the organization's founders, entrepreneur Peter Ackerman, has kicked in several million dollars of his own money to the effort. Ackerman is no stranger to the online world, having started FreshDirect.com, an online grocery service in the New York metropolitan area. He is also the Managing Director of Rockport Capital in Washington and on the Board of Overseers at the Fletcher School at Tufts University.

Ackerman's son Elliot, a decorated Marine veteran who served in Iraq and Afghanistan, is the chief operating officer of Americans Elect. He says the group reflects Americans' frustration with the two political parties and is utilizing the evolving online tools and social networks which have made an effort like this really possible for the first time. Ackerman, who is himself an independent voter, says, "I don't feel I fit in with either party and I feel that registering as an Independent is me advocating my voice."

Ackerman insists the founders of Americans Elect do not have a particular candidate in mind, and the organization exists solely to win the ballot access and host the website to facilitate the nomination of a candidate to run on the Americans Elect ticket. It is merely a facilitator allowing every registered voter to participate in a totally online process to directly nominate a presidential candidate. "It's not a party—it's just a line on the ballot—we're not trying to start a third party," Ackerman says. He also stresses the effort is not an advocacy group, simply a nominating process.

The founding principles of the group included the ideas that the political system is broken and cannot solve the nation's most pressing problems; the pressure on elected officials to attract primary voters and get reelected has perverted the system; many Americans feel disenfranchised; bitter hyper-partisanship is eroding the trust between elected officials and the people; the explosion in the number of Independent voters shows that Americans want something different; laws are written by and for party activists, campaign contributors, and special interests, and moderate views from both sides of the political spectrum consistent with a majority of American voters need to be represented.

The original idea for the effort began with several political consultants who worked for Presidents Gerald Ford and Jimmy Carter, and the Americans Elect board consists of Democrats, Republicans, and Independents. They tried to get the movement off the ground in 2008 but ran into legal problems about the definition of the organization and whether they could accept political contributions. In March of 2010, a federal court cleared the way for Americans Elect to organize and fundraise but as a social welfare group not a political organization. That means once a candidate is selected in June 2012, the organization will cease to exist, Ackerman says. The nominee will inherit the ballot access Americans Elect has worked and paid for but the group won't give any money to the candidate. For the general election the candidate will be on his or her own.

The questions potential voters are asked when they log on to www. AmericansElect.org[12] focus on the economy, foreign policy, energy, education and health care. The idea is for those who log on to the site and participate to nominate fifty potential candidates who will be asked to respond to questions they select. The candidates will then be winnowed down in three rounds of website voting to just six. These six candidates—who can be Republicans, Democrats, or Independents, must pick a vice presidential running mate from a different party. In June 2012, the Americans Elect e-delegates will select their nominee from the group.

Americans Elect hopes to have the participation of millions of registered voters around the country and why wouldn't they? For the first time it puts the power to select a presidential candidate directly in the hands of all voters. And the entire process won't involve that much of a time commitment, much less than maintaining an average Facebook page. And because it's an online process there is a good chance it will have particular appeal and participation by younger voters.

No matter what happens with the American Elect effort, or who is nominated by it, the process is bound to have a significant impact on the 2012 race in the same way that the candidacy of Ross Perot did in 1992. And by raising the money and getting the ballot access ahead of time, Americans Elect has insured that an independent presidential candidate does not have to be a self-financed millionaire. If the Americans Elect ticket can get at least five percent of the vote in most states, it will qualify for automatic ballot access in 2014 and 2016, which could potentially create the framework for a future third party with candidates not only on the national but state and local levels.

Another, much smaller, online effort to mobilize Independent centrist voters is something called the National Centrist Party organized by two guys in Des Moines, Iowa. Their goals and funding are significantly more modest than Americans Elect. Scott Ehredt is a forty-six-year-old married father of two young boys and a database administrator for Wells Fargo bank. Ehredt was a registered Republican who was growing increasingly disenchanted with the party. His partner in the effort is his friend Brad Schabel, a Democrat. Neither of the men had been politically active before.

Not long after the 2010 election, they started talking about politics and realized they agreed on most issues. They began making a list of everything they thought was wrong with the system—things like special interest influence, how candidates financed their campaigns, and Independent centrists not really having a choice about who runs for office. They felt most politicians weren't willing to work together and were most interested in reelection and defeating the other side. "We lamented the lack of civility, honesty, and representation that our current political process offers and decided that we would seek out a moderate party to work for. To our surprise, no party met our criteria," said Ehredt. "We decided that if we were really serious about working for such a party, we would have to start our own."

The National Centrist Party's website went up on the internet, Facebook and Twitter in July 2011 and within just a few weeks several hundred people had signed up and were willing to kick in ten dollars a month to fund the effort. They were from all over the country and had found the group by searching online.

Ehredt says he's not sure if the group's goal will be to create a formal third party or just to support moderate Republicans and Democrats who are willing to work together. But he does know they want to change the political system. Ehredt hopes to affiliate with groups like No Labels, but isn't sure if it will really be possible to organize center and Independent voters.

The feeling that extreme partisanship and incivility are ruining our political system and a desire to offer an alternative to the Tea Party movement is also what motivated Annabel Park to launch the Coffee Party on Facebook in early 2010. Park says what unites the Coffee Party's supporters is a frustration with the inability of the Democrats to get things done, the Republican's obstructionism, and the heightened political polarization in Washington. Almost immediately, the Coffee Party message caught fire and swept across the Internet in a way Park never imagined. A year after its creation, there were Coffee Party chapters around the country, more than 350,000 Facebook followers, and 80,000 regulars signed up for Coffee Party emails.[13]

Park admits that the whole thing was initially "whimsical" on her part and she had no idea it would take off the way it has. "I feel like Kevin Costner in *Field of Dreams*. I didn't know if I build it, will they come?" The grassroots organization's slogan is "Wake Up and Stand

Up," and it encourages its followers to be more involved in the political process and make their voices heard. Although they haven't really been working together and are mostly doing their own thing, the Coffee Party, No Labels, and IndependentVoting.org are aware and supportive of each other and essentially share the same mission.

On a cold, rainy Saturday morning in mid-March 2010, at one of 350 Coffee Party gatherings around the country that day, about two dozen people showed up at the small town hall in Haymarket, Virginia, forty miles west of Washington in Prince William County. They were diverse in age, sex, political party, and philosophy. What they all had in common and what brought them together for coffee, doughnuts, and discussion that morning was a frustration with the current political situation and the partisan fighting in Washington, along with a desire to do something about it. Everyone in Haymarket seemed to be in agreement that the two-party system isn't working and, instead of representing the people, is primarily serving the needs of special interests.

There was plenty of populist frustration expressed in Haymarket over a ruling class of politicians and business leaders who seem to be doing well while everyone else is struggling. A middle-aged man dressed in jeans and a ball cap said, "I belong to the NRA and I love my guns. I consider myself a conservative, a Tea Partier, and a Coffee Partier. I feel like our economy is going down the tubes."

Another man said he took off from work to attend the meeting. "We're working six days a week, twelve hours a day to stay afloat," he said, adding that he is sick of corporate influence over political decisions and lies from public and business leaders who believe there is one set of rules for the rich, who have ample access to elected officials because of their campaign contributions and high-priced lobbyists, and another for everyone else.

Alan Alborn, sixty-two, a retired executive and former army officer who lives in Northern Virginia and voted for both George W. Bush and Barack Obama, says he has always been an Independent/centrist who votes for the candidate not the party. "There's a lot of guys like me out there," he says—disaffected Democrats, liberal Republicans, centrists, and Independents—who are feeling left out and disappointed in the system. "Our government is broken. We've forgotten how to come together in the middle."

Morris Davis is a former air force lawyer from Gainesville, Virgina, who served as chief prosecutor at Guantánamo during the Bush Administration for several years until he resigned over the issue of torture. Davis says the opportunity to have a civil conversation about important national issues is what attracted him to the Coffee Party. He is a ticket splitter who decides his vote based on issues and the candidate. Davis says we've created a "professional ruling class" that is totally disconnected from the citizens. He is particularly concerned about the amount of money it takes to get elected and the Supreme Court *Citizens United* decision and the negative effect that could have on the system.

Economic equity and the reform of tax policy and campaign financing have emerged as the issues of greatest importance to the members of the Coffee Party, which has become increasingly populist in its focus. Its first big project was pushing for passage of Wall Street reform, and Park and other members spent a day on Capitol Hill visiting Senate offices, meeting with staff members, and dropping off petitions signed by Coffee Party members from the home states of senators. Park said the group was trying to counter the influence of lobbyists.

> We feel that the interests of ordinary Americans are not being represented well enough, because we have a democracy with a loophole. Corporations have the resources to pay thousands of lobbyists to spend their time influencing our government. This is fundamentally unfair and undemocratic. The only way to close the loophole is for voters to rise to their civic duty. They have money, but we have the votes. No one gets elected without votes.

She and her Coffee Party cofounder Eric Byler, who are both documentary filmmakers, have also created videos posted on the group's website and YouTube channel that talk about corporations not paying taxes and feature people holding up signs that say, I PAY TAXES and I DID NOT CAUSE THE RECESSION. Park says corporations can get away with not paying taxes and instead spend millions lobbying Congress for more tax loopholes.

There were growing pains and disagreements among Coffee Party members over its mission and goals as the group evolved. Several board members resigned, and in March 2011, they were replaced with a transition team tasked with creating a permanent board of directors. Park expressed frustration to me over trying to grow the group, get media coverage for its efforts, and keep people active and involved.

"I feel we are where a majority of Americans are at, but there's no political road map," said Park.

How do you get the people to have more impact on government? We're trying to organize congressional district by congressional district into a voting bloc to achieve real reform and kick both parties in the butt. . . . We need to figure out how to drum up the interest and get millions of people involved and saying we need to change our power structure. Short of that, we're not going to have real reform. We're trying to figure out that tipping point that will motivate people. I don't know what's going to get people so worked up that they do something. At what point are they going to draw the line? We're trying—but it's so hard.

It's not easy to start a social movement or exert pressure on the political system from the outside. New social media outlets make it less difficult to reach out, but it is extremely hard to convince people who are disappointed with the political process, don't really believe change is possible, and don't think they have a direct stake in the system to get involved.

That is the central question for all these groups. How do they do that? Their very creation and existence speak to the public's desire and need for something outside of the two-party political system. But how do they break out from being just fringe groups of several thousand Internet followers to a significant political movement? How do they get the attention of the millions of Independent voters? It's a question without an obvious or easy answer.

11

Changing the Rules of the Game

If liberty and equality, as is thought by some are chiefly to be found in democracy, they will be best attained when all persons alike share in the government to the utmost.

—ARISTOTLE

MOST AMERICANS, IF ASKED, would probably say that the U.S. system of government is one of the most democratic in the world. And yet, it's not. It is controlled by the Democratic and Republican Parties, who have a stranglehold on the process, making it almost impossible for Independent voters and candidates to participate fully and compete fairly. On a host of issues ranging from who gets to vote in primaries, how congressional and state legislative districts are organized, ballot access and fund-raising rules for Independent and third-party candidates, and campaign financing, the rules are stacked against Independents and in favor of the two parties.

Political parties and their supporters would argue there's no problem with that—it's just the way it should be—but that ignores the fact that more voters now identify themselves as Independents than either Republicans or Democrats and they are being shut out of the political process. Until this changes, and Independents can participate fully, U.S. elections will not be totally democratic.

Voter Registration and Voting Rules

In many states, voter registration and election rules seem designed to discourage rather than promote voter participation. In twenty-nine states and the District of Columbia, voters must register by party, and if you are not a registered Democrat or Republican, you cannot vote in the primary, shutting out millions of Independent voters who have no voice in selecting the candidates who run for local, state, and national office, even though their tax dollars pay for those elections.

In the other twenty-one states, including Ohio and Virginia, voters do not have to declare their party affiliation and can vote in primaries of either party. Only about half a dozen states have same-day voter registration, including New Hampshire, which does have registration by party but allows Independent voters to show up at the polling place, request a Republican or Democratic ballot, and then change their registration back to undeclared if they want to do so.

Harry Kresky, a New York attorney specializing in election law and general counsel of IndependentVoting.org, believes all states should have open primaries but says the open primary system is "under attack." "As more and more people become Independent voters, parties have less and less support and they become more aggressive in trying to control the process. Is it right to have a society where more and more people are Independents and the parties have more and more control?"

Kresky represented IndependentVoting.org in two legal cases in which the Republican Party in Idaho and South Carolina, both states with open primaries, sought a court ruling to allow the GOP to close their primaries to anyone but Republican voters. In the legal briefs filed in those cases, Kresky argued that "For the non-aligned voters represented by IndependentVoting.org, the outcome of this litigation will determine whether or not they can continue to fully participate in the electoral process" and maintained the outcome of the cases could impact voters across the country. If the Republican Party in those two states is permitted to close its primaries, political parties in other states could follow suit. "They want our votes in November, but they don't want us to participate in the primary elections where the candidates are determined," Kresky told me.

One of the states leading the way in terms of election reform is California. In June 2010, the state's voters approved Proposition 14, known as the "open primary initiative," which created a "top two" primary election system, in which all candidates for office would appear on a single ballot, and all voters would be able to vote in the primary.[1] The top two vote-getters in that election would then go on to the general election. The measure, which effectively ends party primaries, was supported by former Republican Governor Arnold Schwarzenegger and Lieutenant Governor Abel Maldonado, who felt that it would increase the chances of more moderate candidates being nominated. Top-two even eliminates the requirement that candidates must list their party affiliation on the ballot, although they can do so if they choose.

The top-two system was endorsed by IndependentVoting.org as an innovation to open up the electoral process to all voters, and the group supports its adoption nationwide.

I am not so sure, however, that top-two will accomplish what its supporters claim and I believe it actually has the potential to make the problem of access worse, resulting in elections that are less open for third party, Independent, and less well financed candidates. Qualified parties like the Green Party had the guarantee they would have a candidate on the general election ballot before the top-two system was adopted. And Independent candidates could get on a general election ballot by collecting signatures. But under the top-two system Independents and third parties must fight it out in primaries against Democratic and Republican candidates backed by their parties and will have an extremely difficult time prevailing. And the top-two system is likely to be even more expensive for candidates than the current system. In a huge state like California, where candidates routinely spend millions of dollars on their campaigns, it seems likely the only candidates who will be able to survive a top-two election will be those chosen and financed by the two major parties or self-financed millionaire candidates.

The other states that currently have a top-two system—Louisiana and Washington—have not seen much change since top-two was enacted or an increase in the number of moderate or Independent candidates who make it past the first round of voting. In fact, in some districts in those states, the top two candidates wind up being from the same party, actually narrowing the general election choices for voters.

Simply opening existing party primaries in all fifty states to unaffiliated voters would achieve most of the same goals as top-two in a much simpler way, with much less risk of unintended consequences.

Election laws vary from state to state, and rules on ballot access and fund-raising limits can be quite different, but the one constant across the country is that they usually disadvantage Independent candidates. As Colorado's Kathleen Curry found out, some states require a year or more notice if a candidate wants to change their registration from Republican or Democrat to Independent and then run for office. New York is another state with similar restrictions. Independent candidates are also often disadvantaged because in some states they are not permitted to accept campaign contributions as large as those Republican and Democratic candidates can receive, and of course they have no party machine funding them. And when it comes to administering election laws and counting ballots, most county clerks, election officials, and secretaries of state are either Democrats or Republicans.

Since election law is created by state legislatures, it is written to benefit the two parties, who operate a virtually closed system in which they make all the rules; Independents have no representation on any of the bodies that regulate elections, from the Federal Election Commission to state and local boards of elections. One other inequity—Republican and Democratic candidates and party officials can get free lists of registered voters to use for campaign purposes, mailings, and phone calls, but Independent candidates usually have to pay for them.

All of this means that the only Independent candidates who are successful, especially on a state or national level, are those who are already famous or rich enough to pay for their own campaigns, like New York

Mayor Michael Bloomberg, who has spent more than $250 million of his own money on his campaigns.

Bloomberg knows how hard it is to run as an Independent. "In the end, when you have an Independent candidate, not always but almost always, it is the two major parties that get most of the votes," Bloomberg said at the New York launch of No Labels. Because Democratic and Republican politicians are in the business of getting reelected and supporting the current two-party system, Bloomberg said, "I don't think you can expect much change" in campaign finance and election laws that would open up the system to challengers. Bloomberg pointed out that he was "resoundingly beaten" when he tried to adopt an open-primary system in New York City. "It was hard to find anyone that was in favor of it."

The nation's only current Independent governor is Lincoln Chafee of Rhode Island, who agrees with Bloomberg about the challenges of trying to get elected as an Independent.

Chafee was named for Abraham Lincoln because his father, John, a former governor who served in the U.S. Senate for two decades and was a towering figure in Rhode Island politics, was a Civil War buff. Like his father, Chafee was a moderate Republican and was appointed to his father's Senate seat when he died in 1999. Lincoln Chafee often voted with the Democrats and was a fierce critic of President George W. Bush's tax cuts and the war in Iraq. Many Republicans didn't even think of him as one of their own, and he faced a conservative primary challenge when he ran for reelection to the Senate in 2006. "I won the primary—but it cost $2.6 million, and after the primary I was broke and didn't have anything left to spend on the general election," which he lost to Democrat Sheldon Whitehouse.

Chafee decided to leave the Republican Party after that loss because he felt the party had changed too much and didn't fit him anymore. "I've watched it happen over the years. I was an eleven-year-old at the Cow Palace at the Republican National Convention in San Francisco in

1964, watching the supporters of Barry Goldwater boo Nelson Rockefeller," who was seen by the conservative wing of the party as far too liberal to be a Republican. "They booed and booed and booed—they shook the rafters—during Rockefeller's speech. Right from then, I saw the party changing."

When he announced his candidacy for governor, Chafee said, "I believe that running as an independent will free me from the constraints that party politics impose on candidates." One of those constraints is a seeming inability to tell voters the truth about tough issues, something Chafee was willing to do in his campaign. Like so many states, Rhode Island faced a budget deficit, and Chafee thought part of the way to deal with it was to expand the state's sales tax to include items like food, clothing, and services that had previously been exempt. Despite telling voters that's what he intended to do, Chafee won the election. But after Chafee took office, the Democratic state legislature fought his proposal to deal with the $300 million plus shortfall by lowering the overall sales tax rate to 1 percent, but extending it to include more items and services.

Soft spoken and thoughtful, Chafee told me he used to think creating a third party was the answer to the paralysis of our political system, but after his experiences, he's not so sure it's possible.

"My race was so hard, it sobered me to the difficulties of mounting an Independent challenge," Chafee told me. "You don't have a party apparatus behind you . . . and raising money is so hard. The whole thing is just hard." Chafee wound up spending $1.5 million of his own money to win his 2010 gubernatorial race.[2]

If someone with such a deep and rich political lineage, a popular figure with a name extremely familiar to his state's voters and willing to spend seven figures to get elected, has such a hard time as an Independent candidate, it really makes one wonder about the prospects for an average Independent without those advantages who tries running for office in the current system.

Redistricting

A big reason the Democratic and Republican Parties have such a stranglehold on the political system is the way state legislative and congressional districts are drawn—for the benefit of the two parties. In most states, the process is handled by the state legislature and the governor. If one party controls both branches of government, there is usually a struggle and ultimately legal challenge by the minority party to try to assert its rights on the process. Sometimes a deal is struck to protect both parties' incumbents, which is inevitably what happens if the legislature is divided or one party controls the legislative and the other the executive branch. But the public is almost always left out of the equation. The two parties do what they can to ensure as many safe seats for Republicans and Democrats as possible and try at all costs to avoid the creation of competitive "swing" districts.

Redistricting has become as partisan and almost as expensive as campaigning. The Federal Election Commission, run by Democrats and Republicans, has determined that politicians can raise an unlimited amount of money from anonymous donors for the drawing of congressional district maps and the legal fights to defend them and that individual members of Congress can hire their own lobbyists and legal teams to help protect their seats.[3]

Only a few states, including New Jersey, California, Washington, Arizona, Idaho, and Hawaii use independent commissions to handle their legislative redistricting, although most commission members are still appointed by the governor and members of the legislature or by the political parties. Independents, nonaffiliated voters, and in most cases the public have almost no input in the process.

California, also a leader on redistricting reform, has created a Citizens Redistricting Commission approved by voters through a ballot measure, the same way the top-two primary system was adopted. The fourteen-member independent panel, which includes five Democrat, five Republican, and four Independent members, will handle the job of drawing the legislative districts for the state's fifty-three members of Congress, forty state senators, and eighty Assembly members.[4] The process, which has never been tried before, has its critics and could ultimately be subject to legal challenge, but the commission could hardly do worse than state legislatures and governors have done.

"Redistricting should be done by people who don't have an inherent conflict of interest," said Gerald Hebert, a voting rights lawyer who worked for the Department of Justice for twenty years and now heads Americans for Redistricting Reform.

> State legislators want to draw their own seats—want to draw a district that helps them so they can get reelected and move up to Congress. How can you expect them to act against their own political self-interest? They're not going to give up that kind of power unless the voters are willing to take it away from them, and the only way the voters are going to get that chance is in a state with a referendum process, where they can vote for a redistricting commission.

The state of Virginia is pretty typical in the way it handles redistricting, which is to say Republican and Democratic politicians fight and horse-trade over how to best draw the map to protect their own interests. Virginia was also under more time pressure than most states to finish redistricting quickly because the entire General Assembly was up for reelection in November 2011. The House of Delegates, controlled by Republicans, came up with a plan advantageous to them, the Democratic Senate did the same, and the congressional delegation cut its own deal, with House members mostly protecting their own seats. But the legislature's plan was vetoed by Republican Governor Bob McDonnell, who was, no surprise, especially critical of the Democratic Senate plan. The response from the Senate majority leader? "We're not going to change one period or one comma."[5]

McDonnell did appoint an independent bipartisan redistricting commission, but when the commission presented its plan, the proposal was greeted by laughter from state officials, who promptly ignored the commission's recommendations. Olga Hernandez, president of the state's League of Women Voters, said her group has been pushing for redistricting reform in Virginia and around the country for years. The league even ran a competition, featuring fifteen teams of political science students from Virginia colleges who came up with their own redistricting plans that did not include crazily shaped districts that divided communities. Those plans were "proof that we can do better," Hernandez asserted. She said most voters may think of redistricting as boring inside baseball that has little to do with them, but they don't realize the fundamental impact redistricting has on the democratic process. "It all starts with those lines."

As in most states, the partisan gerrymandering of districts has severely limited the number of competitive seats in Virginia. The League of Women Voters calculates that in 2007, almost half the forty incumbent state senators had no opposition and only nine races were "competitive." In the one hundred House of Delegates races that year, fifty-seven incumbents had no opposition and only twelve races were "competitive." In 2009, it was the same story—only twelve out of a hundred General Assembly races were considered truly "competitive."[6]

"The more districts that are ultra-safe, the less compromise you get," says Hernandez. "Everybody goes to their corners and it's ultra-partisan. Problems aren't being dealt with, because everybody is screaming at the edges. This is not good governance. It leads to that polarization . . . which depresses voter turnout and increases the cynicism of our politics."

Redistricting in Virginia is also complicated by the fact that it is one of the states governed by the 1965 Voting Rights Act, which sought to address discrimination and improve minority access to voting and elected office, primarily in Southern states. Virginia's redistricting map must be approved by the U.S. Justice Department before it can be implemented, although the state's conservative Republican Attorney General Ken Cuccinelli has declared that he believes Virginia has "outgrown" institutional racism and no longer should be subject to the Voting Rights Act.[7]

Texas, also subject to the Voting Rights Act, has a history of redistricting scandals, including the controversial map drawn by Republicans led by former GOP House Majority Leader Tom DeLay after the last census. A portion of that congressional map, which led to the ouster of four Democrats from Congress, was ultimately thrown out by the Supreme Court, after a series of court challenges. Texas is bound to be a center of controversy and legal challenges again this time around, since the legislature and governor are Republican and will control the process, but the state's population gains have been in more Democratic areas. Texas is picking up four congressional seats, the most in the country, primarily due to the increase in the Hispanic population. Hispanics accounted for two-thirds of the state's growth during the last decade and now make up 38 percent of the state's inhabitants.[8]

Former congressman John Tanner, a moderate Democrat from Tennessee and a cofounder of the congressional Blue Dog coalition, introduced legislation in the past three congresses to reform and increase public participation in the redistricting process, but he couldn't even get a hearing on the bipartisan legislation, which was cosponsored by moderate Republican Mike Castle. The legislation would have required states to appoint independent bipartisan commissions to draw congressional districts, hold public hearings, and post redistricting maps on the web.

"The right to vote is pretty well rendered meaningless" by gerrymandered districts, Tanner told me. "The Corps of Engineers has to have a hearing before they dig a ditch, but entire legislative districts can be redrawn with no public input." Tanner said if he could have gotten the legislation out of committee and to the floor for a vote, which he couldn't, it would have been pretty hard for members of Congress to vote against it. But, of course, that was the point—they didn't want to have to vote on the measure.

Tanner retired from Congress in 2010, but fellow Tennessean and moderate Democrat Jim Cooper has taken up his effort, introducing the Redistricting Transparency Act in 2011.[9] Cooper removed the requirement that states must appoint independent commissions to handle redistricting. His legislation would simply increase public information about the process and require states to hold public hearings and post information about redistricting on the web, something that common sense dictates should be going on already, without having to mandate it.

"When politicians carve up congressional districts for partisan interests, democracy suffers," said Cooper. "Gerrymandering is backroom politics at its ugliest: it protects incumbents, increases partisanship, and stifles the will of the people."

But there is no reason to believe the two parties will release their stranglehold on the redistricting process, which is a guaranteed incumbency and party-protection plan.

Campaign Finance

One of the biggest reasons cited by many citizens for a lack of trust in government is the pervasive influence of lobbyists and big donors. If you asked a dozen former members of Congress about the impact of money and fund-raising on politics, you would hear the same thing from all of them—members are forced to spend way too much time dialing for dollars and attending events to raise all-important campaign cash. The reliance on political action committees and big donors for this money gives them access to the political process at the expense of the less moneyed average voters.

Jesse Unruh, a former California state official, is known for making two colorful quotes about money and politics. He famously called money the mother's milk of politics, but his even more descriptive quote about the relationship between lobbyists and legislators is a legend: "If you can't eat their food, drink their booze, screw their women, and still vote against them, you have no business" being in politics.[10]

Perhaps. But because of the incredible influence of money on the political process, the appearance of impropriety is everywhere. "Many good people enter politics only to find that the system causes the low road to become the one most traveled," says former Republican Congressman Jim Leach.

This is a feeling that is expressed over and over by angry voters who feel shut out and don't know how to get elected officials to listen to them. I heard this complaint again and again as I talked to Independent voters around the country.

And the Supreme Court's infamous 2010 *Citizens United* decision on campaign spending by corporate interests has the potential to make things much worse. In its 5–4 ruling, the court said that corporations can spend as much as they want to support or oppose candidates for president and Congress, undoing decades-old limits on corporate spending in federal campaigns.[11]

The court overturned a twenty-year-old ruling blocking corporate interests from producing their own campaign ads. But it did leave in place a prohibition on direct contributions to candidates from corporations and unions. In his dissent, Justice John Paul Stevens said, "The court's ruling threatens to undermine the integrity of elected institutions around the nation."

The 2002 McCain–Feingold campaign finance reform legislation, at the center of the court ruling, was an attempt to limit money and influence on politics. But it has proved a toothless tiger in that effort and has pretty much failed. Rather than a stemming of direct contributions by special interests, there has been an explosion of unregulated, independent expenditures for campaign advertising since the passage of McCain–Feingold.

Democratic Senator Chuck Schumer called the Supreme Court's ruling one of the worst decisions in the court's history. "At a time when the public's fears about the influence of special interests were already high, this decision stacks the deck against the average American even more." In response, Schumer and Democratic House member Chris Van Hollen introduced the DISCLOSE Act, which would require full disclosure of any corporate interests funding campaign ads and activity. It would also bar foreign-controlled corporations and government contractors from spending money on U.S. elections, and prohibit political spending by companies that received government bailout money.

The measure was strongly opposed by Republicans and their supporters like the U.S. Chamber of Commerce. Although it passed the House, the DISCLOSE Act couldn't get a vote in the Senate before the 2010 election. In April 2011, the Obama Administration said it was considering an executive order that would put in place part of the DISCLOSE Act's rules by requiring current government contractors and those seeking government contracts to disclose their political donations.

Most campaign finance reform advocates support public financing of campaigns, but given the current economic climate and the public's mood about politics and Washington, such an approach would probably be a very hard sell. And it's not at all clear public financing would solve the problem. For example, in the presidential campaign, Barack Obama chose simply to opt out of public financing so he could raise and spend more than the legal limits for candidates accepting federal funds.

Common Cause, a nonprofit, nonpartisan, good-government advocacy group, and other reform groups are working on different possible fixes to the system, including trying to find ways to increase the number of small political donations, rather than trying to limit large donations from corporate and special interests. Reform advocates want to create a system where big money and independent expenditures won't matter as much because they are counterweighed by small contributions from individuals.

That's the idea behind a joint study released by the Campaign Finance Institute, the Brookings Institution, and the American Enterprise Institute called "Reform in an Age of Networked Campaigns: How to Foster Citizen Participation Through Small Donors and Volunteers." Thomas Mann of Brookings and Norman Ornstein of the American Enterprise Institute were involved in the project, which proposes to expand the playing field of campaign donors by creating a new system of partial public financing in the form of matching funds for small contributions.[12]

Former Congressman Jim Leach acknowledges something must be done.

As the gap between rich and poor is widening in America, so the political gap between the powerful and the powerless is heightening. . . . At a time when the country needs to pull together, the Supreme Court has chosen a path to magnify public cynicism. Citizens should be allowed to exercise free speech in such a way as to be heard by candidates whose ears are not plugged by special interest money. It is the individual voter rather than institutional influence peddler that should be listened to and empowered.

These are the biggest problems with the political system and the most significant obstacles to participation by Independents and third-party groups. The two political parties and incumbents have a lock on the system. The huge amount of money it takes to mount a campaign, increasingly even on the state legislative level, means challengers are significantly disadvantaged.

Independent voters do not have equal access to primary elections, and it is more difficult for Independent candidates to run for office and raise money. Congressional and, in many cases, state legislative districts are gerrymandered to protect Democratic and Republican incumbents and prevent challenges from Independent or even centrist candidates who would appeal to voters in both parties.

These critical things need to be addressed to increase voter access and participation and improve the political system.

12

Battle Cry

We have it in our power to begin the world over again.
—THOMAS PAINE, *COMMON SENSE*

J UST AS THOMAS PAINE called for independence from England more than two hundred years ago, Independent voters today must assert their rights and demand true democracy from their leaders. They must make their voices heard, they must insist that the two political parties listen to them, and they must take back the system.

Paine's message of democracy and independence still lives today—it is at the heart of what makes this country so exceptional. But in the crush of everyday responsibilities, we have lost sight of how important it is for citizens to be vigilant and active to safeguard our democratic institutions. We must decide as a nation and a people if we will continue down the path of division and dysfunction or if we will rise up and take back our government from the parties and specials interests that control it.

In order for change to happen, the voters, especially Independent voters, must get involved. They must make it clear what they want from their leaders and insist on action. They cannot wait for a prophet to suddenly appear and lead them out of the political wilderness, and they cannot expect that the two political parties, professional politicians, and moneyed special interests that have a stranglehold on the political system will voluntarily change that system, which serves their interests.

What may be required is a collective moment like that in the 1976 movie *Network*, written by Paddy Chayefsky and directed by Sidney Lumet, in which a network news anchor played by Peter Finch encouraged people across the country to stand up and say they were mad as hell and they were not going to take it anymore.

Over the past twenty years, there have been only a few, brief times when our political leaders have moved away from partisan warfare toward cooperation and consensus. After the attacks on 9/11, the threat to our national security brought the nation and its elected officials together, but that moment of unity was far too short lived. The election of Barack Obama and the warm fuzzy feeling that followed about the power of our democracy to change was fleeting. The euphoria over the inauguration of the nation's first African American president quickly faded in the withering heat of the realities of our political system. Even our recent financial crisis hasn't served to unite the country, rather it has resulted in even more finger-pointing and political gamesmanship.

The real problems this nation faces—our massive national debt and deficit; our aging population, which will strain our financial resources and require changes to entitlement programs including Medicare and Social Security; our crumbling infrastructure; our loss of a manufacturing base; our need to create good paying jobs in this country and to invest in research and technology so that we can compete globally; our need to do away with our reliance on foreign oil and find new, sustainable energy sources—we cannot solve these problems by fighting and blaming each other.

These are extremely difficult challenges, and what is required of all of us is the kind of effort, resolve, and joint sacrifice Americans showed during World War II. What this country proved then is that there is no crisis to which we can't rise together and surmount as a nation. Finding solutions to our current problems again requires our working together—Democrats, Republicans, and Independents.

Too many Americans, especially Independent voters, are frustrated and disillusioned with the political system and resigned to its current state. They think it's impossible to change anything and there's no point trying. But change is what democracy is all about, and we *do* have it in our power to begin again. The United States has always been a beacon of freedom for the rest of the world and risen to the challenges it faced. We cannot cede our leadership position and the future because it seems too hard to try.

Voting is not enough. Concerned citizens must get involved in civic life. The Internet and the wealth of information available there makes staying informed about what government is doing easier than ever. Every town, city, state, and federal agency has a website loaded with information.

Here is what every citizen can do.

- Insist that public officials make even more information about what they are doing readily available.

- Push for election reform that would make it easier to register and vote, and fight for open primaries for all registered voters everywhere in the country.

- Demand that the creation of state and congressional legislative districts be done fairly and in a nonpartisan way to give Independents, centrist candidates, and challengers a chance to represent you.

- Press for changes in the way our political campaigns are financed to lessen the influence of big money donors and special interests.

- If you can afford it, give small contributions to candidates you support. That will mean you have some skin in the game and will also improve your access when you want to talk to them about issues you care about.

- If you live in a state with a ballot initiative process, use it to force changes to improve election laws.

- Show up at public meetings, testify, call and write your elected officials, let them know how you feel.

- Support candidates and officials who offer solutions and are willing to work with all sides to solve our problems. Oppose those who are interested only in furthering partisan warfare and political advantage.

- If you agree with the mission and methods of No Labels, the Coffee Party, IndependentVoting.org, or another group pushing for change—join them. Or start your own group of friends and neighbors to talk about local and national political issues and the changes you would like to see.

There is power in numbers. The political parties have always known this, and the only way change will happen is if enough people demand it. As Jim Leach says, it requires the commitment of all Americans.

The choice for leaders is whether to opt for unifying statesmanship or opportunistic partisanship. Likewise, the challenge for citizens is to determine whom to follow: those who respect diversity but favor a united country, or those who press debilitating cultural wars or extreme ideological agendas. . . . Citizenship is hard. It takes a commitment to listen, watch, read, and think in ways that allow the imagination to put one person in the shoes of another.

On that tragic and fateful day when Congresswoman Gabrielle Giffords, a moderate Democrat from a swing district who had been subject to extreme partisan attacks, held her "Congress on Your Corner" meeting at a Tucson shopping center for constituents—January 8, 2011—a nine-year-old girl named Christina Green wanted to go and meet her. From ballet to baseball, Christina had many loves, and one of them was this country. Born on September 11, 2001, Christina had been elected to the student council at Mesa Verde Elementary School in Tucson, and she was starting to develop an interest in government and politics, which is why she wanted to meet the congresswoman that morning. She was a patriotic girl who liked to wear red, white, and blue and often talked about how lucky we are in this country.

Christina's young life was tragically cut short that day. Who knows what she might have achieved had she lived to adulthood. Perhaps she would have chosen a career in public service. But her life can still have great meaning for all of us who never had the chance to meet her. As Barack Obama said at the memorial service held a few days after her death, Christina saw our democracy "through the eyes of a child, un-dimmed by the cynicism or vitriol that we adults all too often just take for granted. . . . I want our democracy to be as good as Christina imag-ined it. I want America to be as good as she imagined it."[1]

We can be. But it will take the efforts of all of us.

On June 17, 1825, fifty years to the day after the Battle of Bunker Hill, the first major battle in the Revolutionary War, Daniel Webster spoke at the ceremony to lay the cornerstone for the Boston monument that commemorates that battle. "Let our age be the age of improvement," Webster said. "Let us develop the resources of our land, call forth its powers, build up its institutions, promote all its great interests, and see whether we also, in our day and generation, may not perform something worthy to be remembered."[2]

Let *our* age be the age of improvement. Let us vow to address our most pressing problems and move ahead as a nation. We can do it to-gether.

ACKNOWLEDGMENTS

While I was writing this book, we lost a giant in the world of journalism. As he had been to so many others, David Broder was a mentor and friend to me, generous with his time and advice. When I was formulating the idea for this book, I sought him out to get his thoughts. As I was finishing this book, I looked over the notes I kept from that last meeting with David. He agreed with me that voters have become increasingly disillusioned by their political leaders and the two political parties. He supported the idea for this book and the way I intended to go about it and also made some excellent suggestions. He told me he looked forward to reading it, and recommended I think about including Minnesota and Missouri as two of my swing states. I hope he would forgive me for not doing so.

I think David would have liked this book and its focus on the voters. Throughout his career, in both his *Washington Post* news articles and columns, he frequently wrote about what the voters were thinking. He was a shoe leather, door knocking reporter long past the age when most journalists, or most people of any profession, opted for a more relaxed lifestyle. David, who died at the age of eighty-one and who continued writing until just a month before his death, was an inspiration and a tremendous example to me and to all journalists. He really loved being a reporter.

"I've learned that the most undervalued, underreported aspect of politics is what voters bring to the table," he once said in an interview about his work.

"Given the American people's deep skepticism about our political system today, we can raise their faith some if we give them the feeling that, at least at election time, the press and candidates are responding to their thoughts and views."

At his memorial service at the National Press Club held about a month after his death in March 2011, a video was shown of David in New Hampshire covering the primary there in 2008. He was in his element, a big smile on his face. David said what made covering the New Hampshire primary "really fun" was the "level of energy that comes straight from the people."

His *Washington Post* colleague and friend Dan Balz said at the memorial that David "believed that elections belonged to the voters" and that "When the campaign ended the politicians had a responsibility to do what they could to solve the nation's problems and that good journalism made the machinery of government work better."

I hope that David would have thought this book helps to advance those goals, which are truly at the heart of good political journalism.

This book would not have been possible without the help and cooperation of all of the Independent voters I spoke with—those whom I talked with on the phone, the ones who showed up at focus groups around the country, and those who allowed me to talk to them a number of times in depth about their thoughts and feelings about politics and this country. They were candid and thoughtful and I will always be indebted to them. This book is for them. Many of them are quoted, but there are many more who informed my reporting and who are not named, and I hope they will feel equally a part of this enterprise.

I also interviewed hundreds of other people for this book. It wasn't possible to use everyone's comments, but please know that I appreciate all of your time and contributions. You added to my knowledge and the book is stronger because I talked with you.

There are many people who deserve special thanks. In the earliest stages of conceptualizing this project I met with several editors, including Alice Mayhew at Simon and Schuster. As she always is, she was direct and thoughtful with me, and offered good advice. She suggested I focus on the concerns of the Independent voters and try to capture their voices as well as consider the forces which created them. I hope she feels I have addressed those important questions.

I also talked with several sage experts in the field of politics—Norman Ornstein at the American Enterprise Institute, Larry Sabato at the University of Virginia, and Bill Schneider at Third Way.

Kevin Merida, the national editor of *The Washington Post*, is also a longtime friend and expressed healthy skepticism and peppered me with good questions, as any terrific journalist would do, in the early stages of this project but also offered support and some excellent lunches along the way.

David Tamasi, a former student of mine and now the head of a successful public relations and lobbying office in Washington, also offered good suggestions over several lunches. As a former professor of journalism, there is nothing as satisfying as seeing David's success and the success of so many other former students in Washington and around the country. As I have taken so much pride in their accomplishments over the years, I hope they will feel a bit of pride in this effort of mine.

Brad Todd, a Republican consultant and media strategist, was an incredible help with my first book, *The Freshmen*, on the 1994 Republican Revolution and the 104th Congress, during his tenure with Congressman Van Hilleary. He was also helpful this time around. I was a novice when it comes to trying to organize focus groups, something Brad knows a great deal about, and he offered help and advice as well as his spin on the 2010 election and Independent voters. Although I didn't always agree with him, he was always full of good information.

There were so many people who aided me in finding particular facts I was looking for. Scott Keeter at the Pew Research Center was especially helpful with polling data.

I also want to offer a special thanks to Trey Grayson, the director of the Institute of Politics at Harvard's Kennedy School; and Dan Glickman and Elliot Gerson at the Aspen Institute.

Robert Schlesinger at *U.S. News & World Report* is a friend and colleague and I am appreciative for his long friendship. Several small pieces of this book appeared in columns I wrote for *U.S. News*.

In the course of reporting and writing this book, several other small sections about the 2010 campaign appeared in what was, at the time, *Politics Daily* and I want to thank its former Executive Editor Carl Cannon and the ever charming Walter Shapiro, a fount of political history and information and an excellent dinner companion.

I thoroughly enjoyed the time I spent in Colorado reporting this book and wish I could have spent more time there. I want to thank former Senator Hank Brown for welcoming me into his home and giving me so much of his time. The country would be better off if more people like Brown were still serving in the Senate.

Former State Representative Kathleen Curry was also extremely generous with her time and I enjoyed traveling her former district with her. I also want to thank Marilyn Marks, who welcomed me into her beautiful home in Aspen and provided shelter even though she had never met me.

I enjoyed meeting and talking with former governor Bill Ritter, who was also generous with his time. Former Congressman David Skaggs provided an early primer on Colorado politics when I was just beginning this project and I'll never forget his amusement when he made reference to the state's Front Range and Western Slope and I didn't know what he was talking about.

Several Colorado academics offered good background information including Robert Duffy at Colorado State, John Straayer at the University of Colorado, and especially Tony Robinson at UC Denver, who not only helped me get a room at the university to hold my focus group but offered his students extra credit for participating.

Former Denver television journalist Adam Schrager was extremely helpful and *Denver Post* Washington Bureau Chief Mike Riley also provided good early background information.

Ron Gagnon and Naomi Cranford in Denver offered me lodging when my travel budget was stretched thin, and I am extremely appreciative of their hospitality.

One of the best things about doing a book like this is all of the interesting people you get to meet, and no one I met along the way was more interesting than Norma Anderson, who was full of terrific political gossip and information and a great deal of fun. She has been a trailblazer for women in Colorado politics and I hope I am exactly like her when I am her age.

In Ohio, I was particularly thankful to Columbus television journalist Bob Kendrick, who helped with a focus group that didn't go exactly as planned, and to John Green, the Director of the Ray C. Bliss Institute of Applied Politics at the University of Akron. He was particularly generous in helping to organize a focus group in Akron and I am indebted to him. I also want to thank Michelle Henry and her team at the Center for Marketing and Opinion Research.

Another of my former students, Kevin Joy, now at *The Columbus Dispatch*, helped me in tracking down some people and information and I am appreciative of his efforts.

I also want to thank former Governor Ted Strickland, who was very generous with his time in the middle of a tough campaign. I am glad I got the chance to meet him and get to know him a bit.

In New Hampshire, Ann Camann at the New Hampshire Institute of Politics at Saint Anselm College was helpful along with James Pindell of WMUR in Manchester.

I also am extremely thankful to Andy Smith, the director of the University of New Hampshire's Survey Center who offered both lots of good information on New Hampshire politics as well as help in putting me in touch with New Hampshire voters for my focus group.

There were many extremely fine people I got to meet and talk with in New Hampshire, especially Doug and Stella Scamman, who are genuinely committed to public service.

I interviewed many members of Congress for this book and am appreciative to all of them and to their staffs for their time, but I feel I owe a special thank you to Senator Mark Warner and his extremely fine Communications Director Kevin Hall, who provided me with lots of help and good information.

I also want to thank Julia Pfaff for opening her home for a focus group and spending so much time talking with me.

Throughout the time I was writing this book I enjoyed a relationship as a senior scholar at the Woodrow Wilson International Center for Scholars in Washington and I am thankful for all of the resources and help I received there. I particularly want to thank former director Lee Hamilton as well as Kent Hughes and his assistant Elizabeth Byers.

Sonya Michel offered support and advice at many junctures and I am extremely thankful for her friendship and good humor.

I had a number of very fine research assistants throughout this project and I want to offer them a special thanks. I don't know how I could have completed this book on its accelerated schedule without their help. Aldo Prosperi helped in the early stages. Amanda Andrei and Chelsea Radler helped with a number of things, especially transcribing the recordings of focus groups, a tedious but essential task. Aleschia Hyde was with me in some of my last months and was extremely helpful, and Avram Billig helped me put together the footnotes for the book. The incredibly organized and efficient Sally Reasoner was a tremendous help in the earliest stages of reporting this book and got me going when the task ahead looked formidable. I also want to thank her parents Irl and Joan Reasoner, who were gracious hosts when I visited Columbus on a reporting trip.

I am very thankful to everyone at St. Martin's Press, especially my editor Matt Martz, who improved this book with his comments and was patient when I continued to ask for more time to make ever more additions.

I have saved the best and most important for last. I want to thank everyone at Lippincott Massie McQuilkin, but most especially my agent Will Lippincott. I have no doubt this book would never have been written without Will's help and support. He was always patient and consistently offered good advice as well as occasional nagging to keep me on the straight and narrow. For my money he is the best literary agent in New York, or anywhere else for that matter, and I feel lucky to have met him and to have his friendship as well as his professional association.

NOTES

Interviews

Senator Tom Coburn, R-Oklahoma
Senator Ron Wyden, D-Oregon
Senator Lisa Murkowski, R-Alaska
Congressman Walter Jones, R-North Carolina
Congressman Jason Altmire, D-Pennsylvania (4)
Governor Lincoln Chafee, I-Rhode Island

Former Indiana Senator Evan Bayh
Former New Jersey Governor Christine Todd Whitman
Former Florida Governor Charlie Crist
Former Kansas Congressman Dan Glickman
Former Iowa Congressman Jim Leach
Former Congressman Ralph Regula, R, Ohio
Former Congressman John Tanner, D, Tennessee
Former Congressman Michael Forbes, New York
Former Congressman J. C. Watts, R, Oklahoma
Former Congressman John Shadegg, R, Arizona

Trey Grayson, Director, Harvard University Kennedy School
    Institute of Politics
Annabel Park, Founder, Coffee Party

J. Gerald Hebert, Americans for Redistricting Reform
Harry Kresky, IndependentVoting.org
Nancy Jacobson, Cofounder, No Labels
Matt Bennett, Cofounder, Third Way
Elliot Gerson, Aspen Institute, Executive Vice President,
    Policy and Public Programs
Jackie Salit, Founder, IndependentVoting.org

New Hampshire
Senator Jeanne Shaheen
Former U.S. Senator Judd Gregg
Andrew Smith, UNH Survey Center
John Stephen, Republican candidate for governor
Walter Peterson, former governor and former president of
    Franklin Pierce College
Former Congressman and Senate candidate Paul Hodes
Ann McLane Kuster, candidate for Congress
Former Governor John Sununu
Doug and Stella Scamman

State Legislators
Ken Gould
Carolyn Gargasz
David Kidder

Voters
Betty Hall
Dr. James Squires
Cynthia Dokmo
Elizabeth Hager
Paul Spiess
Rita Lamy
Steve Marchand

Colorado
Governor John Hickenlooper
Senator Mark Udall
Senator Michael Bennet
Former Governor Bill Ritter
Former Senator Hank Brown
Former Senator Ben Nighthorse Campbell
Former Governor Richard Lamm
Norma Anderson, former state House and
    Senate majority leader
Dick Wadhams, former Colorado Republican Party Chairman
Ken Buck, U.S. Senate candidate
Steve Fenberg, New Era Colorado
Kathleen Curry, former state legislator
Bruce Christensen, Mayor of Glenwood Springs
Joelle Riddle

Voters
Adam Gray
Jeanna Grasso
Elizabeth Wright
Richa Poudyal
Ken Weber
Joanne Clements
John Nemmers

Virginia
Senator Mark Warner
Senator Jim Webb
Congressman Gerry Connolly
Former Congressman Tom Davis
Virginia Delegate Tom Rust
Former Congressman Tom Perriello

Tom Capps, Owner, Capps Shoe Company
Olga Hernandez, Virginia League of Women Voters

Voters
Michael Sciulla
Sue Thomas
Julia Pfaff
Steve Richardson
Sally Frodge

Ohio
Former Governor Ted Strickland
Governor John Kasich
Senator Sherrod Brown
Senator Rob Portman
Former Congressman John Boccieri
John Green, Director, Bliss Institute at the University of Akron

Voters
Scott Clinger
Ryan Ayers
Allen Wells
Roy Gibson
Keith Reisdorf
Chris Weigand
Jerry Cupp

Chapter 1: Who Are the Independent Voters?
1 In September 2010, the Pew Research Center released a study of almost three thousand registered voters around the country, which was an extensive look at the views of voters, especially Independent voters: http://people-press.org/2010/09/23/independents-oppose-party-in-power-again/.

NOTES

2   This *New York Times* national map shows each state and the number of votes and percentage of the vote that each candidate received in the 2008 presidential election: http://elections.nytimes.com/2008/results/president/map.html.

3   2010 Pew Research Center Study: http://people-press.org/2010/09/23/ independents-oppose-party-in-power-again/. In May 2009, Pew released a study that focused on voters who consider themselves Independents: http://people-press.org/2009/05/21/independents-take-center-stage-in -obama-era/.

4   The American National Election Studies, an effort between Stanford University and the University of Michigan that conducts and produces survey data on voting and on public participation and opinion found that in 2008, 40 percent of voters self-identified as either Independents, Independent-Democrats, or Independent-Republicans.

The *Party Identification 7-Point Scale (revised in 2008) 1952–2008* chart is located at: http://www.electionstudies.org/nesguide/toptable/tab2a_1.htm.

More information can be found at http://www.electionstudies.org/.

5   The 2010 Pew Research Center Study found that the number of Independents and nonpartisans stood at 37 percent, one of the highest levels in the past twenty years of Pew Research Center polling. The proportion of independents has fluctuated in recent years, but the current number is sharply higher than it was several years ago (32 percent in 2002): http://people-press .org/2010/09/23/section-3-trends-in-party-affiliation/.

6   The 2010 Pew Research Center Study found that 18 percent of voters thought of themselves as neither a Democrat or Republican in the last five years: http://people-press.org/2010/09/23/section-3-trends-in-party -affiliation/.

7   The Pew Research Center released a study in June 2004 about the size of the swing vote in four presidential elections: http://people-press.org/ 2004/06/24/swing-vote-smaller-than-usual-but-still-sizable/.

8 In February 2011, the policy group Third Way published a study called *The Still-Vital Center: Moderates, Democrats, and the Renewal of American Politics*, by William A. Galston and Elaine C. Kamarck. This information is located on pages 4 and 5 of the study: http://content.thirdway.org/publications/ 372/Third_Way_Report_-_The_Still_Vital_Center.pdf.

9 The information about Independent voters in the 2010 election is taken from polls conducted by two Democratic pollsters. Stan Greenberg of Greenberg Quinlan Rosner, who conducted a poll of voters in November 2010, and Celinda Lake of Lake Research Partners, who did a post-election poll. Both revealed the change in support for Democrats among Independent voters. Data can be found on page 7 of the Greenberg poll at http://www.gqrr.com/ and page 18 of the Lake Poll: http://www.lake research.com/people/.

10 Lake Research Partners post-election poll, page 23: http://www.lake research.com/people/.

11 The political significance of swing voters who are less partisan, more moderate, and have a blend of ideological positions is discussed in detail in *The Swing Voter in American Politics*, by William G. Mayer, published in Washington, D.C., by Brookings Institution Press, 2008.

12 The 2010 Pew study found that nearly six in ten (58 percent) Independents say a major reason they are nonpartisan is that they agree with the Republicans on some issues and the Democrats on other issues. More independents say the Republican Party comes closer to their views than the Democratic Party on economic issues (43 percent Republican versus 34 percent Democrat) and foreign policy and national security (44 percent Republican versus 30 percent Democrat). But the Democrats have an edge over Republicans on social issues among nonpartisans (39 percent Democrat, 33 percent Republican): http://people-press.org/2010/09/23/section -3-trends-in-party-affiliation/.

13 2010 Pew study: http://people-press.org/2010/09/23/section-4-indepen dents-under-the-microscope/.

14 Information about the views of Independent voters can be found on page 97 of the Pew Research Center's 2009 study *Trends in Political Values and Core Attitudes: 1987–2009 (Independents Take Center Stage in Obama Era)*: http://people-press.org/2009/05/21/independents-take-center-stage-in -obama-era/.

15 Results about the 2010 election behavior of former Obama voters is con- tained in a Third Way study released in November 2010 called *Droppers and Switchers: The Fraying Obama Coalition*, by Anne Kim and Stefan Hankin: http://content.thirdway.org/publications/352/Third_Way_Report_-_ Droppers_and_Switchers-The_Fraying_Obama_Coalition.pdf.

16 Figures for voter registration can be found on the websites of secretaries of state. This is a link to the Massachusetts Secretary of State's office, where registration data is located: http://www.sec.state.ma.us/ele/elepdf/ st_county_town_enroll_breakdown_08.pdf.

17 Maine Secretary of State website where voter registration data is located: http://www.maine.gov/sos/cec/elec/2010/20101102r-e-active.pdf.

18 Connecticut and New Hampshire voter registration figures: http://www .sots.ct.gov/sots/lib/sots/electionservices/registration_and_enrollment_ stats/2010_registration_and_enrollment_statistics.pdf and http://www.sos .nh.gov/Purge%20Numbers%202011-08-31.pdf.

19 Figures include both undeclared and nonpartisan registered voters as indicated by the Alaska Secretary of State's Elections Division statistics from the 2010 general election. Data can be found at: http://www.elections .alaska.gov/statistics/vi_vrs_stats_history_2010g.pdf, with more Alaskan voter registration information at: http://www.elections.alaska.gov/vi_vrs.php

and http://www.elections.alaska.gov/statistics/vi_vrs_stats_party_2010
.08.03.htm.

20 New Jersey Secretary of State's office website where voter registration
data is located: http://www.state.nj.us/state/elections/election-results/2011
-state-summary-report.pdf.

21 Arizona Secretary of State website where voter registration data is located:
http://www.azsos.gov/election/voterreg/Active_Voter_Count.pdf.

22 Both the Pew Research Center's 2004 survey and William G. Mayer's *The
Swing Voter in American Politics* discuss the public's increasing lack of confidence in government: http://people-press.org/2004/06/24/swing-vote
-smaller-than-usual-but-still-sizable/.

23 Both Gallup and Rasmussen polls in 2010 and 2011 confirmed the dissatisfaction with the performance of Congress: http://www.gallup.com/
poll/143225/trust-legislative-branch-falls-record-low.aspx and http://www
.rasmussenreports.com/public_content/politics/mood_of_america/right_
direction_or_wrong_track.

24 Third Way 2010 report: http://content.thirdway.org/publications/352/
Third_Way_Report_-_Droppers_and_Switchers-The_Fraying_Obama_
Coalition.pdf.

25 This quotation is on page 20 of *Disconnect: The Breakdown of Representation
in American Politics*, written by political scientists Morris Fiorina and Samuel Abrams and published by The University of Oklahoma Press in 2009.

26 This quotation is on page 19 of *Culture War: The Myth of a Polarized
America*, written by Fiorina, a senior fellow at the Hoover Institute and
the Wendt Family Professor of Political Science at Stanford University,
with Samuel Abrams and Jeremy Pope and published in a third edition by
Pearson Longman in 2010.

Chapter 2: A Brief History of the "Passionate Center" and How the Two Parties Lost It

1 This is a link to George Washington's Farewell Address at the Avalon Project, a collection of legal, historic and diplomatic documents at the Lillian Goldman Law Library at Yale Law School: http://avalon.law.yale.edu/18th_century/washing.asp.

2 The Democratic Leadership Council–Greenberg study can be found at http://www.dlc.org/documents/94DLCpoll.pdf on page 48. For more information on the Democratic Leadership Council, refer to its website at: http://www.dlc.org/ or the Greenberg research center at: http://greenberg research.com/.http://www.greenbergresearch.com/articles/1935/3173_r_ the_perotproject_0693.pdf.

3 This is a link to The Perot Project Report written by Stanley Greenberg for the Democratic Leadership Council in June 1993 to study the outcome of the 1992 election and the Perot voters: http://www.greenber gresearch.com/articles/1935/3173_r_the_perotproject_0693.pdf.

4 *The New York Times* and CBS study was published in April of 2010 and can be found at: http://documents.nytimes.com/new-york-timescbs-news -poll-national-survey-of-tea-party-supporters.

5 This is a link to a *New York Times* story about Michael Bloomberg's campaign spending: http://www.nytimes.com/2009/10/24/nyregion/24mayor.html.

6 This is a C-SPAN link to the video of the Future of Independent Politics event that took place in December 1995 in Minneapolis: http://www .c-spanvideo.org/program/FutureofInd.

7 This is a table detailing split ticket voting in Presidential/Congressional elections from 1952-2008 from the American National Election Studies ANES Guide to Public Opinion and Electoral Behavior: http://www .electionstudies.org/nesguide/toptable/tab9b_2.htm.

8 ANES split ticket voting information: http://www.electionstudies.org/
nesguide/toptable/tab9b_2.htm.

9 This is a link to the January 2009 Gallup poll on the importance of religion, and a state by state comparison: http://www.gallup.com/poll/114022/
state-states-importance-religion.aspx.

10 Pew 2009 survey on Independent voters, page 4: http://people-press.org/
http://people-press.org/files/legacy-pdf/517.pdf.

11 Pew 2009 survey, page 4: http://people-press.org/2009/05/21/section-1
-party-affiliation-and-composition/.

12 Pew 2007 study on religion and social attitudes: http://pewresearch.org/
pubs/614/religion-social-issues.

13 2008 *New York Times* exit polling and Pew Research study: http://elections
.nytimes.com/2008/results/president/exit-polls.html and http://pewresearch
.org/assets/pdf/dissecting-2008-electorate.pdf.

14 Coffee Party website: http://www.coffeepartyusa.com/.

15 No Labels website: http://nolabels.org/home.

Chapter 3: Our Broken Political System—
"Ridiculous and Embarrassing"

1 This is a link to the speech on civility given by Jim Leach at New York
University in 2010: http://www.nyu.edu/brademas/resources/video.leach
.jim.4.html.

2 2010 Pew research study: http://people-press.org/files/legacy-pdf/658
.pdf.

3 Three Greenberg Quinlan Rosner/Democracy Corps surveys conducted in November 2010: http://www.democracycorps.com/strategy/2010/11/democracy-corps-campaign-for-americas-future-post-election-survey/ and http://www.democracycorps.com/strategy/2010/11/19942010/ and http://www.democracycorps.com/strategy/2010/11/what-next-for-president -obama-and-democrats/.

4 The Pew Research Center's *More Conservative, More Critical of National Conditions: Independents Oppose Party in Power . . . Again* data can be found on page 29. An overview of the 2010 data can be found at: http://pew research.org/pubs/1739/independent-voters-typology-2010-midtersm-favor -republicans-conservative.

5 E. J. Dionne's book, *Why Americans Hate Politics*, was published in 1991 by Simon and Schuster in New York, and is a study of party polarization and how both conservatives and liberals have failed voters.

6 This is a comment a reader named Larry from California posted to a column I wrote for U.S. News and World Report.com in March 2010: http://www.usnews.com/opinion/blogs/linda-killian?PageNr=3.

7 Fiorina, *Disconnect*, page 73.

8 Gallup Poll on Congress's job approval rating: http://www.gallup.com/poll/145238/Congress-Job-Approval-Rating-Worst-Gallup-History .aspx.

9 Pew 2010 poll, page 42: http://pewresearch.org/pubs/1739/independent -voters-typology-2010-midtersm-favor-republicans-conservative.

10 *The National Journal* is a weekly magazine that covers Congress and the federal government. Senate rankings are located online at: http://www .nationaljournal.com/2010-vote-ratings-senate-20110225. House rankings

can be found at: http://www.nationaljournal.com/2010-vote-ratings-house-20110225.

11 Link to Barack Obama's speech to Wall Street executives: http://www.whitehouse.gov/the-press-office/remarks-president-wall-street-reform.

12 Link to Barack Obama town hall meeting on the economy: http://www.whitehouse.gov/photos-and-video/video/town-hall-meeting-economy.

13 ABC News video of Bill Clinton–Paul Ryan conversation backstage at the Peterson Foundation fiscal summit on May 25, 2011: http://blogs.abcnews.com/thenote/2011/05/bill-clinton-to-paul-ryan-on-medicare-election-give-me-a-call-.html.

14 Third Way post-election poll: http://content.thirdway.org/publications/372/Third_Way_Report_-_The_Still_Vital_Center.pdf.

15 November 11, 2010, Gallup congressional approval poll: http://www.gallup.com/poll/144419/Congressional-Approval-Elections.aspx.

16 Story written by Ginger Gibson and posted on Delaware Online: http://www.delawareonline.com/article/20100320/NEWS02/100902061/Delaware-politics-O-Donnell-faces-campaign-debt-back-tax-issues.

17 As of the time this book went to press the Federal Election Commission had not yet decided this case.

18 Alaska primary election results, posted on the Alaska Secretary of State's website: http://www.elections.alaska.gov/results/10GENR/data/2010_General_Election_Results_Book.pdf.

19 This is a link to the Senate Conservatives Fund website: http://senateconservatives.com/.

20 This is the C-SPAN link to Blanche Lambert Lincoln's Senate farewell address: http://www.c-spanvideo.org/program/297094-4.

21 The Center for Responsive Politics is a nonpartisan, nonprofit research institution that conducts research on campaign and political spending and hosts a website called Opensecrets.org: http://www.opensecrets.org/overview/index.php.

22 The Campaign Finance Institute is a think tank on campaign finance policy: http://www.cfinst.org/pdf/vital/VitalStats_t1.pdf.

23 Michele Bachmann video of speech on the House floor in which she calls the Obama Administration a "gangster government" and a video of her saying Barack Obama and Democrats in Congress have anti-American views: http://www.youtube.com/watch?v=thR-lVuztIY and http://www.msnbc.msn.com/id/27288019/ns/politics-capitol_hill/t/anti-american-comments-hurt-reps-campaign/.

24 Bachmann's campaign spending: http://www.opensecrets.org/races/summary.php?id=MN06&cycle=2010.

25 *Politico* story written by Jonathan Martin and Kendra Marr about Bachmann's visit to New Hampshire: http://www.politico.com/news/stories/0311/51179.html.

26 Link to Tim Pawlenty's July 10 appearance on "Meet the Press": http://www.msnbc.msn.com/id/43710592/ns/politics-decision_2012/t/pawlenty-blasts-bachmanns-nonexistent-record/.

27 Video of Sarah Palin's remarks about Paul Revere: http://www.msnbc.msn.com/id/21134540/vp/43274699.

28 Link to Palin's bus tour website: http://www.sarahpac.com/bus_tour.

29 Fiorina, *Culture War*, page 2.

30 Study by Professors Justin Grimmer and Gary Kin about partisan taunting in congressional press releases: http://gking.harvard.edu/sites/scholar.iq.harvard.edu/files/gking/files/201018067_online_1.pdf.

31 CNN video with comments by Arizona Sheriff Clarence Dupnick: http://politicalticker.blogs.cnn.com/2011/01/08/giffords-had-history-with-palin-tea-party.

Chapter 4: The NPR Republicans and the "Live Free or Die" State: New Hampshire

1 Gallup poll: http://www.gallup.com/poll/114022/state-states-importance-religion.aspx.

2 Links to 2010 U.S. Census data on New Hampshire. Employment: http://www.uscensus2010data.com/33-new-hampshire-employment-statistics-and-income-demographics. Education: http://www.uscensus2010data.com/33-new-hampshire-household-education-immigration-demographics.

3 Link to C-SPAN video of Senator Judd Gregg's farewell speech: http://www.c-spanvideo.org/videoLibrary/clip.php?appid=599279040.

4 *Concord Monitor* story written by Ben Leubsdorf: http://www.concordmonitor.com/article/222231/350000-of-lynchs-money-to-campaign?

5 University of New Hampshire Survey Center Poll on New Hampshire social issues: http://www.unh.edu/survey-center/news/pdf/gsp2011_winter_issues020911.pdf.

6 *Concord Monitor* editorial: http://www.concordmonitor.com/article/241964/reject-bizarre-state-defense-force-bill.

7 *Nashua Telegraph* editorial: http://www.nashuatelegraph.com/opinionedi torials/909872-263/a-big-thumbs-down-to-college-voting.html.

8 This is a link to an American University Law Review article on the Supreme Court decision: http://www.wcl.american.edu/journal/lawrev/21/ reynolds.pdf?rd=1.

9 This is a link to video of New Hampshire House Speaker William O'Brien talking to a New Hampshire Tea Party group about young people voting: http://www.washingtonpost.com/wp-dyn/content/article/2011/03/06/ AR2011030602662.html.

10 This is the story in the New Hampshire news site Seacoast Online about the legislature and Walter Peterson's funeral: http://www.seacoastonline .com/articles/20110608-NEWS-106080373.

11 This information is on page 955 of the *2010 Almanac of American Politics*, published by *National Journal* and written by Michael Barone and Richard Cohen.

12 This is a link to a *New York Times* story by Abby Goodnough about the New Hampshire Republican Party: http://www.nytimes.com/2011/01/ 23/us/politics/23hampshire.html.

13 University of New Hampshire poll: http://www.unh.edu/survey-center/ news/pdf/gsp2011_winter_primary021511.pdf.

**Chapter 5: The Facebook Generation
and a Rocky Mountain High: Colorado**

1 Link to Colorado State Demographer's Office with census and population data: http://dola.colorado.gov/dlg/demog/census.html.

2 Harvard University Kennedy School's Institute of Politics voter's guide: http://www.iop.harvard.edu/var/ezp_site/storage/fckeditor/file/pdfs/ Research-Publications/IOP_Voters_Guide.pdf.

3 Rock the Vote in Colorado 2010 poll: http://www.rockthevote.com/assets/ publications/research/2010/2010-rock-the-vote-colorado.pdf.

4 Institute of Politics voter's guide: http://www.iop.harvard.edu/var/ezp_ site/storage/fckeditor/file/pdfs/Research-Publications/IOP_Voters_ Guide.pdf.

5 IOP voter's guide: http://www.iop.harvard.edu/var/ezp_site/storage/fckedi tor/file/pdfs/Research-Publications/IOP_Voters_Guide.pdf.

6 Nevada population data: http://quickfacts.census.gov/qfd/states/32000 .html.

7 Arizona Population data: http://quickfacts.census.gov/qfd/states/04000 .html.

8 New Mexico population data: http://quickfacts.census.gov/qfd/states/ 35000.html.

9 Colorado Demographer's office census data: http://dola.colorado.gov/dlg/ demog/census.html.

10 CNN 2008 exit poll data for Colorado: http://www.cnn.com/ELEC TION/2008/results/polls/#val=COP00p1.

11 Dick Wadhams's email to state Republican Party: http://www.cologop .org/memo-to-colorado-republican-state-central-committee/.

12 *Time* magazine top mayors: http://www.time.com/time/printout/0,8816, 1050214,00.html.

13 Video for Hickenlooper shower ad: http://www.youtube.com/watch?v=3Yv_g7ZyADM.

14 Gretchen Morgenson of *The New York Times* wrote a story about the Denver School bond financing deal that Michael Bennet had been involved in: http://query.nytimes.com/gst/fullpage.html?res=9F01E0DF 1031F935A3575BC0A9669D8B63&ref=michaelbennet.

15 Jane Norton campaign ad, "Man Enough": http://www.youtube.com/watch?v=Ny5wv6cbHzQ.

16 Ken Buck video, "I Do Not Wear High Heels": http://www.huffington post.com/2010/07/21/ken-buck-vote-for-me-beca_n_654990.html.

17 Ken Buck on NBC's Meet the Press, proposing that being gay is like alcoholism: http://www.msnbc.msn.com/id/21134540/vp/39709968#39 709968.

18 February 2006 Greeley Tribune article by Rebecca Waddingham: http://www.greeleytribune.com/apps/pbcs.dll/article?AID=/20060301/NEWS/103010095&parentprofile=&template=printart.

19 Links to financial information about the Colorado Senate race from the Sunlight Foundation and Center for Responsive Politics: http://reporting .sunlightfoundation.com/outside-spending/2010/candidate http://www .opensecrets.org/races/election.php?state=CO.

20 CNN Colorado 2010 exit poll breakdown by ideology, party, race, and sex: http://www.cnn.com/ELECTION/2010/results/polls/#COS01p1.

21 Udall campaign spending and vote total: http://www.opensecrets.org/politicians/summary.php?cid=n00008051 Almanac of American Politics page 278.

22 *Washington Post* article: U.S. Congress Votes Data Base: http://projects .washingtonpost.com/congress/members/U000038.

23 *Wall Street Journal* article by Nancy Keates: http://online.wsj.com/article/ SB10001424052748703775704576162553297928260.html.

Chapter 6: The Old Dominion Is the New Virginia—
Home of the Starbucks Moms and Dads: Virginia

1 *Washington Post* story by Carol Morello and Dan Keating published in February 2011: http://www.washingtonpost.com/local/vas-numbers-of -hispanics-and-asians-skyrocket-as-white-population-dwindles.

2 *Forbes* magazine rankings of the best states for business: http://www .forbes.com/2010/10/13/best-states-for-business-business-beltway-best -states-table.html.

3 *Forbes* ranking of the richest counties in the U.S.: http://www.forbes .com/2011/04/11/americas-richest-counties-business-washington .html.

4 *Washington Post* story on census data and Fairfax County: http://www .washingtonpost.com/local/fairfax-grows-12-percent-in-latest-census -more-slowly-than-previous-decade.

5 *Washington Post* story on Prince William county and census data: http:// www.washingtonpost.com/wp-dyn/content/article/2011/02/09/ AR2011020906632.html.

6 *Washington Post* story on Loudoun County and census data: http://www .washingtonpost.com/wp-dyn/content/article/2011/02/03/AR2011020 305555.html.

7 Story on 2010 U.S. Census data and national suburban diversity: http://
www.denverpost.com/nationworld/ci_16861137?source=pkg.

8 Congressional Quarterly study of congressional districts by Gregory L.
Girou: http://www.redstatebluestatemovie.com/pdfs/Giroux%20A%20Line
%20in%20the%20Suburban%20Sand.pdf.

9 CNN 2010 exit polling: http://www.cnn.com/ELECTION/2010/results/
polls.

10 2008 Virginia state election info for Fairfax County: https://www.voter
info.sbe.virginia.gov/election/DATA/2008/07261AFC-9ED3-410F
-B07D-84D014AB2C6B/Unofficial/00_059_s.shtml.

11 2009 Fairfax County and statewide election info for Bob McDonnell:
https://www.voterinfo.sbe.virginia.gov/election/DATA/2009/37C2EDEB
-FACB-44C1-AF70-05FB616DCD62/UnOfficial/00_059_s.shtml and
https://www.voterinfo.sbe.virginia.gov/election/DATA/2009/37C2EDEB
-FACB-44C1-AF70-05FB616DCD62/UnOfficial/2_s.shtml.

12 *Washington Post* link to McDonnell thesis: http://www.washingtonpost
.com/wp-srv/politics/documents/McDonnell_thesis_082909.pdf?sid=
ST2009082902758.

13 *Washington Post* story on McDonnell declaring Confederate History
Month: http://www.washingtonpost.com/wp-dyn/content/article/2010/
04/06/AR2010040604416.html.

14 *Washington Post* story by Anita Kumar on McDonnell's support for transportation bonds: http://www.washingtonpost.com/blogs/virginia-politics/
post/mcdonnell-announces-900-transportation-projects-to-be-paid-for
-with-3-billion-in-bonds/2011/04/20/AF4bo0CE_blog.html.

15 2010 *Almanac of American Politics*, page 1538.

16 2010 *Almanac of American Politics*, page 1539.

17 Washingtonian Best and Worst of Congress: http://www.washingtonian .com/print/articles/6/0/16736.html.

18 Obama speech about Congressman Tom Perriello: http://projects.wash ingtonpost.com/obama-speeches/speech/471/.

19 *Almanac of American Politics*, page 1528.

20 *Almanac of American Politics*, page 1528.

21 In 2005 *Time Magazine* named Mark Warner one of the nation's five best governors: http://www.time.com/time/magazine/article/0,9171,1129494, 00.html.

22 Lynchburg and Craddock-Terry shoe company: http://www.craddockter ryhotel.com/historic-hotel/index.cfm.

23 Audio recording of November 8, 2010 post-election interview with Mark Warner: http://www.youtube.com/watch?v=gybd_k6Oqb4&feature=player _embedded.

24 Television interview in which Warner calls remarks "in-artful": http://www .youtube.com/watch?feature=player_embedded&v=OCthhr3-w0s#at=15.

Chapter 7: The Ultimate Swing State—
Home of the America First Democrats: Ohio
1 National Association of Manufacturers facts about Ohio manufacturing jobs http://www.nam.org/~/media/685530A8FB0A4A3EB58A866E67872BE1. ashx.

2 National Association of Manufacturers state data: http://www.nam.org/ Statistics-And-Data/State-Manufacturing-Data/Manufacturing-by -State.aspx.

3 Ohio unemployment data: http://ohiolmi.com/laus/CLFE/AnnualAverages/ 2010CLFE.pdf.

4 *Almanac of American Politics*, page 1161.

5 Video of the RGA Strickland ad: http://www.youtube.com/user/RepGovs ?blend=10&ob=5#p/a/u/1/vnvKQMkSsT4.

6 Various polls show Kasich ahead during the campaign: http://www.quinni piac.edu/x1322.xml?ReleaseID=1500 and http://polltracker.talkingpoints memo.com/contests/2010-oh-gov.

7 Ohio exit polling: http://www.newsnet5.com/dpp/news/political/elections _local/why-they-voted-the-way-they-did-in-ohio.

8 *Columbus Dispatch* story by Darrel Roland, September 26, 2010, pg. 1H. "Points of Division: Jobs Dominate, but 'Hot Button' Issues Remain Important in Governor's Race."

9 National Conference of State Legislators link: http://www.ncsl.org/?tabid =22275.

10 *Washington Post* article by Amy Gardner: http://www.washingtonpost.com/ politics/ohio-gop-may-invite-backlash-with-tough-stance-on-unions.

11 March 2011 Quinnipiac poll on John Kasich job approval: http://www .quinnipiac.edu/x1322.xml?ReleaseID=1570.

12 Data from the Department of Labor Bureau of Labor Statistics: http:// www.bls.gov/news.release/union2.t05.htm.

13 http://www.examiner.com/government-in-columbus/gov-elect-kasich-to -ohio-statehouse-regulars-get-on-the-bus-or-get-run-over.

14 John Kasich "I don't need your people" Politico interview with Ohio state Senator Nina Turner by Jennifer Epstein: http://www.politico.com/news/ stories/0111/48362.html.

15 April 18, 2011, *Columbus Dispatch* article by Joe Vardon: http://www .dispatch.com/live/content/local_news/stories/2011/04/28/kasich-workers -compensation-browns-steelers.html.

16 Barack Obama interview with Ohio TV station WKYC: http://www.wkyc .com/video/default.aspx?bctid=921329383001.

17 April 28, 2011 *Columbus Dispatch* article by Joe Vardon: http://www .dispatch.com/live/content/local_news/stories/2011/04/28/kasich-rips -obama-for-sb5-remarks.html.

18 Public Policy Polling Obama/Bush poll: http://publicpolicypolling.blogspot .com/2010/08/previewing-ohio.html.

19 OpenSecrets.org link to 2010 spending in Ohio's 16th District: http:// www.opensecrets.org/races/summary.php?cycle=2010&id=OH16.

20 *Almanac of American Politics*, pages 1200-1201.

21 Rennacci info from his campaign website: http://www.renacciforcongress .com/About_Jim/.

22 http://www.ohio.com/news/ohiocentric/renacci-campaign-explains-tax -dispute.

23 Sherrod Brown anti SB 5 website: http://ohio.sherrodbrown.com/.

24 Roll Call story about Vice President Joe Biden's attending a fundraiser for Sherrod Brown: http://www.rollcall.com/news/brown_and_biden_chow _down_in_ohio.

25 Public Policy Polling March 2011 survey: http://www.publicpolicypolling .com/pdf/PPP_Release_OH_0315513.pdf.

Chapter 8: Can Congress Be Fixed?

1 Dec. 15, 2010 Gallup Poll—lowest rating for Congress in Gallup history: http://www.gallup.com/poll/145238/congress-job-approval-rating-worst -gallup-history.aspx.

2 Rasmussen poll results http://www.rasmussenreports.com/public_content/ archive/mood_of_america_archive/congressional_performance/just_9_ give_congress_good_or_excellent_ratings.

3 *New York Times* article about Sen. Evan Bayh's announcement that he would leave the Senate: http://www.nytimes.com/2010/02/16/us/politics/ 16bayh.html?ref=evanbayh.

4 *Washington Post* U.S. Congress Votes Database: http://projects.washington post.com/congress/members/B001233.

5 Bipartisan Policy Center session on Dec. 16, 2010 with exiting members of Congress: http://www.bipartisanpolicy.org/news/multimedia/2010/12/ 17/exit-interview-what-we-learned.

6 *National Review* article by Robert Costa about potential GOP primary challenges: http://www.nationalreview.com/corner/254252/cornyn-looks -2012-robert-costa.

7 *Washington Post* US Congress Votes Database-Senate: http://projects .washingtonpost.com/congress/111/.

8 *Washington Post* Congress Votes Database-House: http://projects.wash
ingtonpost.com/congress/111/house/members/.

9 Information about 2010 election and House blue dogs: http://www.politico
.com/blogs/glennthrush/1110/Blue_Dog_wipeout_Half_of_caucus_gone
.html and http://ross.house.gov/legislation/bluedogs.htm.

10 Link to health care polls: http://www.harrisinteractive.com/NewsRoom/
HarrisPolls/tabid/447/mid/1508/articleId/651/ctl/ReadCustom%20De
fault/Default.aspx and http://politicalticker.blogs.cnn.com/2010/03/29/
cnn-poll-americans-divided-on-repealing-health-care-law/.

11 Link to story about Dan Maffei's reelection defeat: http://www.9wsyr
.com/political/story/Maffei-concedes-Congressional-seat-to-Buerkle/
Ualcil1MpEuacRwrgh6v_w.cspx.

12 Politico story by David Rogers on 2011 House spending bill: http://www
.politico.com/news/stories/0411/53204.html.

13 Information about federal budget and tax revenues: http://www.whitehouse
.gov/omb/budget/Historicals and http://www.heritage.org/budgetchart
book/current-tax-receipts.

14 Details of Sen. Mark Udall's reform plan: http://markudall.senate.gov/?p=
press_release&id=777.

15 C-SPAN video of Sen. Christopher Dodd farewell address: http://www
.c-spanvideo.org/program/296808-6.

16 C-SPAN video of Sen. George Voinovich farewell address: http://www
.c-spanvideo.org/program/297094-3.

17 C-SPAN video of Sen. Blanche Lambert Lincoln farewell address: http://
www.c-spanvideo.org/program/297094-4.

Chapter 9: A Question of Leadership;
The Presidency of Barack Obama

1 Video of Barack Obama's 2004 convention speech: http://www.youtube
.com/watch?v=eWynt87PaJ0.

2 *Washington Post* votes database: http://projects.washingtonpost.com/
congress/members/O000167.

3 Video of Barack Obama's 2008 DNC acceptance speech: http://www
.youtube.com/watch?v=yZCrIeRkMhA.

4 Barack Obama election night speech in Chicago's Grant Park: http://
elections.nytimes.com/2008/results/president/speeches/obama-victory
-speech.html.

5 Video of Barack Obama's meeting with the *Reno Gazette* editorial board in
January 2008: http://www.youtube.com/watch?v=VIZAuKedoa8&NR=1.

6 Video of *Reno Gazette* meeting: http://www.youtube.com/watch?v=
mbaszmcpesc.

7 Barack Obama *60 Minutes* interview, November 2008: http://www.cb
snews.com/video/watch/?id=4608198n.

8 Barack Obama Inaugural address: http://www.whitehouse.gov/blog/inau
gural-address/.

9 *New York Times* article about lobbyist meetings with White House officials: http://www.nytimes.com/2010/06/25/us/politics/25caribou.html.

10 Barack Obama interview with Denver television anchor Adam Schrager
in December 2010: http://www.9news.com/video/default.aspx?bctid=
709496658001#/Barack+Obama+talks+to+Adam+Schrager/7094966
58001.

11 *The Promise*, Alter, Jonathan. *The Promise: President Obama, Year One*. New York, NY: Simon & Schuster, 2010. P. 399.

12 This is from an interview I conducted with Tennessee Congresswoman Marsha Blackburn, after she attended the White House health care summit: http://www.usnews.com/opinion/blogs/linda-killian/2010/02/04/democratic-leaders-are-obamas-biggest-obstacle-to-bipartisanship.

13 *Reno Gazette* interview Anjeanette Damon; *Reno Gazette-Journal*; Jan 15, 2008; pg. A.4: http://www.youtube.com/watch?v=VIZAuKedoa8&NR=1.

14 Neustadt Neustadt, Richard E., and Richard E. Neustadt. *Presidential Power and the Modern Presidents: the Politics of Leadership from Roosevelt to Reagan*. New York: Free, 1991.

15 *New Yorker* article by Ryan Lizza, May 2011: http://www.newyorker.com/reporting/2011/05/02/110502fa_fact_lizza?currentPage=all.

16 Obama news conference after the 2010 mid-term election: http://www.youtube.com/watch?v=DYFNOGGwbn8 and http://www.whitehouse.gov/the-press-office/2010/11/03/press-conference-president.

17 2010 Gallup poll on Barack Obama, Bill Clinton, and George W. Bush favorability: http://www.gallup.com/poll/141485/bill-clinton-popular-barack-obama.aspx.

18 Barack Obama press conference on December 2010 congressional lame duck session Tax cut deal: http://m.whitehouse.gov/the-press-office/2010/12/06/statement-president-tax-cuts-and-unemployment-benefits.

19 Obama-Clinton press conference: http://m.whitehouse.gov/the-press-office/2010/12/10/remarks-president-obama-and-former-president-clinton.

20 Lincoln Chafee *New York Times* op/ed: http://www.nytimes.com/2010/02/21/opinion/21chafee.html?ref=opinionl.

21 Barack Obama 2010 State of the Union: http://www.whitehouse.gov/the-press-office/remarks-president-state-union-address.

22 Barack Obama remarks at Tucson Memorial service: http://www.whitehouse.gov/the-press-office/2011/01/12/remarks-president-barack-obama-memorial-service-victims-shooting-tucson.

23 Palin statement on Tucson shootings: http://vimeo.com/18698532.

24 Barack Obama 2011 SOTU: http://www.whitehouse.gov/photos-and-video/video/2011/01/26/2011-state-union-address-enhanced-version.

25 Barack Obama press conference on 2011 spending deal: http://www.whitehouse.gov/blog/2011/04/09/president-obamas-statement-bipartisan-agreement-budget.

26 President's Deficit Reduction Commission report: http://www.fiscalcommission.gov/sites/fiscalcommission.gov/files/documents/TheMomentofTruth12_1_2010.pdf.

27 2011 Polls on Barack Obama performance: http://maristpoll.marist.edu/wp-content/misc/usapolls/US110410/McClatchy/McClatchy.

28 David Brooks July 4 column "The Mother of All No-Brainers": http://www.nytimes.com/2011/07/05/opinion/05brooks.html.

29 July 14 Quinnipiac poll on debt ceiling: http://www.quinnipiac.edu/x1295.xml?ReleaseID=1624.

30 Transcripts of presidential news conferences on July 11 and July 15, 2011:

http://www.whitehouse.gov/the-press-office/2011/07/11/press-conference
-president and http://www.whitehouse.gov/the-press-office/2011/07/15/
press-conference-president.

31 Barack Obama 2008 campaign spending: http://www.reuters.com/article/
2011/04/04/us-usa-election-obama-analysis-idUSTRE7330NY
20110404.

32 *New York Times* and *Washington Post* July 16, 2011 stories about Obama
campaign second quarter fundraising: http://www.nytimes.com/2011/
07/17/us/politics/17donate.html?ref=politics and http://www.washington
post.com/politics/obama-fundraising-report-signals-juggernaut-cam
paign.

33 Poll on Barack Obama's performance after killing of Osama Bin Laden:
http://www.nytimes.com/2011/05/05/us/politics/05poll.html.

34 Bill Clinton remarks at Peterson Fiscal Summit, May 2011: http://www
.pgpf.org/FiscalSummit.aspx.

35 Transcript of State of the Union Address Jan. 25, 2011: http://www.white
house.gov/the-press-office/2011/01/25/remarks-president-state-union
-address.

Chapter 10: Trying to Restore Sanity

1 *Daily Show* ratings: http://tvbythenumbers.zap2it.com/2011/01/31/the
-daily-show-with-jon-stewart-tops-all-late-night-cable-series-in-january
-among-total-viewers-persons-18-49-men-18-34-and-men-18-24/80902/.

2 Rally to Restore Sanity video: http://www.comedycentral.com/shows/rally_
to_restore_sanity_and_or_fear/index.jhtml and http://www.rallytorestore
sanity.com/.

3 Frank Rich No Labels Op/Ed: http://www.nytimes.com/2010/12/19/opinion/19rich.html.

4 Transcript of Joe Scarborough on *Meet the Press* Dec. 19, 2010: http://www.msnbc.msn.com/id/40720643/ns/meet_the_press-transcripts/t/meet-press-transcript-dec/.

5 George Will column: http://www.washingtonpost.com/wp-dyn/content/article/2010/12/17/AR2010121704195_pf.html.

6 No Labels website: http://nolabels.org/home

7 Third Way website: http://www.thirdway.org

8 Democratic Leadership Council website: http://www.dlc.org

9 Bipartisan Policy Center website: http://www.bipartisanpolicy.org

10 Aspen Institute website: http://www.aspeninstitute.org

11 IndependentVoting.org website: http://www.independentvoting.org

12 Americans Elect website: www.americanselect.org

13 Coffee Party website: http://www.coffeepartyusa.com

Chapter 11: Changing the Rules of the Game

1 California Secretary of State information about Proposition 14: http://www.sos.ca.gov/elections/npp.htm.

2 WPRI.com story about Lincoln Chafee campaign spending: http://www.wpri.com/dpp/news/politics/chafee-caprio-spent-52m-on-gov-race.

3 Center for Responsive Politics/Open Secrets story about FEC decision: http://www.opensecrets.org/news/2010/05/federal-election-commission-opens-t.html.

4 California Citizens Redistricting Commission website: http://wedraw thelines.ca.gov/.

5 *Virginian-Pilot* editorial about redistricting: http://hamptonroads.com/2011/04/redistricting-mess-overtime.

6 League of Women Voters of Virginia redistricting information: http://www.lwv-va.org/redistricting2011.html.

7 *Washington Post* story about Virginia Attorney General comments on the Voting Rights Act: http://voices.washingtonpost.com/virginiapolitics/2010/12/virginia_has_moved_beyond_the.html.

8 U.S. Census information about Texas population: http://quickfacts.census.gov/qfd/states/48000.html.

9 Information about the Redistricting Transparency Act: http://www.open congress.org/bill/112-h419/show.

10 This quote is on page 166 of Lou Cannon's 2005 book *Governor Reagan: His Rise to Power*, published by Public Affairs.

11 Supreme Court *Citizens United* decision: http://www.supremecourt.gov/opinions/09pdf/08-205.pdf.

12 Brookings-American Enterprise Institute Reform in an Age of Networked Campaigns report: http://www.brookings.edu/reports/2010/0114_campaign_finance_reform.aspx.

Chapter 12: Battle Cry

1 Barack Obama at the Tucson Memorial Service: http://www.whitehouse
   .gov/photos-and-video/video/2011/01/12/president-obama-memorial
   -arizona.

2 Daniel Webster's Bunker Hill Monument speech, June 17, 1825:
   http://www.dartmouth.edu/~dwebster/speeches/bunker-hill.html.

INDEX

Kasich and, 173
mistrust of government and, 264
Obama on, 50
Park on, 251
Schumer on, 265
Voinovich on, 209
"Locating the New Political Center in
America," 34–35
Loeb, William, 74
Longfellow, Henry Wadsworth, 63
Longley, James, 33
Loudoun County (Virginia), 133
Loughner, Jared, 65, 242
Lugar, Dick, 184–85
Lumet, Sydney, 269
Lynch, John, 77–78, 84
Lynchburg (Virginia), 155–56

Madison, James, 29, 131
Maes, Don, 108
Maffei, Dan, 191
Main Street Republicans, 80
Maldonado, Abel, 256
Manchester Union Leader, 74
Mann, Thomas, 266
manufacturing
in Ohio, 160–61, 167–68
outsourcing, 161–62
Markey, Betsy, 105, 106, 175
Massachusetts, 24, 63
McCain, John, 8–12, 16, 34, 52
McCain-Feingold. *See* Bipartisan
Campaign Reform Act
McConnell, Mitch, 201
McDonnell, Bob, 136, 138–39, 261–62
McGovern, George, 36
McInnis, Scott, 105, 108
McKinnon, Mark, 240
McLane, Susan, 87
media, 49
blogs, 61
social, 252
Stewart on, 239
television, 64–65
Medicaid, 189–91, 232
Medicare, 97, 232, 269
Clinton, B., on, 51
Independent/Swing voters and, 230
taxes, 191
Meek, Kendrick, 57

Messina, Jim, 233
Middle East, 227
middle-class
tax code and, 3
voters, 162
Millennials, 94–95
Miller, Joe, 54–55
Mitchell, George, 244
money, 9, 57, 264. *See also* campaign
finance
cynicism and, 59
Leach on, 264
political system and, 137
TARP, 156
Moody's Investors Service and Fitch
Ratings, 202, 203
Moran, Jim, 141–42
Morning Joe, 241
mortgages, subprime, 204, 237
MoveOn, 57, 157
"Mr. Smith Bill," 207
Mr. Smith Goes to Washington, 207
MSNBC, 62, 103, 241
multi-party system, 26, 72
Murkowski, Lisa, 54, 243
on Palin, 55–56
on partisanship, 56
on Tea Party, 55–56
Musgrave, Marilyn, 105
Muslims, 177

Nader, Ralph, 30
name-calling, 182
NASA, 236
National Association of Manufacturers,
161
National Centrist Party, 248–49
National Commission on Fiscal
Responsibility and Reform, 149
2010 Report, 229
National Conference of State
Legislatures, 170
National Journal, 48
National Republican Senatorial
Committee, 185
National Rifle Association, 12
national security, 23, 209, 269
Nemmers, John, 234
Network, 269
Neustadt, Richard, 222

INDEX